Displacing Natives

Pacific Formations
Arif Dirlik, Series Editor

Chinese on the American Frontier
    edited by Arif Dirlik
What Is in a Rim? Critical Perspectives on the Pacific Region Idea, 2nd edition
    edited by Arif Dirlik
Inside Out: Literature, Cultural Politics, and Identity in the New Pacific
    edited by Vilsoni Hereniko and Rob Wilson
Teaching Asian America: Diversity and the Problem of Community
    edited by Lane Ryo Hirabayashi
Diversifying the State: American Grassroots Groups and Japanese Companies
    by Tomoji Ishi
Encounters: People of Asian Descent in the Americas
    edited by Roshni Rustomji-Kerns

Displacing Natives

The Rhetorical Production of Hawai'i

Houston Wood

ROWMAN & LITTLEFIELD PUBLISHERS, INC.
Lanham • Boulder • New York • Oxford

ROWMAN & LITTLEFIELD PUBLISHERS, INC.

Published in the United States of America
by Rowman & Littlefield Publishers, Inc.
4720 Boston Way, Lanham, Maryland 20706

12 Hid's Copse Road
Cumnor Hill, Oxford OX2 9JJ, England

British Cataloguing in Publication Information Available

Library of Congress Cataloging-in-Publication Data

Wood, Houston, 1954–
    Displacing natives : the rhetorical production of Hawai'i /
Houston Wood.
        p.   cm. — (Pacific formations)
    Includes bibliographical references.
    ISBN 0-8476-9140-3 (alk. paper). — ISBN 0-8476-9141-1 (pbk. :
alk. paper)
        1. Hawaiians—Historiography.   2. Hawaiians—Cultural
assimilation.   3. Hawaii—Historiography.   4. Hawaiians in popular
culture.   5. Hawaii—Description and travel.   I. Title.
II. Series.
DU624.67.W66   1999
996.9'007'2—dc21   99-103443
                                                                        CIP

Printed in the United States of America

♾™ The paper used in this publication meets the minimum requirements of American
National Standard for Information Sciences—Permanence of Paper for Printed Library
Materials, ANSI Z.39.48–1984.

For Isaac, Naomi, and Susan

Contents

Contents

Illustrations and Tables

Acknowledgments

This project has been continually nourished by the writing of Edward Said and of Haunani-Kay Trask. Said's example has encouraged me to redirect my literary training toward broader pursuits while Trask's cultural criticism has served as both a guide and a bracer at each step.

Rob Wilson's cultural criticism that has focused on Hawai'i also provides a foundation for my approach here. Rob kindly guided the revision of early drafts of most chapters at a time when I knew what I wanted to do but not how to do it. Jeffrey Carroll, Peter Elbow, John Goss, Vilsoni Hereniko, Laura Lyons, and Cindy Ward were also very influential in the early going. Kahi Wight assisted me with my limited understanding of the Hawaiian language.

Hawaii Pacific University provided a home and support for the final years of my research. I particularly thank Dean John Fleckles and the Committee for Scholarly Endeavors for their financial support down the stretch. Serge Marek of HPU's geography department allowed me to read early drafts of his important master's thesis; many of his insights appear in chapter 5. Mark Tjarks, a colleague in the English department, influenced me in rethinking chapter 3.

Reshela Dupuis gave me encouragement and important suggestions for revising later drafts. I could not, finally, integrate most of her ideas here, for they deserve yet another book, one I hope she will write.

Susan Hamilton listened patiently to my "notions" on many days and, especially, nights, when she rightly expected to hear me talking about more personal matters. Isaac Wood and Naomi Wood, my patient children, enthusiastically encouraged me to indulge my passion when they could have, legitimately, demanded more attention for themselves.

Thanks also go to the following for permission to reprint material: Atlantic Recording Company (Figure 4.2); the Bishop Museum (Figures 2.3, 5.1, 5.2, and 5.3); the British Library (Figure 2.2.); DeSoto Brown Collection (Figures 1.1, 3.1, 3.2, and 6.4); the Hawai'i State Archives (Figure 5.4); the Hawaiian

Historical Society (Coda Tables 1 and 2); the Dixson Galleries, State Library of New South Wales, Sydney (Figure 2.1); Honolulu Publishing Company, Ltd. (Figures 1.2 and 1.3); Luis Reyes and Mutual Publishing Company (Figures 6.1, 6.2, and 6.3); and Bill Hamilton and the University of Hawai'i Press (Figures Disorientation 1 and Disorientation 2).

Orientation:
Recovering Hawaiian Winds

In the spring of 1994, I heard Esther T. Mookini lecture about some of the problems that she and Sarah Nākoa had encountered in their translation into English of Moses K. Nakuina's *Moolelo Hawaii o Pakaa a me Ku-a Pakaa, no Kahu Iwikuamoo o Keawenuiaumi, ke Alii o Hawaii, a o no Moopuna hoi a Laamaomao* ("The Hawaiian Story of Pakaa and Ku-a-Pakaa, the Personal Attendants of Keawenuiaumi, the Chief of Hawaii, and the Descendents of Laamaomao").[1] Mookini described the text, given the English title *The Wind Gourd of La'amaomao*, as "the first novel ever written in Hawaiian." This last phrase caught my attention for I was, at that time, a student in English at the University of Hawai'i preparing to take my Ph.D. comprehensive exams. I had lived in Hawai'i for twenty years, loved reading novels, and had written two of my own—which now reside in drawers. How was it possible, I wondered, that I had never heard *The Wind Gourd of La'amaomao* mentioned before?

Mookini explained that Nakuina had published the book in 1902, and that it was based on a traditional legend that Nakuina had collected from various sources and then shaped into a single, coherent tale. One of the special features of the book, Mookini pointed out, was that while it was written in prose it contained a lengthy chant collecting the names for many of the winds found on the different Hawaiian islands. For O'ahu alone, she said, *The Wind Gourd of La'amaomoa* lists the names of forty-five winds, each with distinguishing characteristics.

Immediately after the lecture I went searching for the book. There were none in the campus bookstore, which was full of books by and about such writers as Shakespeare and Toni Morrison. I finally located one copy in the library, and I noticed it had only been checked out twice in the preceding two years. I took the book to my office in the English department and began to read. Before long I came upon the section that contained the chant describing the winds of O'ahu. There I read, in the Mookini and Nākoa translation:

> From the sea, the storm comes sweeping toward shore,
> The windward Kui-lua wind churns up the sea,
> While you're fishing and sailing,
> The Ihiihilauakea wind blows,

1

It's the wind that blows inside Hanauma,
A wind from the mountains that darkens the sea,
It's the wind that tosses the kapa of Paukaa,
Puuokona is of Kuliʻouʻou,
Ma-ua is the wind of Niu,
Holouhā is of Kehaha,
Māunuunu is of Waiʻalae,
The wind of Lēʻahi turns here and there,
ʻŌlanui is of Kahaloa
Waiʻōmaʻo is of Pālolo,
Kuehu-lepo is of Kahua,
Kukalahale is of Honolulu, . . .[2]

These were the names for winds that inhabited the places where I lived and studied, where I shopped and visited with friends. Here were many names, yet I recognized not one.

I wanted to be outside, to feel these winds against my skin as I biked to my
home where Māunuunu turned the air. I waited impatiently for the elevator to
carry me out of Kuykendall Hall, a charmless office tower named for Ralph
Kuykendall, the single most influential Euroamerican historian of Hawaiʻi; his
three-volume chronicle, I have since determined, mentions the name of not a single wind.[3] Kuykendall's work focuses on the nineteenth century, when there were
at one time or another nearly one hundred newspapers publishing in the Hawaiian
language. He ignores these sources, too, for Hawaiian history for him is the story
almost exclusively of foreigners in Hawaiʻi, the story of their English-language
newspapers and documents. Hawaiians enter the three volumes of *The Hawaiian
Kingdom* mostly to the extent that they assist or resist what Kuykendall presents
as an inevitable domination by a superior invading culture of American modernity. The building named after Kuykendall now holds a large English department
employing over seventy Ph.D.s. The department is oversized in part because it
was decided twenty years ago, by mostly Asian and Caucasian legislators, that
Hawaiʻi's students, Native[4] and non-Native alike, required extra help so they
might better master a dialect of English associated with an upper middle class
domiciled on a continent twenty-five hundred miles away.

I met my office mate on the ride down in the elevator. He was a fellow graduate student, just then returning from his class in Middle Welsh. I knew that many
of the English faculty could read Latin. Most had at one time also studied Old
English, a language with many fewer written texts than those available in the
Hawaiian language in libraries close at hand. Most of the faculty were experts in
the writing of a group of islands in the North Sea, about eight thousand miles away.
A few taught the American literary canon, and then there were the handful of
recent hires with specialties in the minority literatures of African Americans, Asian
Americans, and postcolonials on various continents and in the Caribbean. Every
professor in the building had read Beowulf and Virginia Woolf, but only a hand-

ful, I guessed, had ever heard of *The Wind Gourd of La'amaomao*. If most of the faculty had to look at it, I knew they could produce excellent metropolitan reasons for dismissing it as an ill-shaped, unengaging novel. Most would probably offer learned explanations as to why it should not be considered to be a novel at all.

By the time I stepped out of the elevator I was having disturbing thoughts about the profession I was working so hard to join. In his preface to *The Wind Gourd of La'amaomao*, Nakuina explains that "some songs, improvised chants, and sacred chants have been forgotten, and others will soon be forgotten; we will never remember them if books such as this one are not published." Nakuina also maintains that his book is addressed to "those who truly love the Ali'i and the Lahui [Hawaiian Nation]."[5] As I walked to my bike, Wai'ōma'o gusted loudly, pressing my face, mocking my knowledge and identity. I began to wonder if I could find a way to resist my own colonization and to embrace some methods for subverting the colonizing work I was being educated to do.

This study is, among other things, an exploration of the contradictions and complexities I have unearthed since that day. It is written with the recognition it is necessary in Hawai'i today either to declare oneself for some version of Native sovereignty or against it. To retreat instead to notions of "antiessentialism," "hybridity," "neutrality," or "objectivity" is to make a consequential choice to support the status quo, wherein much of the Native population has been coerced into landlessness, hunger, suicide, illness, and incarceration. (Native Hawaiians, for example—roughly 30 percent of the total population—make up about 60 percent of those prosecuted by the Euroamerican-dominated "justice system."[6] These Natives are incarcerated mostly by Caucasian and Asian American legislators, lawyers, and judges—immigrants and descendants of immigrants who have prospered in postcontact Hawai'i as, generally, the Native people have not.)

The following chapters examining various cultural productions cannot, of course, make much difference, but they are offered with the hope that they will participate in the "struggle over geography" in Hawai'i—a struggle that, as Edward Said explains, "is not only about soldiers and cannons but also about ideas, about forms, about images and imaginings."[7]

As this reference to Said suggests, as soon as I altered the direction of my studies, I discovered there were many scholars throughout the world who had long been seeking to use their scholarship to assist various decolonizations. In Hawai'i itself, I quickly learned, the colonialist histories of Kuykendall and his many successors are being supplanted by an expanding group of Native Hawaiian scholars, including Momi Kamahele, Lilikalā Kame'eleihiwa, George Kanahele, Herb Kane, J. Kehaulani Kauanui, Davianna Pōmaika'i McGregor, Jon Osorio, Amy Stillman, Haunani-Kay Trask, Kanalu Young, and others.[8] These researchers insist that writers in the islands commit to a project that actively opposes the dominant culture's continuing attacks upon Natives. Trask, for example, writes that such a project of decolonization should "unscrew the power of the colonizing force by creating a new consciousness very critical of foreign terms, foreign definitions, and foreign solutions."[9] Just such an interrogation of foreign terms, definitions, and solutions of the rhetoric of non-Natives forms the focus of most of the pages that follow.

Within my own originating area of literary studies, I found there were several scholars in the islands who had been counseling critics for years to undertake decolonizing work. Dennis Kawaharada, founder of Kalamakū Press and publisher of *The Wind Guord of La'amaomao*, and Richard Hamasaki have been and remain two especially important spokespersons for this view.[10] Rob Wilson also, in a series of articles, has exhorted scholars to recognize how the writing of locals, including Native Hawaiians, offers both resistance and alternatives to the dominant Euroamerican culture.[11]

Special notice is also due to R. Douglas Herman, whose research into the colonialist constructions of sociospatial meanings in the islands in many ways parallels my approach in these pages.[12]

One persistent controversy impacts all current decolonizing efforts in Hawai'i. This controversy turns on the question of whether "authentic," traditional, Native Hawaiian cultural practices continue in the islands at the end of the twentieth century. Some influential scholars maintain that no identifiable precontact behaviors still exist, and so they argue there remains today no uniquely Hawaiian culture to reinvigorate.[13]

My view is that it indeed seems likely that most indigenous practices enacted in Hawai'i today have changed significantly since Cook arrived. It should be remembered, however, that in the same period the cultural practices associated with metropolitan cultures have also changed significantly. Still, though everyday life today would often be incomprehensible to the Euroamericans of two hundred years ago, people speak with confidence about a continuous, Euroamerican tradition of family life, religion, economy, philosophy, science, et cetera. We can speak equally sensibly of a continuous, Native Hawaiian tradition as well.

In her article, "Waipio Valley, a Cultural *Kīpuka* in Early 20th Century Hawai'i," Davianna Pōmaika'i McGregor usefully explains for skeptics one of several ways that Native Hawaiian lifeways survived Euroamerican colonization. The kīpuka McGregor mentions in her title are found on the island of Hawai'i and refer to "holes" (puka) or oases of older forests within larger, younger forests. Such kīpuka are usually formed by lava flows that destroy wide bands of the older forest while leaving smaller swaths of unharmed, old forest encircled by a wasteland.[14] As McGregor describes it, "From these natural *kīpuka* come the seeds and spores for the eventual regeneration of the native flora upon the fresh lava. Rural Hawaiian communities may be regarded as cultural *kīpuka* from which native Hawaiian culture can be regenerated and revitalized in the contemporary setting" (196). McGregor identifies seventeen rural areas where, for much of the twentieth century, many traditional Hawaiian practices escaped both urbanization and the plantation system. Non-Native historians of Hawai'i have ignored these kīpuka, she explains, and so "readers are left with the impression that the Hawaiian people have been totally assimilated into American society and have abandoned their own culture" (198).

Much of the richness of the continuous Hawaiian tradition that has survived Euroamerican colonization remains unknown within the dominant society, since it is available most fully within the immense corpus of oral and written Hawaiian-language texts and performances that have never been translated into English. George Kanahele's *Ku Kanaka* provides one especially rich summary of some of this corpus of what Kanahele calls "Native Hawaiian values."[15] I summarize some of Kanahele's study in later chapters, as well as the explanations of several contemporary Hawaiians who were raised within an unbroken Native Hawaiian tradition. These various Natives dispute the claims of metropolitan scholars such as Homi Bhabha, Roger Keesing, and many others, who argue contemporary indigenous cultures are so thoroughly hybridized that appeals to precontact values should be viewed as romanticized fantasies.[16] That such critics both inside and outside Hawai'i deny the claims of Native writers such as Trask, McGregor, and Kanahele suggests many non-Natives remain committed to presenting themselves as experts who can speak on behalf of indigenous people more authoritatively than these people can speak for themselves.

I began this study hoping I could find a way to keep from seeming to present myself as yet another haole (non-Native) expert. At first I tried a strategy of writing without including any mention of Native claims and self-representations. I drafted many pages that focused exclusively on foreign representations of the islands. I hoped this would avoid the dangers inherent in attempting to describe what past and current Native Hawaiians think and do. After several months I realized that this approach was producing a manuscript that encouraged readers to conclude that only Euroamerican cultural productions are interesting, worthy of study, and currently influential in the islands. My draft manuscript silenced Native Hawaiians as thoroughly as Cook's journals, Twain's letters, Hollywood movies, and the many other foreign representations I meant to interrogate.

To produce yet one more settler text that includes no Native Hawaiian voices finally seemed to be even worse than risking the accusations of appropriation that may be leveled at me now because these pages frequently describe Native Hawaiian cultural practitioners, scholars, and activists. In the face of Euroamerican colonialism, Hawaiians have maintained vigorous alternative views of themselves and their islands. It was the frequent encounters with these Native alternatives in my twenty-five years in the islands that convinced me of the myopia of the hegemonic haole Hawai'i that is now known worldwide.

If I had followed my initial plan and examined only Euroamerican rhetoric, I fear most readers would have remained convinced that monorhetoric accurately displays the reality of the islands. By invoking Native representations as alternatives to those constructed by outsiders and settlers, I hope to better infuse these pages with reminders of practices of interacting with the earth and other humans different from those most Euroamericans embrace.

Part One

From Conquest
to Anti-Conquest

Chapter One

The Violent Rhetoric of Names

If human beings, Native and non-Native alike, are to create an alternative to the planned New World Order, then those who live in the First World must change their *culture*, not only their leaders.

Haunani-Kay Trask[1]

The Euroamerican presence in Hawai'i has been associated with violence ever since one of Captain Cook's lieutenants murdered an unarmed Hawaiian man the first day the English set foot in the islands in 1778. On their next visit, less than a year later, Cook's men massacred dozens more Hawaiians and burned an entire village to the ground at Kealakekua; the number of Native victims was even larger a few years later when the American trader Simon Metcalfe opened fire on unarmed Hawaiians in what is now known as the Olowalu massacre. The pattern was thus established that would see American warships in 1820, a French frigate in 1838, and the British in 1843 aim their separate guns from offshore at Hawai'i's Native government. These varied acts prepared for the day in 1893, when a company of U.S. Marines marched through the streets of downtown Honolulu past 'Iolani Palace to bolster a handful of American businessmen's demand that Queen Lili'uokalani yield her nation's independence to them.

From the outset, foreigners have clothed their acts of conquest in a rhetoric that aims both to justify and to disguise the consequences of their acts. Succeeding chapters examine how journalism, novels, diaries, advertisements, visual arts, museums, films, television shows, and various other types of cultural productions assist the more naked coercion associated with armies, revolutions, and the criminal justice system. When, for example, missionaries transcribe the volcano for geologists, self-proclaimed kama'āinas dance the hula, or Betty Grable (see Figure 1.1), Gidget, and Elvis "go Hawaiian" in the movies, they encourage the destruction of Hawaiians and Hawaiian culture as effectively as the fatal diseases Cook, Vancouver, and other explorers earlier introduced.

Figure 1.1   Betty Grable featured as a hula dancer in *Song of the Islands*

Reprinted with permission of
DeSoto Brown Collection

NAMING AS IMPERIALISM

The mechanisms for naming both Native people and places in the islands have been seized by non-Natives in order to expand the latter's control. Many of the earliest colonizing Euroamericans, for example, were disturbed because Hawaiian personal names did not indicate gender, place children in genealogies of patrilineal descent, or require women at marriage to become wards of their husbands. Foreigners thus pressed for an Act to Regulate Names, a system of naming finally signed into law in 1860. This act required that newly married Native women take their husband's family name, and that all "children born in wedlock shall have their father's name as a family name. They shall, besides, have a Christian name suitable to their sex."[2]

This change in Native naming practices undermined the traditional Hawaiian family system and the tremendous power Native women held within that system. It was, as Patricia Grimshaw shows, yet one more way settlers employed as they "attacked and undermined those very aspects of Hawaiian culture which offered

Hawaiian women some measure of autonomy in their own system."[3] This legally mandated change in naming practices also abraded one central way Hawaiians honored and remained connected with their past. As Pukui, Haertig, and Lee explain, traditional Hawaiian personal names, nā inoa, do not signal gender or link anyone with a father or husband. Each Hawaiian name, instead, is "a kind of force in its own right. Once spoken, an *inoa* took on an existence, invisible, intangible, but real. An *inoa* could be a causative agent, capable of marshalling mystic elements to help or hurt the bearer of the name. And, so went the belief, the more an *inoa* was spoken, the stronger became the name-force and its potential to benefit or harm."[4] By prohibiting the indigenous people from possessing names that enabled them to call upon this ancestral force, Euroamericans weakened the Hawaiians' ability to resist colonization. Such a rhetorical change worked like the threat of physical coercion to enlarge the power of outsiders who did not depend on their personal names to provide "a kind of force."

Native Hawaiian procedures for naming places have also been interrupted by outsiders, with similar devastating effects. Immediately after the overthrow of the Hawaiian monarchy, for example, the Provisional Government actively opposed the use of the Hawaiian language in all public discourse. Native-language schools were abruptly cut off from government financial support, and the newly empowered Euroamericans named streets, companies, parks, and public facilities after their foreign friends and themselves.

The very practice of using personal names as the basis for naming places is a Euroamerican introduction. Traditional Hawaiian place names more often refer to specific geographical features, plants, and/or actions. Like personal names, place names importantly link the present and past.[5] In Hawaiian geographic thought, place names speak the shifting relationships and the narratives that are spoken to create and maintain those relationships. These names participate in a complex and changing history much like Hawaiian places themselves are understood to do. As Abraham Pi'ianai'a explains, such traditional Hawaiian names thus display "a knowledge of place, history, and personal relationships."[6]

Euroamerican settlers disrupted this Native system of naming, replacing it with a system that arrests fluidity and ignores Native history in order to create static symbols suitable for deeds and maps. R. Douglas Herman shows, for example, that beginning with the U.S. Coast and Geodetic Survey of 1903, Euroamericans produced a series of geographical indexes aimed at systematically replacing Native place names with a "logos of Western order and control."[7] The territorial government did use some Hawaiian words in constructing official names, but it so transformed the procedures for designating their meanings that these Native words ended up functioning merely as symbols, no longer resonating with Hawaiian traditions and history.

The loss of their own power to name must have inflicted a terrible wound to the indigenous people of the islands, for, as George Kanahele describes it, Hawaiians "belonged to the land. How could you ever own a place, let alone sell it as a commodity, if its true value is found as the sum of the lives, memories, achievements, and mana of the generations who once dwelled upon it?"[8] This traditional relationship with the land encouraged Hawaiians to name such a multitude of places that Samuel H. Elbert writes in the "Preface" to *Place Names of Hawai'i* that he cannot even make a rough estimate as to whether there were a hundred thousand or a million indigenous place names.[9] Traditional place names helped keep the ancestors alive. With the interruption of the traditional process of naming, many of these ancestors may have died.

After statehood, once the alternative, Native culture no longer seemed to pose as much of a threat, the use of ersatz Hawaiian names increased until their assignment has become today, in some instances (e.g., streets), even prescribed by law. This contemporary governmental use of Hawaiian words gives an impression of respect for Natives, yet ignores the Hawaiians' radically different set of cultural naming practices. As Herman observes, "the cultural capital of things Hawaiian increase [sic] in value at the same time that Hawaiians themselves remain at the bottom of society."[10]

The effective but subtle power that comes with the control of naming apparatuses is evident in the very word "Hawaiian," which I have used repeatedly in these early pages. As Kekuni Blaisdell points outs, both this word and the general idea it invokes are of Euroamerican and not Native invention.[11] The letter "n" gives the word's origins away, since "n" is not one of the thirteen letters the nineteenth-century missionaries assigned to the Hawaiian alphabet. The indigenous people had separate names for each island but, it seems likely, no common name or seeming need for a word that applied to all the islands. Europeans applied the local name for the largest island, Hawai'i, to the aggregate of islands and then, confusingly, started calling even the residents of Maui, O'ahu, Kaua'i, and the other islands "Hawaiians," though most of these people so-called had never set foot on the particular island of Hawai'i that formed the basis of their new name.

"Kanaka Maoli" is a better term, Blaisdell argues: "It is preferred to *'ka po'e Hawai'i'* (Hawaiian people) because the latter depends on the Western, not Hawaiian, generalization from the island of Hawai'i. Further, *kanaka maoli* was *the* term by which our noble ancestors identified themselves."[12] Both Marshall Sahlins and Valerio Valeri, probably the two most widely known non-Native contemporary "authorities" on Hawaiians, have adopted the convention of referring to all the islands as "Hawaii" while saving "Hawai'i" with the glottal stop for denoting what is otherwise commonly known today as the Big Island.[13] Very few if any Natives or non-Natives in the islands have adopted this distinction. That such experts living in places far away would attempt to establish new names for Native places illustrates how little the colonialist practices of too many Euroamericans have changed. (For more on Sahlins's rhetorical production of the islands, see chapter 7.)

In the nineteenth century the newly coined English word "Hawaiian" came to stand for the Euroamerican concept of "race," one of a varying number of so-called types that were claimed to form a hierarchy—with, of course, the creators of these names, the Caucasians, placed at the top. This view continued generally unchanged until after World War II, when "race" began to acquire its current popular reference to "blood quantum" and/or "genetic makeup." When Euroamericans speak of Hawaiians today, then, they usually mean people who possess certain scientifically determined, physiological characteristics.

Many contemporary Hawaiians reject both the English name and concept to assert instead that Kanaka Maoli should be identified as *a people with a particular relationship to specific places and people*. Thus, for example, Blaisdell writes of himself and other Kanaka Maoli in a 1998 letter to a Honolulu newspaper: "kalo is our hiapo (elder sibling), Haloa, who feeds us. Without wai (water) and 'āina (land), we have no kalo, and, therefore, we kanaka maoli (Native Hawaiians) perish as a distinct people and nation."[14]

The differences between these separate names and definitions of "Hawaiian" and "Kanaka Maoli" are destined to become increasingly consequential. Currently, for example, the Euroamerican race-based definition is used by the federal government in allocating the 200,000 acres of lands known as the Hawaiian Homelands. These lands were supposed to be returned to Kanaka Maoli through the 1920 Hawaiian Homes Commission Act of the U.S. Congress but, as is common in the islands, non-Natives controlled the mechanisms of allocation and so kept about 80 percent of this land for themselves. The Euroamerican racial concept of Hawaiian is employed by judges, legislators, experts, and the general public to discredit Native claims that, as Blaisdell says, Kanaka Maoli will perish without access to land and water. The Euroamerican blood-quantum definition makes it reasonable for foreigners to claim that Hawaiians will continue to exist even if, for example, they are all forced to relocate and live far from their ancestral islands. The Kanaka Maoli definition of themselves, however, experiences such displacements as genocide, as effective as disease and guns in destroying what it is to be Native. Separating Kanaka Maoli from the land murders Haloa, Blaisdell explains, destroying the brother, "our hiapo, who feeds us."

One additional naming practice will be the focus of much of chapter 3 in which I show that Euroamericans in the islands were generally still known as "foreigners" even in the early decades of the twentieth century. Rankled by this label, settlers born in Hawai'i began to appropriate the Hawaiian concept of "kama'āina." They transformed the meaning of this word so they could apply it to themselves and assert a right to be thought of as Natives, too. The newly christened kama'āinas resisted Kanaka Maoli counterclaims that only Hawaiians were true Natives. The newly named kama'āinas even began to claim that they, as much or even more than the Kanaka Maoli, possessed special relationships not only with the sea and land but even with many traditional Hawaiian practices such as the hula. Figures 1.2 and 1.3 show two photographs with captions that appeared side by side in a 1936 issue of the settler-dominated magazine *Paradise of the Pacific* that illustrate one instance of this claim.

14

Figure 1.2 "Two girls of the old school"

Source: Paradise of the Pacific (May 1936): 9
Reprinted with permission of the Honolulu Publishing Company, Ltd.

Figure 1.3 "Two girls of the new school . . . of genuine hula"

Source: Paradise of the Pacific (May 1936): 9
Reprinted with permission of the Honolulu Publishing Company, Ltd.

THREE RHETORICAL SITUATIONS

Since names, concepts, and discursive practices are foundational in the many conflicts erupting in Hawai'i today, it is useful to recognize that these conflicts often take place in the borderlands linking three distinctive rhetorical situations. One rhetorical situation is associated with non-Natives like myself. Another involves Kanaka Maoli using mostly non-Native rhetoric. A third situation is created by Kanaka Maoli using some variant of a traditional Hawaiian rhetoric. Though there is overlap among these three, they do denote configurations with distinct characteristics that construct alternative truths.

Most of this study participates in the first rhetorical situation, employing Euroamerican assumptions, tropes, and narratives to analyze how Euroamericans have represented Hawai'i to themselves, to Hawaiians, and to the rest of the world. Chapter 2 begins with an analysis of the various eighteenth-century volumes associated with Captain James Cook, as these volumes were the first to apply foreign terms, definitions, and development plans to the islands. Subsequent chapters analyze the related rhetoric produced by later Euroamerican arrivals to the islands, focusing particularly on the missionaries, scientists, travel writers, journalists, novelists, painters, photographers, film and television producers, lyricists, advertising executives, and others who, together, produced the "Hawai'i" that is now well known worldwide. I examine a range of historical circumstances surrounding various productions, but point to continuities in this rhetoric as well. I argue these productions form a *monorhetoric*, a body of symbolic acts that identify the islands with a linear, irreversible history associated with visible phenomena. Most of this monorhetoric reflexively maintains that the islands so constructed exist independently of these practices and, further, that these islands can best be represented not by Kanaka Maoli but by Euroamerican representational forms.

A second rhetorical situation exists when Kanaka Maoli use Euroamerican languages to challenge the validity of the representational practices used by Captain Cook and his two centuries of successors. This second situation includes those texts that Mary Louise Pratt describes as "autoethnographic," texts "in which people undertake to describe themselves in ways that engage with representations others have made of them."[15] Haunani-Kay Trask's diverse and influential work offers a vivid example of this second rhetorical situation, for her political essays, scholarly articles and poetry rely far more on Euroamerican than on Hawaiian tropes. She writes back against empire, to adapt Salman Rushdie's suggestive phrase, by adopting monorhetorical styles of argument, narrative, and the tradition of English lyric poetry, with only occasional invocations of Native Hawaiian ideas and forms. Trask's writing, as Pratt writes of autoethnographies in general, involves "a selective collaboration with and appropriation of idioms of the metropolis or the conqueror. These are merged or infiltrated to varying degrees with indigenous idioms to create self-representations intended to intervene in metropolitan modes of understanding" (139).

The interventions of most other Native Hawaiian activists, scholars, writers, and poets rely similarly upon Euroamerican rhetoric. As Arif Dirlik argues in *After the Revolution* and elsewhere, such adaptations seem to be necessary if indigenous people are effectively to oppose the global dominance of Euroamericans. The very idea of a sovereign Hawaiian "nation" populated by a distinctive group of Hawaiians emerged as a concept in the islands only through the Native people's nineteenth-century experiences with nation- and race-identified outsiders. Now, similarly, at the end of the twentieth century, the growing self-awareness and interest in local, Native, cultural practices have arisen largely as a response to what Dirlik describes as the "unprecedented penetration of local society" by a global, mass-media driven, consumer culture.[16] As Rob Wilson and Dirlik explain, Hawaiian writers, like other indigenous writers, must thus examine how "the global deforms and molests the local" in order to repel this molestation.[17] Such oppositional analyses require some engagement with the Euroamerican monorhetoric that dominates both corporate and cultural forms of globalization, for it seems likely that only through some adaptation of the dominant monorhetoric, as Pratt argues, will indigenous people find a "point of entry into the dominant circuits of print culture."[18]

Though most of the cultural productions of Native Hawaiians who act within this second rhetorical situation make extensive use of Euroamerican tropes and narratives, the work varies considerably in how consistently each writer claims to be speaking as a Native, on behalf of other Natives. This work differs as well in whether these speakers, writers, and artists address mostly other Natives or the dominant culture. Thus, for example, much of the most recent work by Trask and others associated with the Center for Hawaiian Studies at the University of Hawai'i (which I review in later chapters) presents itself as Native scholarship, by and for other Natives; while the poetry of contemporary writers such as Michael McPherson or Joe Balaz, or the recent fiction by Kiana Davenport, seems aimed more at heterogeneous audiences.[19] These variations create tension and lead to disputes within the Native Hawaiian community over legitimacy and authenticity—disputes, happily, of little relevance to our purposes here.[20]

Most of these Native artists and writers, whether writing polemics, essays, novels or poetry, prominently refer to a third rhetorical situation, a situation they associate with those Kanaka Maoli who today continue cultural traditions that predate Cook. The existence of these practices is radically consequential, as many Euroamericans and even some Native Hawaiians claim that the precontact Native culture is extinct or, at best, indistinguishable today from the so-called local culture in Hawai'i, a culture that includes elements contributed by several immigrant groups. In these pages I repeatedly emphasize the counterclaim that distinctive Hawaiian traditions are thriving in the islands. I accept John Dominis Holt's perspective that "it is remarkable that some of what is Hawaiian in the purer terms of feeling, thinking, believing, doing, being, survives to this day from those perilous times of contact."[21] Trask offers a similar view when she writes, "Without doubt,

Hawaiians were transformed drastically and irreparably after contact, but remnants of earlier lifeways, including values and symbols, have persisted."[22] When Holt, Trask, and others write about these "remnants" using a predominately non-Native rhetoric, they are engaged in the second rhetorical situation. When they or others directly engage in the practice of these "earlier lifeways," they enter a third situation, one that is not comprehensible to those who understand only Euroamerican monorhetorical forms. Many Euroamericans, of course, seem determined to continue to produce representations of these lifeways through their apparatuses of anthropology, journalism, film, video, web pages, and many other media. Such cross-cultural representations do not display comprehension, however, any more than a cross-cultural hula or mele (song) depicting atomic theory would be acknowledged by Euroamericans to demonstrate comprehension of physics.

CRITICAL LOCALISM

Trask, like many others, argues that Hawaiians must continue to speak and write within the second rhetorical situation, because traditional practices *by themselves* are not oppositional to the dominant culture and so are not likely to encourage decolonization. In hotels at Waikīkī, say, or on the stages at the Polynesian Cultural Center, traditional practices such as kahiko hula or pule (prayers) to Pele act not as subversions but as commercial entertainment for tourists. It is thus necessary for at least some Kanaka Maoli to effectively learn and employ monorhetoric, embracing the second rhetorical situation, to re-present traditional Hawaiian practices as alternatives to the dominant culture.

It is important for non-Natives within the first rhetorical situation to try to construct oppositional analyses as well, for, as Trask acknowledges, Native peoples probably cannot "resist the planned New World Order by ourselves."[23] Non-Natives are faced with the complicated task of trying to champion alternative Native practices while simultaneously straining to resist the imperialism woven into this monorhetoric. Dirlik and Wilson describe this project as a "critical localism," a program of nourishing "alternative spaces, sub-languages, and local identities grounded in the otherwise and elsewhere."[24] Ashis Nandy's championing of "critical traditionalism" presents an important related program. Nandy insists it is essential that we nourish multiple, alternative, dissenting traditions in "the peripheries of the world where . . . the subjects of anthropology, as opposed to the anthropologists, live."[25] Each of these alternatives must draw upon its own past cultural practices while simultaneously and self-consciously constructing new practices that actively resist Euroamerican definitions of the ethical and real. Nandy points to Gandhi as an exemplar, for Gandhi aggressively marshaled elements of the Indian tradition to construct both a critique of and an alternative to Anglo colonialism.[26] Abdul R. JanMohamed amplifies Nandy's argument in his interview with S. X. Goudie. According to JanMohamed, "In critical theory today there is a large premium on the celebration of differences, which is all very well in itself; nonetheless, unless you articulate antagonisms, unless you identify the stakes and the issues along which lines are going to be drawn, you are not going to have any kind of political movement."[27]

The challenge is especially daunting for Euroamericans who hope to encourage the growth of multiple, separate, critical localisms worldwide. Such scholars must work to clear a space for this plurality of alternative practices but simultaneously avoid representing these practices in the same monorhetorical "categories and systems of knowledge" that, as Nandy remarks, underwrite a continuing Euroamerican hegemony as effectively as "naked political and economic powers."[28] The process of colonization has, after all, often been accompanied by Euroamerican "good intentions" toward Natives that, in practice, did much to hasten their colonization. The contemporary cultural critic's intention to assist Native critical localisms seems just as likely to result in a further valorization of the power and rhetoric of Euroamericans.

Paul Carter's influential *The Road to Botany Bay: An Exploration of Landscape and History* provides a cautionary example. Carter persuasively argues that most histories of Pacific places deny what Carter refers to as "the plural nature of historical space."[29] When confronted with multiple versions, stories, myths, and histories, whether enunciated by Euroamericans or Natives, imperial history turns to procedures that reduce the cacophony of versions to a single "most accurate" account. According to Carter, the resulting mononarrative is then claimed to be the best match with a supposed reality that is asserted to exist independent of the procedures that produced it.

Carter develops an alternative, poststructuralist approach based on the premise that Euroamerican explorers and colonizers in the Pacific created places through their "intentional" cultural practices. Carter concludes, "In truth, the 'objects' of nature did not 'present themselves': rather, they remained invisible and had to be distinguished by the intentional gaze" (305). Though, for example, the rhetoric of the elite class differed substantially from that of convicts and Aborigines, Carter shows that the elite ignored or appropriated parts of convict and Aboriginal narratives to manufacture a single, official, imperial geography and history that the elite then claimed encompassed all of what could be reasonably accepted as real.

There is much value in Carter's approach as well as in the work of many others who are similarly building poststructuralist critiques of colonialism. These critiques, as Carter's book shows, encourage an increased appreciation of the alternative local truths and places created both by Native peoples and by the many nonelite Euroamerican groups who have been systematically ignored or disparaged by imperial histories.

Still, this method presents dangers in its (often implied) claim that all spaces are equally arbitrary human inventions. The method may seem to suggest, for example, that Native Hawaiians created one local place in the islands, imperial historians and Euroamerican colonists another, and more recent immigrants yet another. Such a method implies that there can be no grounds for preferring one rhetorical construction of one place over another, since all places are "merely" the sum of the cultural acts of one group or another.

Ahmad Aijaz, Arif Dirlik, Anne McClintock, Benita Parry, and Robert J.C. Young, among many others, have explored the reactionary implications of histories written within this or similar perspectives.[30] When, for example, Carter claims that "reality" is a "turbulent, unpredictable, rebellious" space, he espouses a metaphysics that can be traced back to Hobbes, and probably earlier. This metaphysics denies the validity of alternative claims about primordial reality contained in the traditions of Native Pacific peoples. Whether one describes these different views in Carter's terms as a difference between solitary or multiple places, or one uses a more general vocabulary to speak of structuralism against poststructuralism, or modernism versus postmodernism, in all cases the discussion remains remote from both traditional and contemporary Pacific islander concerns.

Although structuralism, modernism, and humanism are usually condemned for being context bound and partial, the newer, poststructuralist perspectives falsely pretend to have escaped this myopia. Those in Hawai'i today who participate in this debate often make imperious claims that probably sound as Eurocentric to some Natives as did earlier modernist analyses. Controversies over structuralism and poststructuralism, linear histories and plural histories, however clever and interesting to Euroamerican-trained readers, do little in themselves to encourage decolonization. Such discussions do not invite Native Hawaiian people or issues to become more prominent in the islands' intellectual and cultural life.[31]

Because poststructuralism as a universalizing methodology undermines Native Hawaiian claims, I use it in these pages mostly as a method for interrogating the cultural tradition from which it arose. In looking for substantial alternatives to colonialism, I treat with grave suspicion all Euroamerican cultural traditions, no matter how progressive or liberating they claim to be. As Nandy reminds us, "One day there will have to be post-modern societies and a post-modern consciousness, and those societies and that consciousness may choose to build not so much upon modernity as on the traditions of the non-modern or pre-modern world."[32] In Hawai'i, surely, it is best to insist that the people who have inhabited these Pacific islands for several thousand years lead in forging this new society and consciousness.

Chapter Two

ᐧ

Captain James Cook, Rhetorician

Apotheosis it was. Making Cook a God it was. But it was Europeans who made
Cook a God, not the Hawaiians.

Herb Kawainui Kane[1]

Seldom has any book published in any country at any time created more excitement than did *A Voyage to the Pacific Ocean*, which appeared in print in London
four years after Captain James Cook's two ships *Discovery* and *Resolution* returned home.[2] The initial, four-volume edition of two thousand copies sold out in
three days, and second and third editions swiftly followed. Pirated editions were
soon generally available, and a French translation in 1785 excited Parisian readers. Public forums and newspapers could not seem to satisfy the demand for opportunities to discuss the volumes. Plays loosely based on the reported events
filled London theaters.

The eighteenth-century excitement was so great that historians in our own century remain affected by the hyperbolic prose that was associated with these events.
So, for example, Anthony Murray-Oliver gushes about these 1784 volumes that
through them the "whole civilized world thrilled to the vicarious voyaging so
many took with Cook."[3] O. A. Bushnell's recent account is only slightly less ef-
fusive: "Once again, as after his first two voyages, in an effusion of Polynesian-
mania, London's versifiers, playwrights, composers, and dancing masters, drawing more upon fancy than upon knowledge, produced a spate of epics, odes, and
elegies, gaudy pantomimes, dramatic spectacles, and grand ballets, in which the
brave deeds and gory murder of Captain Cook were the dominant themes."[4]

It was already well known in England and Europe prior to the volumes' publication that Cook had been killed by the so-called Indians of Hawai'i. Cook's official artist, John Webber, had issued his watercolor of Cook's death as a mass-
produced engraving in 1782. This image, as David W. Forbes points out,
extensively "mythologized what actually occurred."[5] Though he had not witnessed the stabbing, Webber continued in this watercolor the careful practice

21

shown in his other images; Forbes explains he depicted "Cook as the embodiment of the enlightened eighteenth-century explorer in his ceremonial progress through the Pacific" (18–19). Webber's *The Death of Cook* (see Figure 2.1) focuses on a Cook dressed in white and not in the canvas he actually wore. He stands on a beach, although there was no beach at Ka'awaloa. Webber's martyr offers his vulnerable back to a mob of fierce, armed Hawaiians. He raises a naked hand in an effort to order his own men to cease firing. As Forbes concludes, Webber thus skillfully represents Cook "as a victim of his own humanity" (54).[6]

Webber's engraving, released two years before the official volumes appeared, helped make those few sections of the volumes that described Hawai'i of particular interest. Authorship of the first two volumes was ascribed to Cook, and the third volume detailing Cook's death and the subsequent return home of the two ships was offered as the writing of James King, who took command of the *Discovery* after Cook's second in command, Charles Clerke, also died.

Though now more than two hundred years old, Webber's many images remain among the most influential representations of Hawai'i ever produced. The folio volume, titled *An Atlas of Illustrations*, contained the still often-reprinted plates that were based mostly on Webber's watercolors and drawings. (Webber's already famous *The Death of Cook* was not offered as part of this volume. Forbes speculates that the Admiralty might have decided that the plate would detract from the impact of the others depicting Cook as the master of his domain.) In *European*

Figure 2.1   *The Death of Captain Cook* by **John Webber**

Reprinted with permission of the Dixson Galleries, State Library of New South Wales, Sydney.

Vision and the South Pacific, the pioneering and still standard work on this eighteenth- and nineteenth-century art, Bernard Smith argues that Webber's work became "the chief source for illustrations concerning the Pacific in all kinds of publications—travel books, geography texts, missionary tracts, and articles on the Pacific in journals, newspapers, encyclopedias of costume and exotic wallpapers."[7] While Smith focuses on Webber's overwhelming impact in earlier centuries, art historian Forbes surveys the twentieth century and maintains that the 1784 Webber-inspired plates "so effectively fixed in the minds of the world the image of the Hawaiian islands at the period of first contact with the West that popular knowledge of Hawaiian culture is still largely dependent on his drawings and watercolors and the engravings made from them" (7). It is only in several of Webber's drawings, for example, that it is possible to view examples of the Kanaka Maoli helmet that has become such a prominent icon in contemporary Hawai'i. Webber's representations associate this helmet with Lono, a god of the season of peace, but most modern reproductions on T-shirts and hanging from the mirrors of cars link the helmet with warriors.[8]

Forbes probably overestimates Webber's influence, but it does seem clear that Cook and King's 1784 text as well as Webber's illustrations continue to impact contemporary perceptions of Hawai'i. It may be useful then, and not merely for historical reasons, to interrogate the assumptions upon which these first representations of the islands were built.

In a search for titillation, many early readers probably skipped directly to King's pages describing Cook's demise. Interest in Cook's death was so great that numerous artists and playwrights produced multiple versions of the event. Fascination with it has remained so strong that at the close of the twentieth century one still finds new accounts appearing. Most prominent of late has been a quarrel between the anthropologists Gananeth Obeyesekere and Marshall Sahlins over what Hawaiians were thinking as they killed Cook.[9] That Cook, a foreigner, remains the focus of this dispute among scholars supposedly interested in Hawaiians illustrates how narcissistic Euroamerican scholarship remains. One cannot imagine these metropolitan scholars becoming as exercised over the still unresolved issue of what Kamehameha was thinking as Keōua was killed at the dedication of Pu'u Kohola Heiau near Kawaihae in 1791. Yet the consequences of this event were far more consequential for the people then living in Hawai'i than the death of an English captain.[10]

Though hundreds of Euroamerican scholars and many thousands of pages have examined Cook's death, there has been no Euroamerican interest in any century in the Hawaiian man that Cook murdered shortly before he himself was killed.[11] There has been, likewise, next to no writing or discussion even in contemporary Hawai'i about the dozens of unarmed women, children, and men that were slaughtered and dismembered by the English in the twenty-four hours after Cook died.

This disproportionate interest in Euroamerican subjects and subjectivities is a constant in the two hundred–year tradition of Euroamerican representations of

Hawai'i. It is a reminder of why it is useful to view foreign representations of Hawai'i like the comparable early cultural productions of the Americas, productions Stephen Greenblatt describes as "representations that are relational, local and historically contingent. Their overriding interest is not knowledge of the other but practice upon the other."[12]

FASHIONING RATIONALITY

It is not only through their obsessive self-absorption that Euroamerican representations expose their inadequacy. The very practice of composing descriptions of the other is best understood not as a method of knowledge production but as a method of fashioning a particular, historically situated "self." Cook, for example, used several rhetorical techniques in what Paul Carter calls his "explorer's discourse."[13] Carter focuses on a single technique, on the ways that Cook's naming practices created a geographical space into which later explorers, merchants, and settlers could venture with confidence. Carter points out that Cook's very first act of naming in the Pacific produced an island called "New Island" because, Cook explained in his log, "it is not laid down in any chart."[14] Such a name emphasizes its "firstness" for Cook and Anglo-Europeans and ignores any qualities of the island itself. As Carter observes, "It is a name that refuses to admit the place was there before it was named, a name that celebrates the travelling mode of knowledge" (9). Cook's hundreds of Pacific namings, along with the explanations he offered in journal and log, helped transform the Pacific for Euroamericans from a vast empty space into a place with a history defined by its relationship to England. The central players in that history were not the peoples who had inhabited it for millennia, but rather the newly arrived Englishmen and, particularly, Cook himself. Giving names with Anglo-European stories attached asserted both Cook's own and later Euroamericans' rights to return, to continue the personal and nationalistic narrative Cook began.

Placing these newly bestowed names in the then-still-experimental grid of longitudes and latitudes constituted yet another rhetorical technique to assist in taking possession. The anchor of all Cook's mapping, the prime meridian, refers his discoveries back to England, to Greenwich. Other European navigators would for many decades to come fix this arbitrary point in their own countries, but all, like Cook, anchored their grids in a Eurocentrism that, as R. Douglas Herman points out, encouraged a fetishizing of mathematics while de-emphasizing intimacy with particular Pacific places. Longitudes and latitudes allowed explorers like Cook to write continents and thousand-mile-long archipelagos into their geographic grids without having to step off their boats, without having to meet or learn one thing from the Native peoples who had thousands of years of histories and names for these places.[15]

Cook arranged his journal entries by date, and this sequencing operates as another powerful rhetorical device within his explorer's discourse. For example, under the heading "January 19" in the portion of the journal describing events of

1778, Cook writes of his unanticipated sighting of Hawai'i: "At this time we were in some doubt whether or no the land before [us][16] was inhabited, this doubt was soon cleared up, by seeing some Canoes coming off from the shore towards the Ships."[17] Cook's use of dates as an organizing principle encourages readers to feel as if they are experiencing Cook's travels in linear time, presumably just as he experienced them. This January 19 entry places readers inside Cook's head as he wonders about the possibility that there are inhabitants of this newly discovered land. Readers then seem to watch him as time unfolds and "this doubt" is "cleared up" in the sighting of canoes. A sense of immediacy for readers of the journals is amplified by Cook's tendency to write nearly daily entries and to include within them such copious and minor details, often of interest only to future Pacific sea captains, that readers are encouraged to assume they are being provided with a thorough record of everything important Cook thought and saw.

These senses of immediacy, of dailiness, and of completeness are, in fact, artifacts of Cook's considerable rhetorical art. The journal entries are indeed arranged by dates, but the journal was not in fact written daily. Instead, Cook's biographer J.C. Beaglehole concludes, Cook made notes, then drafts, borrowed from the writing of various others, then carefully crafted further revisions before finally inscribing his journal with prose he knew would be read by others.

Cook's notes and drafts for his third voyage have not survived but, as Beaglehole details in his lecture *Cook the Writer*, the manuscripts remaining from Cook's previous voyages into the Pacific make the impressive progress of Cook's apprenticeship as a writer very clear. On his first voyage, Cook had kept a log "with details of the winds and the ship's behaviour and management," as well as a separate column of events deemed worthy of remark.[18] These compositions were awkward, leaving little doubt Cook "was not a natural-born writer" (6). Cook's log was later expanded into a rough written journal; upon Cook's return, this text and the journals of several others on the voyage were given to John Hawkesworth, who was charged with turning the crude prose of seamen into volumes fit for polite society.

On his second voyage, Beaglehole shows, Cook began shaping his log and his journal differently, with more self-consciousness—aware as he had not been on the first voyage that his shipboard writing would likely later become the basis for a book. Cook wrote and revised much more on the second than he had on the first voyage, as Beaglehole summarizes, "drafting and redrafting, expanding, abbreviating and recasting, correction, substitution, interlineation, a million words or so" (12). Some of these manuscripts were turned over to John Douglas, Canon of Windsor, who further revised, added and edited them into a book. Douglas was still revising the proofs for this manuscript to be published under Cook's name as Cook left England on his third voyage. And so, Beaglehole argues, Cook's method of composition on his final voyage was shaped even more by Cook's determination to return with a final draft that would leave Douglas with little to complain about or change. Cook, no longer content simply to be an explorer, aimed to prove himself to be an author and a gentleman as well. He now understood how his future reputation would be based not so much on what he did on his voyages as on what he and others had written about them. The result, in Beaglehole's words, was "a far cry indeed from the journal of his first voyage to this sophisticated document."[19] Cook's entries representing Hawai'i, then, are no more spontaneous descriptions or casual diary entries than were such other eighteenth-century prose observations as Sterne's *A Sentimental Journey* or Boswell's *Life of Samuel Johnson*, each written about the same time.

Cook's composition apprenticeship included studying and copying into his own journal the writings of others on his voyages. He borrowed from his subordinates—Joseph Banks in his first voyage, William Wales on his second, and from William Anderson on his third. Each of these men had had more formal education and practice in writing polite prose. From each, Beaglehole maintains, Cook learned tricks of the writer's craft as he copied lengthy passages from their writings into his journal.

In addition to this work of imitation, we know Cook gradually learned how to make extensive, "improving" revisions. The length of time Cook took refining his prose on his final voyage seems to have been at least as long as a month, for the last entry in his journal is dated January 17, 1779, four weeks before he died. (Beaglehole observes that the probable multiple versions of notes and revisions Cook had collected preparatory to making these entries seem to have been lost soon after his two ships returned to England.) The surviving drafts reveal Cook scrupulously shaped his compositions by omitting or, in later drafts, removing, most references to his personal thoughts and feelings. As Beaglehole concludes, "Only very rarely did Cook's irritations seep through to his journals" (cliii). Cook's drafts (see Figure 2.2 for a sample) instead show that he fashioned himself to be a creature without desires, pains, hungers and prejudices, as a kind of objective recording machine, as the kind of man that the new Anglo-European science was starting to claim produced universal knowledge.

Beaglehole concludes that Cook probably had planned to revise substantially his entire journal one final time on the long, usually uneventful sail home (clxxiv). Death interrupted this plan, but the draft did receive radical revisioning by Douglas before publication of the 1784 volumes that took Europe by such a storm. Douglas relied much on Anderson's journal, often printing long passages from Anderson as Cook's own. Douglas further added whatever details he thought felicitous or appropriate for Cook's image. Sometimes, as Beaglehole points out, it seems Douglas used Cook's original text as "merely a springboard" (cc). It was Douglas and not Cook or Anderson, for example, who composed what has often been referred to as Cook's final entry before his death, the claim that the discovery of the Sandwich Islands "seemed, in many respects, to be the most important that had hitherto been made by Europeans, throughout the extent of the Pacific Ocean."[20] It was Douglas, as well, who composed most of the passage attributed to Cook I quoted above offering praise of Anderson and Webber. In his journal Cook had written simply: "I left the command to Mr. Williamson who was with me and took a walk up the Valley, accompanied by Dr. Anderson and Mr.

Figure 2.2   A page from Cook's journal

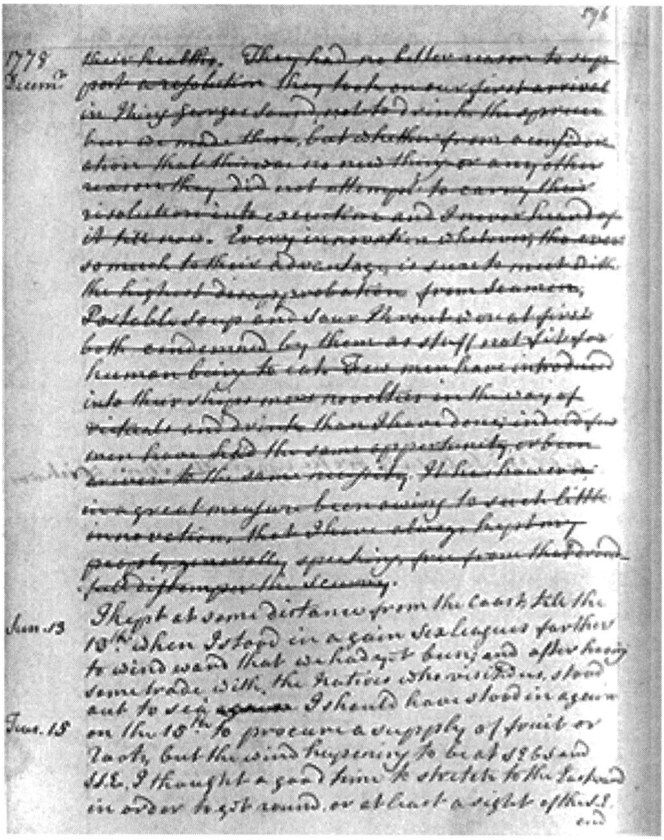

By permission of The British Library, MS Egerton 2177A, f596.

Webber; conducted by one of the Natives and attended by a tolerable train."[21] Douglas revises "walk" to "excursion," expands "up the Valley" to "into the country, up the valley," and attributes to Cook entirely from Douglas's imagination the claim that Anderson and Webber were "well-qualified" with pen and pencil to represent every thing "worthy of observation." Since Cook could not protest, Beaglehole speculates, Douglas felt free to change as much as he wished.

Still, Douglas's revisions share Cook's own general aim to fashion the journals into a trustworthy, gentleman-explorer's discourse. Both writers labored to ensure that the resulting volumes pleased their sponsors in the Admiralty, enticed book buyers, and constructed Cook as a judicious, rational, and heroic man. In each of these aims, the 1784 volumes and the many supporting images (see Figure 2.3) succeeded so spectacularly that now, even at the end of the twentieth century, Cook remains a hero to many throughout the world.

Figure 2.3   *The Apotheosis of Captain Cook* **from a design of P. J. De Loutherbourg, 1794**

Reprinted with permission of the Bishop Museum.

REFASHIONING COOK

A fundamentally different, unheroic representation of Cook appears, however, in the journals and logs composed by those who accompanied Cook on his final voyage. At least thirty of the one hundred eighty men on the two ships on Cook's last voyage at one time or another were busy scribbling in their own logs or journals in apparent hopes of one day cashing in on the notoriety that Cook had won during his first two trips to the Pacific.[22] Some of these texts (William Anderson's, for example) seem to have been as carefully crafted as were Cook's. Most, however, were likely written only once and left unrevised. In composite, these disparate texts depict Cook not as a dispassionate machine producing universal knowledge but rather as a man growing increasingly irrational, unreliable, and violent as a long, frustrating journey stretches on and on.

For example, though Cook's journal makes a pretense of offering an extensive, daily and complete account of his stay in Tonga, Cook's journal and, of course,

Douglas's revised version omit to mention what some others do: how, for petty thievery, Cook ordered one Tongan's ear cut off, another's arm to be mangled, and yet others to be whipped with several dozens of lashes—though, according to British admiralty rules, only twelve lashes per day were legal for seamen. Midshipman George Gilbert wrote about these incidents in his journal:

> Capt. Cook punished in a manner rather unbecoming of a European viz: by cutting off their ears; fireing at them with small shot, or ball, as they were swimming or paddling to the shore and suffering the people [ship's crew] . . . to beat them with the oars, and stick the boat hook into them where ever they could hit them; one in particular he punished by ordering one of our people to make two cuts upon his arm to the bone once across [sic] the other close below his shoulder.[23]

About these events in his revised journal, Cook reported only that "as the crowd was always so great I would not allow the sentries to fire lest the innocent should suffer for the guilty" (132). After days and perhaps weeks of drafting and revising, Cook chose here to lie about what he ordered the sentries to do because, we can surmise, he wished to fashion his image in his journals as a man who acted judiciously.

Weeks later, Cook wrote about events on the island of Moorea that he had twice "sent the Carpenters to break up three or four Canoes" (231) of the Natives as punishment for stealing one goat from him. Alternative accounts by three other witnesses illustrate again how carefully Cook revised his journal to shape his image. William Harvey, the master's mate, wrote in his log that Captain Cook had not simply broken a few canoes but had destroyed the Chief's house and his canoes, "then march'd along shore burning all the Houses and Canoes they met with till they arrived at the Place where the boats lay to take them in, they burnt in all 20 houses and 18 large War Canoes some of which row'd 100 to 200 paddles" (231–232).[24]

Murder was the first notable act of Cook's men after their "discovery" of Kaua'i. The people of Kaua'i seem to have been curious about these strange new men and ships, likely the first of their type that they had ever seen. As William Bayly, the ship's astronomer and an eyewitness to the killing, wrote in his log, it did not seem that the group of Hawaiians that Cook's men attacked "had any ill intention, but rather the contrary. They being over eager to Assist us, in landing thro' the surf" (267n). Nonetheless, John Williamson, the *Resolution*'s third lieutenant, aimed and fired his gun. Cook once again revised his journal to repress any suggestion that he lacked rational control, reporting that Williamson "was obliged to fire, by which one man was killed" (267). Cook's careful choice of "was obliged" turns Williamson's active murder into a passive, suggesting Williamson was forced to kill a man whose only mistake was being "over eager to Assist."[25]

On February 14, 1779, before dawn, Cook once more prepared his men and himself to attack unarmed and friendly Natives. Aboard their ship anchored in

Kealakekua Bay, Cook ordered nine marines to load their muskets with ball rather than with small shot. Shot, at worst, inflicted horrible abrasions, painful and difficult to heal in the humid tropics. Ball, however, as Cook and his men knew, was usually lethal. Cook led his band in a raid on the settlement ashore, though the people there had made it clear to Cook they no longer welcomed such visits. Cook kidnapped for ransom Kalaniʻōpuʻu, a chief who had earlier shown Cook much kindness. Cook was about to load Kalaniʻōpuʻu into a boat to take him away when the Hawaiians standing nearby received news that elsewhere a separate gang of Cook's had murdered Kalimu, another Hawaiian chief. The bystanders, anxious for the safety of Kalaniʻōpuʻu, began to insist that Cook release him. Cook refused and fired a shot at close range at one Hawaiian, who was not much injured because of the thick mats he wore about his chest. Soon after, as Beaglehole tells the tale, "Cook fired his other barrel, loaded with ball, and killed a man."[26]

Pacific scholars have little discussed Cook's murderous act yet they have lavished attention for two hundred years on the fact that, soon after shooting this man, Cook himself was killed. The first official version appeared before the Anglo-European public in the supposed words of Captain James King, in the third volume of the 1784 book that created such a sensation throughout Europe. King's version of Cook's death, like the hundreds that followed and that continue to appear, omits even an allusion to the massacre that Cook's crew inflicted on the Hawaiians to memorialize their Captain's death. At least five chiefs were immediately killed in retaliation, as well as about twenty-five other Kanaka Maoli. John Law, the ship's surgeon whom Beaglehole describes as a "fair, able and humane mind" (cxc), witnessed the events and wrote, "Natives who stayed In their Houses were run thro' by Bayonets & some poor People Making their Escape were Shot" (562). Afterwards, Law continues, "when they had Murdered these Defenceless people they severed the heads and stuck them on the boats as Trophies" (563). Such behavior, of course, undermines the image of Cook that he and his sponsors wished to disseminate throughout the Anglo-European world. This trophy killing and marauding has been similarly absent from the many representations of Cook and of his work that by 1975 had led, by Anthony Murray-Oliver's count, to the erection of more than two hundred statues and memorials to Cook around the earth, "so widespread and lasting is the world's admiration of the great man."[27]

Beaglehole, a great admirer of Cook, was apprehensive that his twentieth-century publication of the various contemporary collateral logs and journals would subvert the gentleman-sailor image that Cook and Douglas first constructed, an image that Beaglehole himself had made a career out of buttressing. ("He was the genius of the matter of fact," Beaglehole proclaims toward the end of Cook's journal [698].) Beaglehole even inserted a two hundred–page apologia as his "Introduction" to the third volume of the journals in an attempt to establish a preemptive explanation for the troubling images the writing of Cook's companions presents. Beaglehole argues his "thesis," as he calls it, that Cook started the third voyage "already a tired man."[28] Cook had not sufficiently recovered from his first two voyages, Beaglehole maintains, and was in poor mental health. This caused the usually rational Captain to make mistakes, at Tonga, Moorea, and Kealakekua Bay, places where Beaglehole argues we can see Cook acting "completely out of character" (cxi) and/or experiencing a "temporary displacement of character" (cliv). Here is a sample of how Beaglehole elaborates this defense:

> the inner tensions of an able mind were set up, and exacerbated. We have a man tired . . . with that almost imperceptible blunting of the rain that makes him, under a light searching enough, a perceptibly rather different man. His apprehensions as a discoverer were not so constantly fine as they had been; his understanding of other minds was not so ready or sympathetic. It was not to be expected that at Kealakekua Bay in February 1779 he should be more subtly master of events, more imaginatively calculating, than he was in Tonga in June 1778. (cliv)

The normal Cook, Beaglehole insists, had an "able mind" and "constantly fine" apprehensions that produced decisions and knowledge that any "reasonable" person in the same situation would recognize as objective. This careful, reasonable man survived within Cook sufficiently for him to pen the third voyage's masterfully controlled journal. When he was not writing, however, according to Beaglehole, a "blunting" caused by fatigue led Cook to leave the realm of reason, to invade lands, cut off ears, administer lashes to people who had never before seen a whip, to burn houses and canoes, to kidnap friendly chiefs, and to murder men trying to protect their beloved chiefs.

Beaglehole's apologia of Cook's rationality invites a thought experiment. Suppose one reverses the roles of the actors in these events. Imagine invaders coming unprovoked to Beaglehole's island, New Zealand. Suppose, with no declaration of war or warning, they burn Beaglehole's house and church, infect his daughters with syphilis, kidnap his father and murder several of Beaglehole's friends. Beaglehole suggests such behavior need not alter our understanding of the invader's "constantly fine" and "able mind" if we understand that this invader is fatigued and under strain. Because Cook was suffering these maladies, Beaglehole advises, even Cook's victims should accept his journal as an honorable and accurate account of Hawaiians and of the other Native peoples he encountered.[29]

SCIENTIFIC COLONIALISM

Viewing Cook, then, not as he writes himself but as he is written about by his shipmates undermines Cook's claims to be a reliable and rational observer. Similarly, when one looks at European arts and sciences in general, not as they present themselves but as they appear when viewed within a broader context, their related claims to universality also appear to be situated.

It is commonly claimed, for example, that Cook's voyages were intended to add to the body of knowledge about world geography, flora, and fauna. The full title of those sensational 1784 volumes included the explanation that the third voyage was undertaken "for making Discoveries in the Northern Hemisphere." The first sentence of the "secret instructions" Cook was given shortly before he left England even seem to support this view, as it states it is "his Majesty's pleasure, that an attempt should be made to find a Northern passage by sea from the Pacific to the Atlantic Ocean."[30] This declaration can be read as suggesting a certain interest in increasing geographical knowledge, though, of course, the commercial and military benefits of such a sea passage were paramount to those funding the voyage. Little in the rest of these secret instructions suggests any interest whatsoever in advancing knowledge, for, once a course and timetable are set, the orders focus almost exclusively on politics. Cook is instructed on how he should deal with "any part of the Spanish dominions" and with "any of the inhabitants or subjects of his Catholic majesty" (ccxxi). He is to keep himself hidden from them, if at all possible, or, if contact is made, to use every means to avoid provoking a war.[31]

Cook's secret orders also direct him to collect "accurate Observations of the nature hereafter mentioned that have not already been made . . . as far as your time will allow" (ccxxii–ccxxiii). The "nature hereafter mentioned" focuses on information that might be useful for future colonies. "You are also, with the consent of the natives, *to take possession*, in the name of the King of Great Britain, of convenient situations in such countries as you may discover . . . but if you find the countries so discovered are uninhabited, you are *to take possession* of them for his majesty, by setting up proper marks and inscriptions, as first discoverers and possessors" (ccxxiii, emphasis added).

Cook followed orders: He took possession of several lands by leaving inscriptions on trees, rocks, and in bottles, and by carefully recording in his journal the dates and locations of these symbols. He took discursive possession as well by placing every site in a grid of latitude and longitude that asserted Greenwich, England, as the cardinal center of the earth. Furthermore, Cook took possession by giving English names to hundreds of Native places and dozens of Native peoples. Strikingly, in fact, Cook's meticulously composed journals describe no single activity more often than Cook's proclamation of what, henceforth, the prominent features of the Pacific should be called.[32]

England's need for new possessions seemed especially acute at the time the three commissioners of the admiralty were composing Cook's secret orders. As Cook sailed from England in July of 1776, British warships were also preparing to sail to confront the troublesome terrorists in the American colonies where earlier explorers, too, had practiced both symbolic and violent acts of possession. War with the American colonists and with the French would erupt as Cook completed his assigned tasks.[33] This context suggests why there was so much expense and secrecy in sending Cook out on yet a third voyage. This perspective also makes more understandable why Douglas in the Cook and King volume would compose for Cook's final journal entry the declaration that the discovery of Hawai'i was "the most important that had hitherto been made by Europeans, throughout the extent of the Pacific Ocean."[34] Douglas makes this claim on Cook's behalf not because of Hawai'i's size, for New Zealand and Australia were known to be larger, nor because of Hawai'i's natural resources, for other places were more amply endowed. Hawai'i's importance was based on its strategic placement as a site for supplying ships on the way to the new Pacific rim colonies England's rulers desired. These new colonies were expected to and indeed did become of paramount importance to imperial England in the nineteenth century after its loss of a large chunk of North America.

Cook was ordered to collect knowledge "as far as your time will allow," but even this part-time occupation was to focus on the acquisition of information that might help establish new colonies and defeat England's Euroamerican enemies. The penultimate paragraph of Cook's orders illustrates rather directly how Cook's work was to aid England's military pursuits: "Upon your arrival in England, you are immediately to repair to this office, in order to lay before us a full account of your proceedings in the whole course of the voyage; taking care, before you leave the sloop, to demand from the officers and petty officers, the log-books and journals they may have kept, and to seal them up for our inspection; and enjoining them, and the whole crew, not to divulge where they have been, until they shall have permission so to do" (ccxxiv). This emphasis on secrecy undermines both the eighteenth- and twentieth-century representations of Cook as a man engaged in the disinterested pursuit of knowledge. The writing of the officers and of the petty officers had to be confiscated and all of them enjoined to silence, for the goal of Cook's so-called scientific work was to use it as a means for symbolically and physically taking "possession, in the name of the King of Great Britain, of convenient situations in such countries as you may discover."[35]

COOK'S MASTER NARRATIVE

Even as Cook fashioned his journal into a careful narrative of Anglo-European superiority, many of Cook's own men mocked this viewpoint. These seamen, and a few of the officers, maintained against Cook's official view that it was not the English but Pacific peoples who possessed a superior life. A few of Cook's men deserted, and many others began to plot desertion, even though such an act likely meant they would never be able to see their own native land or families again.

The danger from desertions became so great at Raiatea, a little over two months before the ships arrived off Kaua'i, that when two men deserted ship on November 24, 1777, Cook wrote in his journal, "As these were not the only two persons in the Ships who wanted to end their days at these islands, it was necessary in order to put a stop to further desertion to have them got back at all events"

(247).[36] Cook sent massive, armed parties to search for and arrest the deserters. When these searches failed, Cook himself went with even more men. He also called the officers and crew of both ships together, an important event that, like many others, Cook carefully omits mentioning in his writing. Luckily, Alexander Home, master's mate of the *Discovery*, wrote in his journal at length that "upon the discovery of this spirit of desertion Captain Cook Turned his men up and Made a Long speech on th[a]t head. He Made use both of Entreateys and Threats and with a Deal of Art and Eloquence. . . . Amoungst Other things he told them they Might run off if they pleased. But they might Depend upon it he would Recover them again."[37]

Home's account of Cook's speech continues with mention of several of the specific threats Cook made. Home ends with a summary of Cook's final words: "They Might fly," Cook told the men, "if they please to Omiah King Ottou or to the Most distant Country known to these people. His authority would bring them back and Dead or Alive he'd have them" (cxiii). Home concludes, "Every man was Convinced and how so ever great Our inclination Might be to taste of these Joys and Bliss that seemed More than Mortal all hopes was now given over" (cxiv).

History in the Anglo-American tradition is still written mostly by scholars who identify with Cook and the educated and propertied classes who funded him. So, for example, such historians analyze Cook's death endlessly, yet rarely mention the fact that four marines died beside their Captain that same morning at Kealakekua. These writers, and most of their readers, naturalize the class inequities upon which Anglo-European explorations depended. Cook's crew, however, like the majority in England and Europe in that time, had little reason to identify with the narrative of Western superiority offered by their Captain and his titled sponsors. Hunger, poverty, conscription, and threats of imprisonment—not hopes for wealth and titles—forced most of Cook's crew to endure his long and dangerous voyages. These men had little reason to suspect they would ever experience much "Joy and Bliss" in their homeland. Thus it was not by appealing to his crew's sense of English superiority but rather through repeated lashings and threats of death that Cook kept his crew from mass desertions.

Though Cook knew better than to try to share his narrative of English magnificence with his own crew, he nonetheless offered it (as best he could, with limited language skills) to try to convince Pacific Islanders to submit. Cook's recurring accounts of his usually futile attempts to impress Pacific Islanders make much of his journal read today like a Shandian farce, though it is clear Cook himself little experienced the humor.

For example, Cook—at considerable expense and bother—stuffed a bulky, ravenous, and odorous menagerie of animals onto his two ships. This collection included mares and stallions, heifers and bulls, sheep, goats, rabbits, and poultry, "all of them," in Cook's words, "intended for New Zealand, Otahetie and the neighbouring islands, or any other place we might meet, where there was a prospect that the leaving of some of them might prove usefull to posterity."[38] The "posterity" Cook had in mind was mostly that resulting from his fellow country-men who would later come on English war and merchant ships and would need food supplies. He knew that the Pacific Islanders themselves already had plenty of their own foods to eat. It was for future countrymen that for over a year Cook forced his unhappy crew of one hundred and eighty to share a tiny living space with large and small animals. At each landfall these same men were required to row the stock ashore and back again, so the animals could forage.

Cook expected the Natives to be awed by his four-legged presents, for they were the centerpiece of his effort to convince Pacific Islanders of the preeminence of Europeans. Many animals died, however, before they could be given away, and many others, once given, were promptly eaten by those Pacific Islanders who received them. As a symbol of his largess and superiority, Cook's troublesome menagerie proved nearly useless. Cook's journals several times lament that though the islanders liked iron and other Anglo-European trinkets, they valued anything red—and red feathers even more. Cook acknowledges he gained some credit among various islanders for acting as an interisland ferry for feathers, but he was displeased to be associated with a narrative that assigned him value principally as a middleman in trade for an item with no intrinsic connection to Anglo-Europeans.

Just as Anglo-European products and animals seldom buttressed the story Cook offered Natives about his supposed superiority, so, too, did Anglo customs and arts generally make a disappointing impact as well. About Tahiti, for example, Cook complains, "Europeans have visited them at times for these ten years past, yet we find neither new arts nor improvement in the old, nor have they copied after us in any one thing" (241).

Cook sometimes tried to support his narrative of Anglo-European supremacy by firing off guns, but even this noise seldom impressed. He and his men were quick to murder Natives, too, as we have remarked, but, again, the results were disappointing. Pacific Islanders seemed to have believed that they already possessed an adequate array of methods for ending lives, so Cook's way of murdering did not strike them as a particularly consequential innovation.

Cook's successes at impressing the Natives are so few that his journal exults when they do occur. He reports excitedly that the Natives in Tahiti had a "Very great surprise and astonishment" to see him ride a horse: "It was afterwards continued every day by one or another so long as we stayed and yet their curiosity was not then satisfied; they were exceedingly delighted with these Animals after they had seen the use that was made of them and I think they gave them a better idea of the greatness of other Nations than all the other things put together that had been carried amongst them" (209). So great was Cook's pleasure that he writes here with no awareness of the absurdity of his equating his supposed superiority—"the greatness of other Nations"—to the display of sailors riding a few, half-starved horses.

One of Cook's favorite demonstrations of Euroamerican magnificence depended upon displays of a Chinese art. As he writes of some "sky and Water Rockets" set off in Tonga, Natives were "astonished and pleased . . . beyond measure and [the fireworks] intirely turned the scale in our favour" (110). Unfortunately for Cook, by the time he was blown to Hawai'i, he had used up most of his pyrotechnical supplies and could only set off a single weak aerial display, to little effect.[39]

Then as now, Hawaiians and other Pacific Islanders resisted the foreign narrative Cook inaugurated, the narrative that places Natives in a chain of being closer to dumb beasts than to the Euroamerican, educated classes that Cook and his successors thought they represented. The more the Natives would resist, however, the more Cook would insist. And so, on February 14, 1779, Cook marched forth once again to try to enact his narrative of superiority. Some Hawaiians that day silenced Cook's imperious demands with lethal blows and dismemberment.

Cook's death, of course, did not silence his master narrative of European superiority or the explorer's rhetoric of possession of which it was a part. These have been elaborated in various media for two hundred years, so that now Euroamerican representations of Hawai'i are annually disseminated to billions of people worldwide. Resistance to this imperious worldview has persisted, however, among some Euroamerican inheritors of the tradition of Cook's mutinous men. As later chapters will detail, resistance persists in the islands as well, more prominently and poignantly among the descendants of those people who yanked Cook's heart from his chest.

Chapter Three

The Kama'āina Anti-Conquest

From a distant camp came a snatch of Hawaiian music, the outpourings of the
sad, confused hearts of a destroyed people. Breathlessly, terrifyingly, it swept
Hamilton and Patricia together.

Armine Von Tempski[1]

During the decades following the death of Cook, numerous explorers from many
Euroamerican nations arrived in the islands, probably drawn almost as much by
the notoriety of Cook's murder as by the strategic placement of the islands near
the center of the world's largest ocean. Most of these explorers followed Cook's
example in composing their logs and journals, and many of these documents later
formed the bases for books that further disseminated the self-aggrandizing rhetoric so effectively employed by Cook. In 1820, however, fourteen extremist, New
England missionaries settled in the islands to begin the promulgation of a substantially different rhetoric. The islands these uninvited zealots invaded were
claimed to be important not for their strategic location but rather because they
were home to many thousands of purported heathen in need of a "salvation" the
missionaries proclaimed they were uniquely equipped to provide.

The missionaries introduced a rhetoric of revulsion, and this rhetoric struggled
for dominance in the islands for many decades against alternative rhetorics produced by explorers, sea captains, merchants, and, of course, Kanaka Maoli themselves. The missionary rhetoric of revulsion labeled even the simplest of Native
acts as "depraved."[2] The worse this rhetoric could make Hawaiians seem, the
more the missionaries could present themselves as courageous, righteous, and
worthy of the continued remittances they required be sent for their support from
home. Remarkably, only a few generations after the missionaries arrived, their
own descendants led a movement to replace the rhetoric of revulsion with a rhetoric that emphasized the need to preserve many of the same cultural practices the
missionaries had so doggedly opposed. This latter rhetoric, what I call here the
rhetoric of the kama'āina anti-conquest, is the focus of most of this chapter. We

begin, however, with a brief review of the earlier missionary rhetoric that provided the discursive context out of which this later rhetoric arose.

THE RHETORIC OF REVULSION

Missionary Charles S. Stewart described in his journal his feelings upon first seeing the people he had traveled halfway around the world to save:

> A first sight of these wretched creatures . . . was almost overwhelming. Their naked figures and wild expressions of countenance, their black hair streaming in the wind as they hurried over the water, with all the eager action and muscular power of savages, their rapid and unintelligible exclamations, and whole exhibition of uncivilized character, gave to them the appearance of half man and half beast, and irresistibly pressed on our mind the query, *"Can they be men—can they be women—do they form a link in the creation, connecting man with the brute?"*[3]

Hiram Bingham had a similar reaction upon his arrival, claiming many "were ready to exclaim, 'Can these be human beings! . . . Can we throw ourselves among these rude shores, and take up our abode, for life, among such a people, for the purpose of training them for heaven?'"[4] Repeated emphases on such hyperbolic revulsion, however sincere, seem calculated to increase sympathy and support from coreligionists left at home.

Subsequent years of living with Kanaka Maoli little altered most of these New Englanders' claims that they were now living among beasts. Sheldon Dibble, for example, the influential founder of Lahainaluna School, wrote about Hawaiians in the February 1833 edition of the *Missionary Herald*, "As to the multitude, they are without feeling, without serious reflections, and without thought. Their minds are dark, their hearts insensible."[5]

The missionary men took the lead in making contact with Hawaiians, but their wives relied on a similar rhetoric when they represented their Native hosts to each other or to family and supporters back on the continent. Patricia Grimshaw points out that though these women were increasingly restricted to their houses and discouraged from undertaking the very proselytizing they had hoped to do, few "were long in the islands . . . before giving voice to negative responses—no matter how mild, hospitable, or 'harmless' Hawaiians may have seemed at first."[6] Hawaiians are "naked, rude, and disgusting to every feeling," Mary Parker complained in 1831 in a letter to another missionary. Similarly, a few years later, Clarissa Armstrong wrote to her relatives in America: "Week after week passes and we see none but naked, filthy, wicked heathen with souls as dark as the tabernacles which they inhabit. The darkness of the people seems to destroy the beauty of the scenery around us."[7]

Cook and most other early explorers and sea captains valued Kanaka Maoli as trading partners and generally worked within the existing indigenous social formations to increase foreign access to supplies. The missionaries, however, condemned these social formations and worked tirelessly to alter every aspect of Hawaiian society. For these Americans Christianity entailed much more than simply committing to a certain sect and attending services to listen to official doctrines. It also required they instill their own early nineteenth-century, middle-class, New England customs into the lives of the Natives. As Grimshaw concludes from her study of the missionary archives, "anything that was not customary for Americans was deemed wrong for Hawaiians."[8] The missionaries thus repeatedly exhorted Kanaka Maoli to abandon both small everyday customs, like the wearing of flowers, and broad traditions, like communal land tenure and the independence of women.

The missionaries sometimes tempered their rhetoric of revulsion by representing Hawaiians less as beasts and more as children. "They are but 'babes in Christ,' who can neither stand nor go for themselves, for a long while," one missionary wrote in the *Missionary Herald* in 1829. "When we preach," another missionary wrote in 1836, "we feel that we preach not to children, but to infants in knowledge." As Herman points out, "The infantilising maneuver positions the missionaries into the paternal role that establishes their right and duty to guide and transform the lives of Hawaiians."[9] Whether depicted as animals or as children, Kanaka Maoli remained in the missionaries' rhetoric as beings who required the supervision of settler Americans.

Many others have told the story of how the island-born descendants of these missionaries subsequently instigated economic and political revolutions that impoverished Kanaka Maoli in their own lands.[10] I want to focus here on a less noted revolution, on the radical transformation in settler rhetoric that enabled the economic and political upheavals. This discursive revolution led the children and grandchildren of missionaries to begin calling for the preservation of the same "beastly" and "infantile" cultural practices their parents had fought to destroy.

RACE IN THE ANTI-CONQUEST

These missionaries' descendants constructed a new rhetoric that, first, emphasized a supposed hierarchy of races and, second, separated cultural practices from the supposed "races" that originated them. Both of these rhetorical constructions emerged in tandem with and were supported by the new specialized Euroamerican rhetorics that today are known as the social and behavioral sciences.[11]

Much writing about and originating from Hawai'i from the mid-nineteenth century on seems, in retrospect, obsessed with trying to specify the "essential characteristics" of what became known among settlers in the islands as the "kanaka" race. Though the precise essentials were never decided upon, every attempt to name these essentials further strengthened the assumption that the Kanaka Maoli possessed certain, definite, race-determined behavioral characteristics.

Mark Twain's effort to define Hawaiians in an 1866 article for the then-powerful Sacramento *Union* presaged much of the racial rhetoric soon to follow:

> They are a strange race, anyhow, these natives. They are amazingly unselfish and hospitable. To the wayfarer who visits them they freely offer their houses, food, beds, and often their wives and daughters. If a Kanaka who has starved two days gets hold of a dollar, he will spend it for poi, and then bring in his friends to help him devour it. When a Kanaka lights a pipe, he only takes one or two whiffs and then passes it around from one neighbor to another until it is exhausted. The example of white selfishness does not affect their native unselfishness any more than the example of white virtue does their native licentiousness. Both traits are born in them—are in their blood and bones, and cannot be educated out.[12]

Three months' residence in the islands seemed sufficient for Twain to believe he had discovered racial traits of Hawaiians that would never be educated out. These inborn traits, Twain makes clear elsewhere in his letters for the newspaper, proved Hawaiians would make great servants but poor capitalists.

Four decades later, in a series of widely read short stories, Jack London offered yet more proclamations about the essence of the Hawaiian race. London's "Koolau the Leper," for example, includes the musings of a Hawaiian waiting as Euroamerican troops under the banner of the 1893 illegal Provisional Government climb a mountain to try to kill him. London's Koolau surprisingly concludes he "could not but admire" these haoles determined to murder him: "There was no gainsaying that terrible will of the haoles. Though he killed a thousand, yet would they rise like the sands of the sea and come upon him, ever more and more. They never knew when they were beaten. That was their fault and their virtue."[13] For London's audience, this supposedly racially determined lack of perseverance suggested one more reason why such an inferior race should be colonized by a race that "never knew when they were beaten" (53).

Twain's and London's representations of the "kanaka race" were widely consumed in America and beyond, but their Euroamerican perspective on race was disseminated within the islands more influentially by American settlers and immigrants. The increasingly frequent use of the rhetoric of race by these expanding groups helped disguise their violent displacement of Kanaka Maoli. Mary Louise Pratt describes a similar rhetorical effect in her study of early Euroamerican representations of both Africa and South America. According to Pratt, early explorers and visitors to these continents tended to represent their actions unambiguously: They baldly admitted that they sought conquest through the acquisition of land, power, and/or wealth. Later, however, Euroamerican settlers often continued to conquer Natives while simultaneously claiming to have the Natives' best interests in mind. Pratt labels this discourse a rhetoric of anti-conquest. It is a rhetoric that she says employs "strategies of representation whereby European bourgeois subjects seek to secure their innocence in the same moment as they assert European hegemony."[14] This dual work of asserting innocence while securing hegemony became common among Euroamerican settlers and immigrants in Hawai'i toward the last third of the nineteenth century. It is a practice that still in Hawai'i flourishes today. The practice of pretending innocence while securing hegemony, for example, informs common usage in the islands of the word "kama'āina." According to Pukui and Elbert's *Hawaiian Dictionary*, before Euroamericans arrived kama'āina referred to Kanaka Maoli who were born to a particular locale.[15] Early explorers, missionaries, and settlers left this meaning unchanged, but later immigrants and Euroamericans born in the islands increasingly desired to possess land not only by deed and lease but also through the claim that Hawai'i was their "home." "Kama'āina" was thus transformed from a concept denoting Native-born into a term meaning "island-born," or even merely "well-acquainted with the islands." By adopting a Native word to describe themselves, Euroamericans obscured both their origins and the devastating effects their presence was having on the Native-born.

The transformation of the meaning of kama'āina can be observed in the pages of the Eurocentric Honolulu-based magazine *Paradise of the Pacific*. This influential periodical, which began monthly publication in January 1888, aimed at dual audiences—Euroamerican residents in the islands and Euroamericans on the American continent who might be prospective investors and visitors. The subheading for the first few issues, *Hawaii for Health, Pleasure and Profit*, announced the magazine's intentions. The term "kama'āina" rarely appears in the five hundred or so annual pages of *Paradise of the Pacific* in its first few decades. "Foreigner" remains a common term for Caucasians there, or "white," whether referring to Euroamericans born in the islands or elsewhere. One finds, for example, this declaration in the February 1909 edition in an article pleading for more respect for the sophisticated literary tastes of resident Euroamericans: "The standard of personal intelligence, especially among the white, or as it is still called, *'the foreign population,'* has advanced steadily from the days of the first missionaries to the present so that it now would not be possible, perhaps, to assemble elsewhere, on the same area, as many persons of exceptional attainments as may be brought together at short notice in Hawaii, and especially in Honolulu."[16] Later issues show the term "kama'āina" gradually usurping the semantic space that "white" or "foreigner" occupied in 1909. By the 1930s, at least for the mostly Euroamerican writers in the pages of *Paradise of the Pacific*, kama'āina referred to Caucasians who had lived long in the islands, or who claimed to know much about "island ways." Many of these newly self-named kama'āina were now even asserting they knew more about "authentic" Hawaiian culture than did Kanaka Maoli themselves.

ARMINE VON TEMPSKI

Probably the single richest site available for exploring the kama'āina anti-conquest is the thirteen books of Armine Von Tempski, a writer widely read by the general public but seldom discussed by critics. Several of Von Tempski's eleven novels (eight for adults, three for juveniles) and two autobiographies remained in print for decades, and many are now back in print some seventy-five years after their first appearance. Her work displays the many rhetorical practices kamaʻāina use to disguise their colonialism from themselves, Hawaiians, and metropolitan publics worldwide.

Von Tempski's grandfather, Major Gustavus Von Tempsky, killed Maoris in the Maori land wars until he himself was killed in 1868. Von Tempski writes proudly of Gustavus in her first of two autobiographies: "Today children studying history in the Antipodes find him rated as one of the great heroes of New Zealand."[17] Gustavus's son Louis, Von Tempski's father, left New Zealand when he was eighteen and eventually immigrated to Hawaiʻi, where he became the manager of an immense cattle ranch on Maui. In *Born in Paradise*, Von Tempski says of her father, "When he sang or danced *hulas* with Hawaiians, he was Polynesian; when he talked with Whites, his keen mind and vision enabled him to see through immediate problems to goals of the future" (6). In a single generation, then, Von Tempski asks her readers to believe that the Von Tempski men have evolved from slaughtering Polynesians to practicing their arts and, on occasion, experiencing themselves as Polynesian. In brief, such is the difference between the early conquest and the subsequent anti-conquest phases of colonialism. The imperialism of the first phase is based on frankly acknowledged violence and conquest; in the next phase, colonists continue their "expansionist project," as Pratt explains, but "in mystified fashion."[18]

Claims that kamaʻāina can become Polynesian often appear in Von Tempski's and other anti-conquest rhetoric, along with the associated claim that kamaʻāina are not only experts *about* but also themselves living representations *of* things Hawaiian. Kamaʻāina describe themselves as "Hawaiian at heart," suggesting that they are intimate with the Kanaka Maoli experience.

Kamaʻāina rarely embrace the reciprocal claim that Hawaiians are "Caucasian or haole at heart" and so to be accepted as living representatives of authentic Euroamerican traditions. Kanaka Maoli "blood" supposedly restricts such Native achievements. Sometimes kamaʻāina do admit that Hawaiians of the highest royalty, or those possessing substantial amounts of Euroamerican "blood," experience life like white people. Much more often, though, the "taint" of even the slightest amount of Hawaiian blood is claimed by kamaʻāina to render a person incapable of "rising" to the level of Euroamericans.

Like Twain and London, Von Tempski grapples endlessly with the quixotic task of establishing the supposed essential characteristics of the Hawaiian race. Her first novel, *Hula*, sets the pattern for the many books that followed. Published in 1927, *Hula* served as the basis for a popular silent film of the same name staring Clara Bow. (See chapter 6 for further discussion of this film.) In the novel, Edwin notices one young cowboy standing among a group of Hawaiians. Something about his appearance catches Edwin's attention: "His features were too fine to be purely Hawaiian."[19] Later Edwin divines the young man's parentage from looking closely at him once again. "The imagination of some white progenitor, who should never have intruded himself into the making of him, tricked him" (238). The trick, we soon learn, has ruined the young man by giving him to possess "what his [pure Hawaiian] mates did not—imagination" (239). Such a trait can do the young, mixed-blood cowboy no good, according to Edwin and Von Tempski's reasoning, for imagination mixes poorly with the essence of what a Hawaiian's nature predestines her or him to be.

A more complex meditation on racial difference appears in one of Von Tempski's last and most popular novels, *Ripe Breadfruit*, published first in 1935. David Birthwood, a kama'āina through length of residence though not of birth, meditates for several pages on the people who act as laborers and servants on the vast ranch he manages. He concludes that "primitive peoples appeared to have the gift of listening with their minds" so as to hear "nature's vast whispers" better than ears dulled "by the noises of civilization."[20] Von Tempski writes: "From years of association with Polynesians, David knew that primitive people were more acutely aware, more attuned to forces working behind and through nature. Crippling concepts of the universe did not hamper their minds. In them, as in children and animals, the subconscious was alert" (240). Birthwood concludes there is a difference between the visible and invisible worlds (242; cf. 252), and that, because he is white and possesses "reason, logic, commonsense" (241), access to the invisible world will always be denied to him.

In this formulation of essentialized racial differences, Hawaiians are lauded for possessing "faculties, keen as those of animals" (96) while, simultaneously, they are condemned as being incapable of understanding "concepts of the universe" associated with reason and logic. Such primitive Hawaiians, we are told, have their charms, even their virtues, much like children and animals. A race enthralled by the invisible, however, exists to serve more advanced races who better understand how to organize and manipulate the visible. Animalistic races like the Hawaiians, can be expected to disappear as more "advanced" races expand around the globe.

The rhetoric of the kama'āina anti-conquest not only includes claims that Native Hawaiian primitiveness necessitates Native servitude, but it also maintains that Hawaiians are personally fulfilled by serving whites. Twain was only one of many early writers to begin to construct the notion that generosity, later to be glossed as "aloha," was at the core of the Hawaiian's innate nature. This claim had become so widespread by the turn of the century that *Paradise of the Pacific* could coo in 1903: "The Hawaiian is one of the most sociable and hospitable of beings. He is always ready for a good time and when he is enjoying himself he wants his friends to share his pleasures."[21] Von Tempski, decades later, explored some of the intricacies of this claim as it became a key element in the rhetoric of those who were imposing an accelerating industrialization and urbanization upon Kanaka Maoli throughout the islands.

Most of Von Tempski's books prominently feature Hawaiian cowboys, whom she repeatedly praises for their skilled ranching labor, for their loyalty to their white bosses, and, perhaps surprisingly, for their superior caretaking of white children. So, for example, in the opening section of *Ripe Breadfruit*, Von Tempski describes the childhood of her protagonist Walter Hamilton: "Like the majority of children born in Hawaii, each day when his nurse had fed and dressed him he had been placed in the care of a Hawaiian cowboy, appointed to ride, rope, and swim. From the age of four he had been in the saddle all day, riding with his guardian and the other *paniolas* as they went about their work. The impressionable and formative years of his childhood had been largely spent in the company of a race keenly attuned to nature" (4). By a "majority of children," Von Tempski expected her readers to understand she meant white children only. The children of her heroic cowboys themselves are not often thought worthy to appear in her books. When Von Tempski does refer to nonwhite children, it is usually to make clear why they are inappropriate friends for whites or why they must never be treated as possibly suitable mates.

In both her novels and two autobiographies, Von Tempski's Hawaiian cowboys are delighted to work six and seven days a week, to ride long miles on thirsty trails, to sleep outside in rain and wind, to round up lost cattle and mend fences, while simultaneously tending to the rearing of their boss's children. These saintly cowboys often sing and dance, for the entertainment of their employers as much as for themselves. Typical is Edwin, the Hawaiian "half-white" cowboy who acts as guardian to the kama'āina girl Hula in Von Tempski's first novel. Edwin has spent many years in unpaid labor serving as both mother and father to the neglected girl. His job is made even more difficult by the fact that he is able to be with Hula only when she is out-of-doors, for Edwin, like all cowboys on the vast Hana ranch, is not allowed to step on the porch or inside the white people's main house, except on rare occasions when his employer gives special permission. Edwin cares for Hula, though he regularly has to work late into the night and get up hours before dawn to complete his other full-time ranch laborer duties. The novel climaxes when Edwin is instrumental in the violent death of the only other prominent Hawaiian character in the book. Von Tempski pits these two mixed-race people against each other, the good versus the bad Native, allowing them to express emotions the more civilized whites cannot. Edwin opposes the other half-white's desire to marry Hula, for Edwin, too, does not think Hula should be carnally connected with the dangerous Hawaiian blood.

Edwin's devotion to Hula is explained like that of most of the Hawaiians Von Tempski represents in her books: Giving to others is at the core of the "natural generosity" of the Hawaiian race. In *Ripe Breadfruit*, for example, Von Tempski describes the Hawaiian King Kalākaua as shaking hands "without affectation, with the quick sincere, easy affection of his race" (104). Claims for this natural Native "aloha" helped colonizing whites explain to themselves, to visitors, and to Hawaiians as well why Polynesians should be expected to give freely their natural resources, land, and labor to kama'āina. Hawaiians then and now who do not yield their nation and lives with smiles are accused of being "bad" Hawaiians.

KAMA'ĀINA AS PRESERVERS AND PRACTITIONERS OF HAWAIIAN TRADITIONS

In their first decades in Hawai'i, homesick American settlers filled their small houses with reminders of the homeland they had abandoned. Later, beginning in the last quarter of the nineteenth and continuing through the twentieth century, kama'āina added Hawaiian tools and artifacts to the decor of their now frequently much larger houses. Hawaiian servants were often employed in these houses, to dust and polish Kanaka Maoli creations few Hawaiians themselves now used or owned. These various tools and artifacts served as memorials to the Native traditions the kama'āina were industriously displacing. So, for example, *Paradise of the Pacific* described an elegant, mid-twentieth-century "kamaaina beach home" as presenting such artifacts in several rooms as "authentic and fascinating reminders of Hawaii's colorful historical past."[22] Such anti-conquest rhetoric places Hawaiian culture in a distant past while mystifying Euroamerican responsibility for the violent changes associated with that past. The rhetoric also positions kama'āina as enlightened moderns who sometimes kindly serve as curators for exotic Native artifacts that the Natives themselves cannot properly take care of.

The elegant, island-style kama'āina home of earlier decades is today the basis for the decor of many of the more expensive Hawai'i's hotels. These hotels exhibit such artifacts as kapa, bowls made of Native wood, fine mats, tapa sticks, tiki, poi boards and pounders, spears, gourds, and related crafts, including quilts of "native" design based upon the Euroamerican introduction of the "useful domestic art" of sewing.[23] The hotels present themselves, as kama'āina once did, as the guardians and preservers of Kanaka Maoli culture while simultaneously employing dozens of security personnel to make sure most contemporary Hawaiians do not "trespass" on the hotel's carefully manicured beaches and lawns.

Kanaka Maoli then and now have vigorously resisted this fetishizing of physical objects and their use by others to generate profit. Some Kanaka Maoli insist that Hawaiian cultural productions acquire their importance only if they participate in a network of reciprocal relationships among people, particular places, and specified behaviors. When such objects are owned and/or displayed in kama'āina houses, hotels, or museums, they validate Euroamerican and not Kanaka Maoli cultural traditions. Such displays make it seem settlers are honoring Natives, when in fact the very practices of ownership and of display without traditional use invalidate the purpose and meaning these objects possess within Kanaka Maoli traditions.[24]

The kama'āina anti-conquest tends to transform Native lifeways into a collection of discrete Native crafts. Each such craft can then be appropriated by settlers without regard for Kanaka Maoli genealogies and histories. Kama'āina thus do featherwork, carve koa canoes, and dance hula for kama'āina pleasure and profit (see Figure 3.1), without the need for any land remaining within Hawaiian hands. The preservation of such Hawaiian practices so conceived does not even require Native Hawaiians. Von Tempski's observation that her father "became Polynesian" when he danced hula displays the anti-conquest assumption that Hawaiian practices are isolated behaviors and therefore "traditions" that can, for example, be practiced in Euroamerican parlors by ranch managers as authentically as by a Kanaka Maoli hālau (hula group) on traditional Hawaiian lands.

Just as kama'āina have appropriated the hula and other Native Hawaiian practices and crafts for themselves, so too have they often claimed a privileged relationship with Native lands. It was not enough to many kama'āina to possess only the settler-introduced leases and deeds; increasingly, kama'āina wanted to claim ownership of the Hawaiian spirits associated with their new properties as well. Because the land is said to speak to whomever owns it, anti-conquest rhetoric represents these spirits as communicating unrestrainedly with kama'āina, showing

Figure 3.1   Haole hula girl

Reprinted with permission of DeSoto Brown Collection.

little loyalty or concern for the Native Hawaiian people the kama'āina are displacing. Kama'āina do not feel the need for the presence of any actual Kanaka Maoli in order to experience the supernatural thrills kama'āina have often maintained made Hawaiian colonialism especially emotionally rewarding.

As Von Tempski explains in *Ripe Breadfruit*, any Euroamerican settler could experience "the damnable enchantment of the islands" (171), since this enchantment was not generated by Hawaiian people but "by vegetation growing out of soil that had lava underneath it" (78). Von Tempski continues: "The vibrations which were created shook people loose inside themselves." When Kanaka Maoli were shaken loose from Euroamerican normality, they were often called brutes or children and were said to have demonstrated their racial inferiority. When Euroamericans were similarly shaken, they were elevated by "the imperious beckoning, the hypnotic pull, the mysterious promise of Hawaii" (86).

Kama'āina often sexualized this "shaking loose," associating the supposed enchantment of the land with seduction and lust. Von Tempski uses this trope often, though it can be found as well in Cook, Vancouver, Twain, London, and many other early writers. (We will see when we examine Hollywood's Hawai'i in chapter 6 that a similar, sexualized landscape became a staple of commercial films.) Von Tempski sometimes describes her island landscapes as "throbbing" in such a way as to incite kama'āina hearts and genitals to throb synchronously with them. "Some force surging up from the earth beneath them vitalized her," she writes in *Ripe Breadfruit*, "an impulse magical and vast that emanated from the soil, from the ocean teeming with life, a force against which she could not fight" (84). Kama'āina women, for example Hula in *Hula* and Lynette in *Ripe Breadfruit*, often become symbols of this sexual force in Von Tempski's books, though she makes it clear in *Ripe Breadfruit*, as elsewhere, that non-Native men and women are also susceptible to the persuasion of the "voices of hidden things" (145) in the land, voices that seduce them to give "rein to their lesser natures in a wholesale way" (23). The rhetoric of the kama'āina anti-conquest claims that the Natives are fortunate now to have the civilizing influence of people like Von Tempski and her father, who can employ Kanaka Maoli in wage labor and keep them from indulging their "lesser natures" day and night.

When settlers appropriate Native spirits, they transform them into expressions of Euroamerican traditions with only incidental connections to indigenous people. In *Ripe Breadfruit*, for example, the ex–sea captain settler Hi-ball Trevellyan returns after death to haunt his old ranch. Though he acts like a Victorian ghost and not a Kanaka Maoli spirit, Von Tempski's characters refer to him as an *akua*, and one even asserts "ghosts are only little *akuas*" (326). In her first autobiography, *Born in Paradise*, Von Tempski provides a more detailed account of the kama'āina spiritual view: "Even if there were no *akuas* and *kahunas* in England, there were in Hawaii. The Great Ancient Dead and Mighty Invisible Ones hadn't withdrawn from the Pacific as they had from other lands where doubting folk let their limited consciousness shut them off from realms and forces they could not touch and see. They didn't feel the Great *Akua*'s breath in the wind, sense his Presence in the ebb and flow of tides, and in the pulse of growing vegetation" (135).

Even the most superficial examination of Kanaka Maoli traditions would show that Von Tempski's conceptions here express settler and not Native views. "The Great Akua" has no cognates in Kanaka Maoli pantheism—certainly not in any patriarchal form like the one Von Tempski's "his Presence" implies.[25] Such rewriting of Kanaka Maoli spirituality into Euroamerican conceptions illustrates once again how the rhetoric of the anti-conquest radically transforms the very traditions it claims to perpetuate. Unfortunately, as we shall see in chapter 4, this tendency to misappropriate Hawaiian spirits for Euroamerican theologies has become increasingly common in recent years.

THE ANTI-CONQUEST AND LOCAL LITERATURE

Kama'āina dreams came true in 1959 when Hawai'i was illegally proclaimed the fiftieth state.[26] The by-now-familiar rhetoric of anti-conquest dominated the explosion of representations of the islands that followed. James Michener's *Hawaii*, for example, published in 1959 and still widely read, roots its narrative in the supposed genetic differences among races, which Michener conceived to be much like the essentialized racial types that Twain, London, Von Tempski, and other earlier writers used.[27] Similarly, producer Hal Wallis's widely viewed 1961 production of *Blue Hawaii* featured Elvis Presley as a kama'āina fighting like a character in a Von Tempski novel against the "dangers" of "going native." The limited dramatic tension produced in the film arises from Elvis's parents worrying he will become a "beach bum" and fail to follow in his father's footsteps as a white man profiting from the labor of Asian immigrants and of the Natives in their ancestral land.[28]

Statehood produced changes in the rhetoric of the anti-conquest. The rapidity with which outsiders could supposedly become kama'āina or, at least, have experiences like kama'āina was accelerated. Government and businesses supporting mass tourism combined to disseminate the conceit that even visitors could, like Von Tempski's father, "become Polynesian," if only for an afternoon or an evening. Director Paul Endkos's 1961 film *Gidget Goes Hawaiian* depends upon this conceit. On vacation with her family at the Royal Hawaiian Hotel, Gidget (played by Deborah Walley—see Figure 3.2) quickly learns to surf, to hula, and even to desire to become sexually active under the "spell" of the Hawaiian landscape and of the Native Hawaiian employees who surround her at the hotel. Though the older rhetoric of the kama'āina anti-conquest required a more "authentic" and lengthy encounter with the islands before such a transformation, Gidget's cinematic "going Native" encouraged the notion that every tourist can experience the throbbing sensations described by Von Tempski and other non-Native writers of Hawai'i.

Statehood also encouraged an increased emphasis on the mostly kama'āina-invented claim that "giving to others" is the core Native Hawaiian cultural value.

Figure 3.2   *Gidget goes Hawaiian*

Reprinted with permission of DeSoto Brown Collection.

The many possible alternative Hawaiian values, such as those elaborated in George Kanahele's *Ku Kanaka*, were systematically ignored. Instead, as Haunani-Kay Trask points out, "the Hawaiian values of generosity and love such as *aloha*" were misappropriated to make it seem as if they are "particularly suited to the 'visitor' industry which, in turn, encourages, and preserves Hawaiian culture."[29] Trask concludes: "The truth, of course, is the opposite: the myth of the happy Hawaiians waiting to share their culture with tourists was invented to lure visitors and to disparage Native resistance to the tourist industry" (53). Von Tempski's books suggest the myth of the happy Native was constructed earlier by kama'āina as one way of disguising their complicity in an ongoing colonialism. One accomplishment of the tourist industry since statehood has been to make this representation of happy, giving Hawaiians into a cliché familiar to metropolitan people around the globe.

Another change in the kama'āina rhetoric of the anti-conquest results from the ascent of Japanese Americans to positions of power throughout the state. During World War II, many people of Japanese ancestry suffered discrimination, property seizures, and imprisonment in internment camps. In postwar Hawai'i, many of these same people were determined to acquire political power and/or to assimilate into the American cultural mainstream. Within a few decades of the end of the war, county, state, and middle-level management positions throughout the state were dominated by Americans of Japanese ancestry in proportions far in excess of their numbers in the general population. Whites still dominated the media, higher education, foundations, and major corporate boardrooms, but island-born Japanese Americans were now the single most influential group in shaping public discourse on all aspects of island life, including discussions of Native Hawaiians.

In general, these new discussions perpetuated the tropes of the older kama'āina rhetoric of the anti-conquest. Now, however, it is as often kama'āina Asians as kama'āina Caucasians who claim to "become Polynesian" while dancing the hula or while fishing at ancient Native Hawaiian fishing spots. Beginning in the 1970s, a significant body of writing emerged from Bamboo Ridge Press, founded by several island-born Asian Americans and named for just such a fishing place that Native Hawaiians know in their own language as Hālona. This writing resisted the representations of Hawai'i found in the work of such short-term visitors as James Michener, Hal Wallis, Francine du Plessix Gray, and others. Rob Wilson provides a sympathetic reading of this literary movement and argues it was a source for "cultural resistance, projected community, and the *coalitional recovery* of counter-history and multi-voiced critique (by the local) of Euroamerican domination."[30] When Native Hawaiians authored or appeared as subjects or characters in these texts, they were usually seen as sharing a local identity like that associated with non–Kanaka Maoli locals. Richard Hamasaki argues that there was probably a moment when this inclusion of Native Hawaiians within the rhetorical construction of "local" helped to place them "in opposition to 'mainland' and white cultural domination."[31] Still, the cultural and political interests of Native Hawaiians and non-Native locals have rarely been the same. Though Kanaka Maoli writers, artists, and politicians once sought assimilation, they are increasingly seeking separation and a recognition of Native differences. (Many, for example, who once wrote under English names now use their Hawaiian language names instead or as well.) "Local does not translate into 'indigenous,'" Haunani-Kay Trask pointed out a decade ago. "Publishing for the indigenous writer, then, is not only an ambitious dream, as it is for most writers. It is a necessary struggle against extinction."[32]

Darrell H.Y. Lum's definition of local writers as "writers whose work reflects the multicultural composition of the islands" encourages the image of Hawai'i as a mixed plate where different ethnic groups with similar interests live and mingle.[33] Such a perspective, however, obscures the reality that this literature typically defines the local in relation to plantation memories and tensions between Asian and American traditions, themes with only an indirect relevance for Native Hawaiians. "When you read this local Asian American literature," Dennis Kawaharada points out, "you won't learn much about the land, sea, seasons, or cultural traditions which developed in Hawai'i previous to the plantation days."[34] As the rhetoric of the anti-conquest associated with such writers as Twain, London, Von Tempski, and Michener is supplanted by local Asian Americans Eric Chock, R. Zamora Linmark, Darrell H.Y. Lum, Gary Pak, Lois Ann Yamanaka, and others, Native Hawaiians remain represented once more largely by others and not by themselves.

In earlier decades, local writers—both Native and non-Native—contributed to the confusion of the local with the indigenous, but now most are careful to grant Kanaka Maoli their unique status as the First People of the islands. Confusion is still plentiful, however, especially among critics and readers. One especially influential instance of this conflation is found in Stephen H. Sumida's *And the View from the Shore: Literary Traditions of Hawai'i*, an influential study that Henry B. Chapin describes as "the definitive critical history of the literature of Hawai'i, and his commentary will henceforth set the terms of local literary discussion."[35] To the extent this is accurate, it signals the continuation of the Euroamerican anti-conquest rhetoric. Sumida builds his analysis on the concepts of "the pastoral and the heroic," as if these very culture-specific terms provide a neutral frame for interpreting both precontact oral and postcontact written literatures created in the islands. As Wilson queries, "why should Hawaii's writers aspire towards works of the 'heroic,' that most Eurocentric, male-based and even imperialist of forms as these literary prototypes come down 'from da mainland' through Homer, Milton, and Whitman to these Polynesian shores?"[36]

In a pivotal chapter on what he calls "Hawai'i's Complex Idyll," Sumida links island-born, Asian American novelist Milton Murayama's highly praised *All I Asking for Is My Body* with Native Hawaiian John Dominis Holt's less often read *Waimea Summer*.[37] The problems of Murayama's Japanese American and Holt's Hawaiian protagonists are similar, Sumida maintains, for these novels both express the same "polyethnic synthesis" that guides contemporary writing in Hawai'i: "Each one [novel] is a *Bildungsroman* plotting the development of the narrator's psyche and values. Both begin in the childhood idyll; yet both include elements of the heroic. . . . Though their central themes differ, these works share a way of looking at several dimensions of the past. . . . They share, that is, an important element of local sensibility" (110). Readers who accept that Murayama and Holt exhibit a common "local sensibility" are encouraged to believe that Japanese American and Hawaiian experiences are much the same—that, for example, the Japanese American's and the Hawaiian's relations to their families and to Hawaiian land are the same. Such rhetoric linking the Hawaiian people's experience of having their land colonized and their nation overthrown with stories of immigrant plantation struggles undermines claims for indigenous rights and reparations.

Sumida follows his long and confident summary of *All I Asking for Is My Body* with an equally long and confident summary of Native Hawaiian Holt's *Waimea Summer*, reflecting his assumption that as an Asian American he can penetrate the core of Holt's work as easily as he can Murayama's. Sumida claims Holt's novel is a guide "through a powerful and troubling exploration of a profound 'dark side' to the Hawai'i idyll" (137). Sumida's confidence in his Euroamerican critical

concepts emboldens him to offer an unequivocal interpretation of the novel's ending, which Sumida correctly acknowledges perplexes most non-Native readers.
Sumida claims this climax demonstrates that the young protagonist Mark has become wise enough to know that the ancient history of Native Hawaiians may be
studied but that it cannot any longer be lived (158). He concludes that Holt was
using this novel to offer his personal judgment about these issues to Native
Hawaiians and to declare the same opinion Sumida cites Wayne Chang as also
maintaining, "that the hula, mele, and oli of today are for art and entertainment,
not for worship" (160). Sumida thus uses Holt's novel as an opportunity to memorialize the passing of a supposedly dying or dead culture—a tactic that Von
Tempski and other earlier kama'āina writers too often used.

Holt, though deceased, remains a central figure in the intellectual and literary life
of contemporary Hawai'i. Sumida's reading of Holt's only full-length novel thus
begs for alternative interpretations lest it seem that Holt actually believed Hawaiian
culture now exists more for entertainment than for spiritual practice. I well recall
one illuminatingly convincing reading offered by a Kanaka Maoli student in Rob
Wilson's Pacific Literature class at the University of Hawai'i in the fall of 1993.
This Hawaiian said that it seemed clear to him that Mark Hull's flight back to
Honolulu indicated not that Holt was proclaiming the end of Native Hawaiian lifeways and history but, on the contrary, that Holt was demonstrating that the continuation of that culture cannot be avoided. He further suggested that we are to imagine Mark returns to a life much like the one John Dominis Holt himself lived—a
person in a Euroamerican society but not of it. *Waimea Summer* itself could thus be
understood as an act of participation in still-vital, Native Hawaiian ritual practices.

More dangerous than the particular reading Sumida offers of Holt is Sumida's assumption of the role of Native expert while ignoring that the differentials in access
to power, in land ownership, in ability to publish and to be heard, are almost as great
in the islands today between Japanese Americans and most Native Hawaiians as
they were between Twain, London, and Von Tempski, and the Kanaka Maoli they
presumed to represent. These differences were vividly revealed, for example, when
the U.S. government gave $20,000 to each person of Japanese descent who had
been illegally interned during World War II. These payments were token payments
of restitution for an injustice fifty years old. The illegal overthrow of the Hawaiian
nation, a more egregious injustice one hundred years old, has not yet been seriously
considered by the federal government for a similar type of token payment. The
wronged internees were compensated because the nation of Japan and Japanese
Americans have power in the United States and, particularly, among Hawai'i's del-
egates to the Senate and House of Representatives. This power is reflected as well
in the current flurry of publications of and attention to writing by Japanese
Americans, as well as to Asians with origins in other countries where Euroamerican
companies are seeking new markets. Contemporary Native Hawaiians remain
mostly ignored in these geopolitical and geoliterary games.

Disorientation: Unwritable Knowledge

In an address delivered at the Voices of the Earth Conference in Amsterdam, Native Hawaiian scholar Jon Osorio observed that indigenous peoples had until recently not had to worry too much about Euroamericans stealing their knowledge. Earlier scholars and journalists wrote their "world" histories and universalizing social science theories without consultation with the world majority they were writing about. Now, Osorio lamented, Euroamericans were becoming increasingly fascinated with third and fourth world cultures, creating new dangers: "With the gradual change in scholarly attitudes toward 'indigenous perspectives' it has become necessary to protect ourselves from the academic prospector who comes to us hoping to reveal the wonderful and exotic ways in which we view the world. Telling themselves that they are doing the world and indigenous people a tremendous service, they either ignore or rationalize the fact that not everyone benefits equally when they share our information."[1] Osorio advises Natives to insist these academic prospectors understand that Native knowledge is not public property but is instead the private heritage of the peoples who create and transmit it.

Osorio laments that this guarded attitude is especially difficult for Native Hawaiians to maintain because, traditionally, Hawaiian "knowledge is never sold or traded, it is shared. This custom allows non-Natives to profit from our knowledge as we have found it difficult even in modern times to be suspicious and selfish with what we know." As a result, Osorio points out, there is an increasing number of non-Natives who are using what they learn from Hawaiians to further their own personal, academic and commercial interests.

Cultural and economic globalization, with its tendency to commodify indigenous cultures, is accelerating such appropriations of isolated fragments of Native knowledge. So, in Hawai'i, banks and retailers now regularly emphasize bowdlerized Hawaiian concepts in their advertising, calling their companies "ohanas" (families), for example, or using images of nineteenth-century ali'i (chiefs) and sacred symbols to decorate the very offices in which they sell Native lands at prices few Natives can afford. Misappropriated knowledge about Hawaiians, furthermore, underwrites Hawai'i's economy as the non-Native–controlled tourist industry sells the islands as a site of "aloha." As Osorio writes, "The word Aloha has come to mean the submission of Natives to the invasion of their world." This creates profits for transnational corporations while forcing an increasing number of Hawaiians into homelessness and poverty in their own native land.

Though transnational capitalism drives much contemporary misappropriation of Native knowledge, there are other forces at work as well. R. Douglas Herman, for example, argues that missionary teaching about literacy was influential in the settlers' transformation of the islands and that the complexity of Hawaiian language and thought was "reduced" through writing.[2] Euroamericans in the islands have generally always associated "real" knowledge with writing, a view clearly articulated by missionary Sheldon Dibble in his 1843 *History of the Sandwich Islands*, published on the mission press at Lahainaluna: "The amount of their knowledge on every subject was still more deplorable than their destitution of the arts and means of civilized life. They had no knowledge of writing, or of the use of arbitrary signs to express thought. . . . They had not the least conception of any mode of expressing thought except by the voice and gestures of the living person."[3] The missionaries thus lay the foundation for a process that continues, a process whereby people attempt to "save" and/or "honor" Native knowledge by reducing it to writing. As Doris Sommer points out, even when Natives offer resistance to such translations from the unwritten to the written, Euroamericans tend to treat their protests "as coquettish modesty calculated to incite conquest."[4]

Though significant differences between oral and literate knowledge systems have long been recognized, these differences seldom have been accepted as great enough to slow the translation of Native traditions into written Anglo-European languages. Finally, however, the protests of Osorio and other Natives are being heard, perhaps less out of respect for Natives than because these protests echo the currently fashionable Euroamerican theories associated with Mikhail Bakhtin, Jacques Derrida, Eric A. Havelock, and Walter Ong. In different ways and to different degrees, these theorists encourage the belief that there is an unbridgeable semantic gap between oral and written cultural forms.

Greg Dening explores the gap between the oral and the written in its specifically Pacific context: "It is the outsider, the observer, who says he has seen the last turtle and describes it, draws a model, calls an end to the infinite progression, says he has caught an essence and translates what is particular, active, unbroken and complex into something general, static, structured and simple."[5] What Dening says of models applies as well to all monorhetorical representations. Semantic violence results when "the infinite progression" of orality is translated into static, structured Euroamerican forms.

In opposition to those who continue to insist on their right to translate Hawaiian oral into haole written forms, Osorio offers the University of Hawai'i Center for Hawaiian Studies as "a model that may be useful to other indigenous peoples seeking to preserve and assert their knowledge." The Center, he claims, restricts access to Hawaiian knowledge, discourages non-Natives from enrolling in courses about Hawaiians, and maintains that within the University of Hawai'i system only Native scholars should be allowed to "teach Native subjects in history, art, economics and politics." This approach embodies what I earlier described as the second rhetorical situation, as the Center advises Native scholars to borrow from both Euroamerican *and* Native tropes and narratives, while simultaneously interrogating monorhetoric's imperious assumptions.

Since writing and its frequent translations have played a critical role in colonialism, they seem destined to play a central role in decolonization as well. The efforts of Native scholars working within this second rhetorical situation are essential for the vitality of the critical localism I earlier discussed. Still, there is a grave danger associated with the body of writing that this second rhetorical situation produces, for these texts are likely to be used by non-Natives—and by some Natives as well—to further identify the traditional oral culture with its written translations.

Writing in English, Hawaiian and other languages has no doubt altered the oral tradition in unknown ways, but the tradition today remains dependent primarily upon the many kūpuna (elders) who continue to teach others, face to face, much as Kanaka Maoli have taught each other for many hundreds of years. If the knowledge of kūpuna becomes a corpus primarily associated with writing, the distinction between the spoken and written Kanaka Maoli culture may be increasingly effaced. It may become increasingly easy, for example, for readers to believe that in reading Mookini and Nākoa's translation of Nakuina, or Kame'eleihiwa's translation of the Kamapua'a tales, they are acquiring a knowledge of Kanaka Maoli storytelling that is much like the knowledge of those who learn these stories orally.

In her "Introduction" to *A Legendary Tradition of Kamapua'a, the Hawaiian Pig-God*, Kame'eleihiwa points to some of the unbridgeable differences between the oral and written versions of Kamapua'a's and other Kanaka Maoli stories. Kame'eleihiwa maintains that the kaona, or hidden meanings, that are the foundation of Kanaka Maoli oral literature depend on four levels of simultaneous understanding. First are surface or "face value" meanings, "boy meets girl, falls in love, falls out of love, and so on." A second level is built out of "innumerable allusions to ancient events, myths, Gods, and chiefs that have become metaphors in their own right."[6] A third level depends on the numerous chants and proverbs strewn throughout the telling. These, too, often offer both surface and metaphorical levels of meaning whose understanding depends, in part, upon their specific placement within the story. A fourth level is created "by the manner in which the story is told," as the speaker sometimes aims messages at just a few or even a solitary member of the audience, "while everyone else remains oblivious to the message."

Kame'eleihiwa summarizes the interrelations of these four levels: "These subtle levels of meaning are like strands of *lei* woven together as an object of honor and affection for loved ones and the *Ali'i Nui*. Their function is to remind the audience of something that is similar to the present and at the same time slightly different" (ix). Only oral performers can shift their ways of telling tales so as to remind particular audiences about differences between the present and other times. Only oral performers can shape their speaking at each presentation to honor different loved ones and aliʻi. Only oral performers can arrange their speaking to add new levels of meaning to the lei of understanding by alluding to earlier performers of that day or of the days just before.

After summarizing these unique qualities of orality, Kameʻeleihiwa offers an annotated written English translation of one written Hawaiian-language version of the Kamapuaʻa epic. The result is a spectacular read but not a text that should be too intimately associated with the Kamapuaʻa oral tradition. If such translations are generally accepted as making "available to a wide audience the constellations of meanings that are essential to understanding Hawaiian poetry and storytelling," as one reviewer maintains, then Kanaka Maoli storytelling would seem to be on the way to becoming but one among many literary traditions. As Kameʻeleihiwa herself explains in *Native Land and Foreign Desires*, as well as in the "Introduction" to her Kamapuaʻa translation, Kanaka Maoli storytelling has so far operated as something much different and more important than that.[7]

The dangers associated with offering Kanaka Maoli traditions in translated, English-language versions is also apparent in Malcolm Naea Chun's recent edition of Davida Malo's *Ka Moʻolelo Hawaiʻi: Hawaiian Traditions*. Though Malo's extraordinary text, as Chun writes in his "Introduction," "has been a primary source of information on pre- and post-contact Hawaiian society for the last ninety years," most have read it only in Nathaniel B. Emerson's 1898 translation.[8] The flaws in Emerson's translation have long been apparent. Valerio Valeri, for example, writes: "The comparison between the original and the translation reveals that Emerson often took liberties with a text he sometimes poorly understood. . . . It is thus necessary to consider Malo's Hawaiian text and Emerson's notes as two completely different sources."[9] Chun hopes his new English translation will correct Emerson's mistakes. He concludes his "Introduction" with this explanation:

> So, I believe that we may now have a clearer picture, perhaps not a perfect one of early, transitional Hawaiian society.
> We also have an even better idea of our culture as seen from our own world-view and this is an important point today as many Hawaiian kūpuna [elders] have recently died, who could have instructed and transmitted this Native world-view. This tragic loss is leaving us with an unnerving sense of uncertainty in Native Hawaiian communities. The publication of this new translation may give us a renewed sense of confidence in the knowledge of who we are because Davida Malo's legacy will endure continuing to teach the next generation of Native Hawaiians and those yet to come. (ix)

Certainly all will hope that Chun's translation will help fill the loss of some kūpuna. Still, it remains important to remember that *Ka Moʻolelo Hawaiʻi: Hawaiian Traditions* will most often be read by people within the context of a literate and not of an oral tradition. Though it may point toward the Kanaka Maoli oral tradition, the text in both English *and* Hawaiian versions is not an instance of that oral tradition itself. This seems obvious, but the imperialism of literacy encourages readers to forget it. One reviewer has claimed, for example, that Chun's translation may come to occupy for Hawaiians a place like that "the Bible occupies in the Christian world."[10] This is a category mistake, I believe, for there are no Bibles, no definitive texts, in an oral tradition. Definitive texts depend on assumptions about reality, representations and knowledge that seem in important ways to be radically unlike the worldview transmitted by kūpuna. Once an oral tradition is accepted as being adequately represented by its written versions, it loses much of its force as a radically alternative worldview.

Tejaswini Niranjana usefully explores the implications of this argument in *Siting Translation: History, Post-Structuralism, and the Colonial Conquest*, a study of "translation as a significant technology of colonial domination."[11] Niranjana summarizes some of the assumptions associated with modern Euroamerican literacy. Within this worldview, she explains, "reality is seen as something unproblematic, 'out there'; knowledge involves a representation of this reality; and representation provides direct, unmediated access to a transparent reality" (2). Niranjana points out that the world majority does not share these assumptions about the nature of reality, knowledge, and representation. Niranjana thus counsels Natives to avoid writing about themselves in any way that might seem to suggest that they, as Natives, accept the belief that their worldview can be reduced to more or less accurate written versions. She asks for Native translations and other writings that instead actively undermine Euroamerican assumptions about reality. Niranjana counsels Native translators "to inscribe heterogeneity, to warn against myths of purity, to show origins as always already fissured. Translation, from being a 'containing' force, is transformed into a disruptive, disseminating one" (186).

There are no doubt additional possibilities for Native writers and translators besides the one Niranjana develops. Her discussion is important, however, in that it raises the warning that writing, even when undertaken by Natives, often may further legitimize the colonizer's (literate) traditions at the expense of the Native (oral) alternative.[12]

The ease with which Native Hawaiian self-representations can be absorbed into the colonizer's worldview can be illustrated by an examination of Anne Kapulani Landgraf's *Nā Wahi Pana O Koʻolau Poko Legendary Places of Koʻolau Poko*.[13] This is the inaugural book selected and edited by Native Hawaiians in a series published by the University of Hawaiʻi Press—the first such series to be controlled by Kanaka Maoli and issued by this important regional publisher. Initially, this book presents itself much like thousands of other collections of photographs, with large, black-and-white images filling one page and each facing page containing text in Hawaiian, with an English translation. The texts detail the appropriate place names along with a brief, thirty- to three hundred–word summary of events associated with these places. Readers trained in the Euroamerican tradition will likely view this book much as they do books by Euroamerican photographers such as Edward Weston or Robert Mapplethorpe. They will focus on the images and assume that with sufficient study they will be able to see what the photographer intended them to see. Viewing in this way, then, readers will tend to believe that Landgraf's book provides some intimacy with the legendary places of Koʻolau Poko (see Figures Disorientation 1 and 2).

Both Landgraf's "Preface" and Haunani-Kay Trask's "Introduction" to the book, however, suggest these photographs may be better viewed not as a compilation of representations but rather as what Niranjana seeks for Natives—a text that acts "as disturbance and displacement of hegemonic views" (38). Landgraf writes that the place names "are like kūpuna, linking us to the past" (v). She suggests her photographs be viewed not as visual re-presentations of the places themselves but rather as links between the past and the present. This notion of linkage is radically unlike the relations of reality, knowledge, and representation associated with Euroamerican literacy that Niranjana describes.

Trask explains why she chose Landgraf's work to launch the pioneering Kolowalu series of Native Hawaiian books: "Here, I thought, was a stunning accomplishment: culture, political awareness, and a highly refined technical skill combined to reveal the Hawaiian view of our sacred places." This "Hawaiian view" seems to me to reflect what Trask calls "a cultural context drawn from a period before the arrival of the haole in Hawaiʻi."[14] In this context, the photo-

Figure Disorientation 1   Kukuikāne (Light of Kāne)

Source: Anne Kapulani Landgraf, *Nā Wahi Pana O Koʻolau Poko Legendary Places of Koʻolau Poko* (Honolulu: University of Hawaiʻi Press, 1994). Reprinted with permission of University of Hawaiʻi Press. No other use of the above photo is permitted without written permission.

Figure Disorientation 2   Pōhaku Hiʻiaka (Hiʻiaka's Stone)

Source: Anne Kapulani Landgraf, *Nā Wahi Pana O Koʻolau Poko Legendary Places of Koʻolau Poko* (Honolulu: University of Hawaiʻi Press, 1994). Reprinted with permission of University of Hawaiʻi Press. No other use of the above photo is permitted without written permission.

graphs seem to be *about* but not *of* Hawaiʻiʻs sacred places. Euroamerican sacred places (to the extent any exist) may be literally pictured and represented, for they are closely identified with their visual manifestation. Native Hawaiian sacred places, however, Landgraf and Trask here suggest, are sacred at least as much for what cannot be directly seen as for their visible manifestations.

Through looking at photographs one may gain monorhetorical knowledge of the Washington Monument, Yosemite's Great Dome, or the cathedral at Chartres, but it is probably a category mistake to believe one can know Koʻolau Poko, Kukuikāne, Pōhaku Hiʻiaka, or any other Kanaka Maoli site in "the Hawaiian way" through sight. Diligent study of photographs, scientific instruments, or videos yields only haole—not Kanaka Maoli—knowledge.

In her poem, "Returning the Gift," Trask proffers yet another way to think about the differences between Euroamerican and Hawaiian assumptions concerning the relations among reality, knowledge, and representations. This poem was first published in an anthology, *Returning the Gift: Poetry and Prose from the First North American Native Writers' Festival*, that commemorated the Returning the Gift Festival held in Norman, Oklahoma, in 1993. Joseph Bruchac maintains in his "Introduction" to the anthology that the festival "brought more Native writers together in one place than at any other time in history."[15] The theme of returning the gift was suggested for the festival by Chief Tom Porter of the Akwesasne Mohawk Nation. The festival organizers write: "He remarked that in our avocation as Native writers, involved as we are in taking our peoples' literature back to them in the form of stories and songs, we were actually returning the gift—the gift of storytelling, culture, continuance—to the people, the source from whence it had come" (xxv).

As Cynthia Franklin points out, Trask's poem in this anthology joins with several others to "work to blur the lines between the text and the event, between poet and poem, and also between written literature and Native oral storytelling traditions."[16] Trask's poem aspires to invoke memories of preexisting knowledge and stories in communities where these already exist. "Taking our peoples' literature back to the source from whence it had come" invokes an oral rhetorical situation, a worldview that is monumentally unlike that which most books—including *Displacing Natives*—assume.

Part Two

Displacing Three Hawaiian Places

Chapter Four

Displacing Pele:
Hawai'i's Volcanoes in a Contact Zone

The volcano area of the island of Hawai'i is now occupied mostly by the Hawaii Volcanoes National Park (HVNP), the most popular tourist attraction in the islands. Through numerous signs, maps, dioramas, and a federal government–staffed Visitor's Center, contemporary visitors to the park are offered an official interpretation of the area, which includes some Euroamerican versions of Native Hawaiian beliefs but which primarily offers a layperson's version of contemporary geological science. Much of this science has been produced by the Hawaiian Volcano Observatory (HVO), a research facility sponsored by the U.S. Geological Survey, whose offices and laboratories are prominently located within the park. HVO has set up displays explaining its work, as well as a museum celebrating the history of the people and instruments that created their interpretations. These coherent accounts of volcanism offered to the millions of annual visitors to the area by both the park service and HVO scarcely allude to the long battle that has raged to determine which of several competing rhetorics would dominate representations of this area. This battle boiled throughout the 1800s and into the early twentieth century, subsided substantially in the middle of the twentieth century, and has erupted again with increasing vigor in the past decade. I wish here not only to review the history of this discursive battle but also to bolster those presently nourishing alternatives to the official, government-sponsored view.

NINETEENTH-CENTURY TRAVEL NARRATIVES

Early, non-Native visitors to Hawai'i's volcanoes claimed to be at a loss about how to speak and write about their experience. Their resulting descriptions often included an invocation of an experience of tropelessness, a claim that in the presence of such a site a conscientious visitor could only be silent. William Ellis, the

very first Euroamerican to visit and write about Kilauea, inaugurated this tradition. In the 1825 edition of his journal, Ellis wrote:

> We at length came to the edge of the great crater, where a spectacle, sublime and even
> appalling, presented itself before us—
>   "We stopped, and trembled."
>   Astonishment and awe for some moments rendered us mute, and, like statues, we
> stood fixed to the spot.[1]

Another missionary, C. S. Stewart, penned in his journal that same year that the
view "which here burst on our sight was emphatically of that kind" for which "description, and even painting, can do no justice; and in conveying any adequate impression of which, they must ever fail."[2]

Fifty years later, Isabella Bird viewed Kilauea from a vantage much like Ellis's
and Stewart's: "I think we all screamed, I know we all wept, but we were speech-
less. . . . It is the most unutterable of wonderful things. The words of common
speech are quite useless."[3] Even Mark Twain, writing about his visit to Kilauea in
1866, discovered that the spectacle at night fractured his ironic prose. Twain's
sentences erupted in uncharacteristic exclamation marks, until at last he proclaimed: "You could not compass it—it was the idea of eternity made tangible—
and the longest end of it made visible to the naked eye!"[4]

Those familiar with Euroamerican colonialism will not be surprised to learn
that such protestations of muteness, speechlessness, and an inability to "compass
it" usually preface long passages that nonetheless speak loquaciously about the
volcano. These subsequent descriptions display a persistent disquietude, suggesting that the initial claims of speechlessness have not been entirely shaken off.
Still, the texts of these nineteenth-century writers never conclude that there is
something about this Native place that removes it from foreign understanding.
Multiple rhetorical strategies are used to reassert each visitor's ability to take discursive possession of all she or he surveys.

One recurrent trope found in many of these early texts compares Kilauea to the
fires of the Christian hell. "The smell of sulphur is strong, but not unpleasant to
a sinner" (297), Twain writes at the end of his pages on Kilauea, a section he calls
"The Vision of Hell and Its Angels." Bird similarly invokes images from the book
of Revelation: "Here was the real 'bottomless pit'—the 'fire which is not
quenched'—'the place of hell'—'the lake which burneth with fire and brim-
stone'—the 'everlasting burnings'—the fiery sea whose waves are never weary"
(54). Neither Twain nor Bird nor most other nineteenth-century writers long sus-
tain this metaphor, however, as their texts usually include encomiums remarking
on Kilauea's creative powers. So Bird, for example, follows her invocation of hell
with a declaration that the fire fountains were "dancing around the [lava] lake
with a strength and joyousness which was absolute beauty" (55). This and Bird's
further remarks on Kilauea's "glory, majesty, mystery, and even beauty" (55) col-
lide with her claims that the volcano is an earthly manifestation of hell.

Bird heaps trope upon incongruous trope, often presenting one image only to immediately contradict it with another. "A sound as of the sea broke on our ears . . . but the ocean was thirty miles away" (50–51). Lava is consecutively compared to the columns of Staffa, to waves, and to snakes. Bird several times draws attention to the contradictions within her prose, as if these acknowledgments of incoherence will help create coherence. She declares, for example: "But what can I write! Such words as jets, fountains, waves, spray, convey some idea of order and regularity, but here there was none" (54).

Incoherence is prominent as well throughout what is perhaps the best crafted of all nineteenth-century travel accounts of Kilauea, Charles de Varigny's *Fourteen Years in the Sandwich Islands 1855–1868*. This text, published in French in Paris in 1874, was not translated into English until 1884 because, Alfons L. Korn speculates, it argued against American interests in Hawai'i and for the kingdom's independence.[5] Varigny begins his account as have his predecessors, with the trope of speechlessness, with a claim his words will not be able to convey his experience, then, like those predecessors again, Varigny proceeds to offer copious descriptions. He twice calls Kilauea an "abyss" (76, 77) and once a "whole immense circus" (76). Varigny spews a mixed array of historical, classical, and biblical tropes, creating a confusing swarm. These are examples from a single paragraph: "I seemed to behold from on high a conquered Sebastopol, annihilated in that hellfire celebrated in the annals of war. . . . Then, all of a sudden, I was present at the fall of Sodom. . . . The earth cracked open to swallow the accursed city. Let the Dead Sea sweep in" (76). Varigny declares he is aware of the incongruous swarm of tropes he is offering. He is "a plaything in a world of dreams," he writes. "A thousand fantasies, a thousand confused images, rushed through my brain" (76).

Twain's passage on Kilauea contains a comparable jumble of disharmonious tropes, but Twain deflects attention from his incoherence by invoking the supposed coherence of numbers and by using humor. "I am passably good at judging of heights and distances,"[6] Twain declares, before demonstrating his prowess by offering supposedly exact measurements of much of what he sees. A wall, for example, is "from six hundred to eight hundred feet high" (292), "the far end of the basin, two miles and a half away" (292–3), a path "half a mile" (293), and an illumination "two miles wide and mile high" (293). The numbers seem an attempt to reassure readers that the site is not after all, as Twain had said earlier, "too stupendous" (292) and not to be compassed.

Twain also attempts mastery of the place through humor, and it was in large measure through his success at this in his pieces on Hawai'i that Twain's national reputation as a writer was launched. For example, immediately after suggesting such a natural wonder might be beyond his grasp, Twain eases the sting of this admission by connecting it to this additional claim: "I also know a woman who looks criminally homely at a first glance will often so improve upon acquaintance as to become really beautiful before the month is out" (291). Similarly, soon after beginning his description of the view of the crater at night, following a passage where adjectives and even a final exclamation mark suggest the prose is deteriorating into tropological incoherence, Twain defuses his earnest tone: "The place below looked like the infernal regions and these men like half-cooled devils just come up on a furlough" (294).

Twain's ambivalent prose also dominates the last paragraph he writes about Kilauea. He describes a lava fountain: "I thought it just possible that its like had not been seen since the children of Israel wandered on their long march through the desert so many centuries ago over a path illuminated by the mysterious 'pillar of fire.' And I was sure that I now had a vivid conception of what the majestic 'pillar of fire' was like, which almost amounted to a revelation" (298). Twain seems to be straining to have it both ways—to offer an impressive sight without suggesting that he, himself, was particularly impressed. It is only "just possible" the fire fountain Twain has seen was like that seen by the children of Israel, though it leaves Twain "sure" he has a "conception." This, however, leads only to an "almost" revelation, for the narrator seems determined to admit to experiencing nothing that leaves him long moved or overwhelmed.

Still, even the suggestion here of a near revelation appears to have been too much for Twain. When he revised this 1866 article about Kilauea, first published in the Sacramento *Union*, for inclusion in *Roughing It*, Twain omitted this description of the fountain of fire with its hint of his near epiphany.

In 1865, the year before Twain arrived, the missionary Orramel H. Gulick had provided the newly built Volcano House hotel with a guest register into which, as he wrote, visitors were invited "to note all, or any, volcanic phenomena that may come under their notice."[7] Twain left a long entry, dated June 7, 1866, mocking earlier entries and much of what he himself would soon publish in his newspaper article referring to the wild beauty of this place. Twain wrote in the register that he saw fall a lump of dirt the size of a piece of chalk:

> Oh, God! It was awful!
> We then took a drink.
> Few visitors will ever achieve the happiness of two such experiences as the above in succession.
> While we lay there, a puff of gas came along, and we jumped up and galloped over the rough lava in the most ridiculous manner, leaving our blankets behind. We did it because it is fashionable, and because it makes one appear to have had a thrilling adventure.
> We then took another drink.[8]

This posting in the register is in dialogue with earlier and succeeding accounts therein. "We had been reading old files of Hawaiian newspapers and the 'Record Book' at the Volcano House, and were posted," Twain acknowledges in the letter about Kilauea he published in 1866.[9] So, similarly, would Isabella Bird write ten years later that, before viewing the crater, she had read "seven different accounts in which language was exhausted in describing Kilauea" (54). When, thereafter,

Bird's own prose seems often similarly to exhaust itself, there seems little doubt that she, like Twain, is embracing the conventional rhetoric of confusion familiar to her from what she has read.

The tropological disjointedness of these early travel narratives seems unlikely to have confused nineteenth-century readers, for these texts reflected the then-familiar genre of the romantic sublime, a genre Rob Wilson shows was adapted from Europe and given peculiar American meanings.[10] Many early visitors to Hawai'i's volcanoes explicitly used the word sublime in describing their experiences. So, for example, C. S. Stewart's *Journal* says of the lava lake at Halema'uma'u, "its action was more horribly sublime than any thing I ever imagined to exist, even in the ideal visions of unearthly things" (388). Many other writers invoked the trope of the sublime without including the word. (Garrett Hongo resurrects this term for the "volcano experience" in his contemporary memoir *Volcano*.[11])

Neil Hertz describes how the trope of the sublime operates in most eighteenth- and nineteenth-century English literature. Hertz says writers typically invoke a single observer, usually male, then depict this person sighting and experiencing a natural phenomenon that bewilders and threatens to overwhelm. By writing this experience and representing its threatening sublimity, Hertz says, an author both reestablishes "boundaries between representor and represented and, while maintaining the differences between them, keeps the poet-impresario [the author] from tumbling into his text."[12] Again and again, it seems, early travelers to Hawai'i's volcanoes used their very representations of the supposedly unrepresentable to reassert their mastery and, simultaneously, the universality of Euroamerican rhetoric.

The constructed subjectivity of a single observer-writer within these early travel narratives creates a coherence amid what might otherwise seem to be disoriented and contradictory descriptions. Such an author-function—as Michel Foucault terms it in "What Is an Author?"—allows one to read these nineteenth-century passages, with their jumble of incompatible tropes, and maintain a sense that a comprehensible narrative is being offered.[13] Since Ellis, Twain, Bird, Varigny, and others are writing stories of their separate selves, every trope they offer participates in the time sequence that is their life. "First I saw this," each of them writes, "then I experienced this, next this," and so on. The rhetorical construction of a central self provides a narrative unity for the discordant array of incongruous tropes.

The impact on Euroamerican readers of similar, early, travel narratives focused on central selves is analyzed in Mary Louise Pratt's *Imperial Eyes: Travel Writing and Transculturation*, where she positions such writing within the broader transformation whereby Euroamericans were developing a "planetary consciousness."[14] By producing "other parts of the world for the imagination of Europeans" (18), travel writers invited further visitations and conquest. Their narratives encouraged the belief that Euroamericans could settle in remote places on the earth without losing their familiar sense of self. Even the most incoherent travel writers, describing their experiences at Kilauea or elsewhere, wrote in such a way as to indicate that they had emerged from their visit much the same person they had been before. The transformations of a Lemuel Gulliver or of a Kurtz were practically unknown. The imperial eye of travel writers gazed with impunity everywhere, even on Kilauea's "hellish" fires. What could be visited could be known and described. What could be described, it was implied, could also be colonized and owned.

The early writing about Kilauea encouraged Euroamericans to travel to Hawai'i to view the volcano and other sublime sites in order to experience the pleasurable sensations of confronting and mastering nature's "threats." This tradition of sublime incoherence, however, proved insufficient as a discursive strategy once foreigners settled in the islands to do either God's or their own business. These settlers constructed alternative representations of the volcano for themselves.

THE SYSTEMATIZATION OF THE WORLD

Other rhetorics about Hawai'i's volcanoes were in circulation at the same time that nineteenth-century travel narratives of the romantic sublime were being written. One of these, what has come to be known as geology and volcanology, was new in the nineteenth century not only to Hawai'i but to the world. The unity of these scientific rhetorics is not based on selves, like travel writing, nor does it invoke genealogies, like Native Hawaiian beliefs. Instead, the rhetoric of volcanology claims there are orderly, "natural forces" that exist independent of both selves and ancestors. This natural science rhetoric was offered with special fervor by many of the Calvinist missionaries who immigrated to Hawai'i in hopes of converting the Native people to their sect of Christianity.

The missionaries were assisted in their efforts by several visiting scientific teams and especially by the United States Exploring Expedition, which was in Hawai'i in 1840–41.[15] As Pratt remarks, such international scientific expeditions were "conspicuous instruments of expansion." Her comments on European expeditions hold true for the American expeditions to Kilauea and Mauna Loa: "Scientific exploration was to become a focus of intense public interest, and a source of some of the most powerful ideational and ideological apparatuses through which European citizenries related themselves to other parts of the world."[16] This work expanded and refined Captain Cook's discursive possession through mapping, imaging, and describing (see chapter 2).

The scientific accomplishments of the early expeditions to Hawai'i were reviewed in Thomas L. Wright and Takeo Jane Takahashi's *Observations and Interpretation of Hawaiian Volcanism and Seismicity 1779–1955*, and a companion book by these authors and James Griggs, *Hawai'i Volcano Watch*.[17] Wright and

Takahashi pointed out that, perhaps surprisingly, the most detailed nineteenth-century observations were found not in the texts of professional observers but in the notebooks of missionaries. Of special significance were the records begun in 1833 by Sarah Joiner Lyman and kept up by the Lyman family for almost one hundred years. In addition, according to Wright, Takahashi, and Griggs, the carefully recorded observations of missionary Titus Coan were superior to those observations made by James D. Dana, a man sometimes called America's first volcanologist. The layman Coan's notes about Hawai'i's volcanoes, for example, eventually forced Dana to change his theory of how lava is extruded.

Wright and Takahashi's history of missionary observations looked back from the vantage of contemporary volcanology to place the missionaries in the formative chronology of this modern field. These missionary records take on a very different meaning, however, when considered not as precursors of a later science but rather as acts of rhetoric within their originating context. In the islands in the nineteenth century, they were not so much proto-volcanology as a vociferous counter-narrative offered in opposition to the narrative Hawaiians had spoken for centuries.

The Hawaiian missionary practice of observing nature participated in what Foucault describes as the modern European project of seeking a "description of the visible."[18] Hearing, taste, smell, and, to a large extent, touch, were excluded from this recently invented Euroamerican rhetoric. Places with specific cultural histories, places like Hawai'i's volcanoes, were ignored by a master narrative of scientific enlightenment that constructed such sites as instances of visual universals. As Pratt emphasizes, "One by one the planet's life forms were to be drawn out of the tangled threads of their life surroundings and rewoven into European-based patterns of global unity and order. The (lettered, male, European) eye that held the system could familiarize ('naturalize') new sites/sights immediately upon contact, by incorporating them into the language of the system."[19] In such a narrative, Kilauea and Mauna Loa were seen not as Native Hawaiian places but as instances of a Euroamerican category, volcano, to be grouped and understood along with other volcanoes Euroamerican observers were visiting around the world. Such narratives, Pratt concludes, removed sites "not only from their organic or ecological relations with each other, but also from their places in other peoples' economies, histories, social and symbolic systems" (31).

Such a "natural history" rhetoric protected observers from lapsing into the speechlessness so often invoked by travel writers. There could be no surprise and no silence for the natural history writer for every place offered opportunities for the further recording of observations that supported her or his assumption of a preexisting natural order. The various nineteenth-century expeditions that visited Hawai'i's volcanoes may be seen, then, as in part government-sponsored demonstrations of the "universality" of this recently developed rhetoric. They were exercises in a discursive imperialism, with effects comparable to the imperialism of the gunships that often accompanied them.

The missionaries on assignment in Hawai'i were both constructors and dis-
seminators of this new rhetoric. These texts and observations proved extremely
valuable to scientists—especially since many scientists never even visited the islands, for, in the natural history view, data signify more than actual experience at
particular sites. Natural history rhetoric impacted Hawai'i in the nineteenth century, however, more as a polemical weapon than as science. The missionaries em-
braced natural history to strengthen their attacks on Pele, a vital survivor from the
precontact era whom they thought it most crucial for them to oppose.

OPPOSING PELE

While Euroamericans were circulating both a rhetoric of the sublime and a rhetoric of natural science in their efforts to take possession discursively of the volcano, Kanaka Maoli maintained their centuries-old, alternative rhetoric based
on an understanding of Pele and other Hawaiian ancestors. Nineteenth-century
Kanaka Maoli willingly shared some of their Pele beliefs with Euroamericans,
who seemed to have often been fascinated by her and often tried to integrate
her into their texts in some way. Pele's appeal is evident, for example, even in
the texts of Bird and Twain, who spent only a few months in the islands. In
Varigny's *Fourteen Years in the Sandwich Islands*, the Pele narrative disrupts
the writing of a European who lived considerably longer than most foreigners
near Pele's home.

Varigny served as Kamehameha V's finance minister and also as a foreign minister, negotiating treaties with several European powers. He left the islands in
1868 and published his book in 1874. Varigny offers both a postcontact history of
the islands and a personal memoir, and both these parts of the book are guided by
what his English translator aptly describes as Varigny's "trustful, rational, positivistic religion of progress."[20] In his preface, Varigny writes:

> No, progress is not an empty word. It is the law of humanity, a providential law, laid
> down by God himself, which a whole people as well as individuals obey, sometimes
> without being aware of doing so. It has been my fortune, in a remote corner of the
> earth, in Oceania, and in a country whose very name is scarcely recognized, to record
> the existence and power of that law, to follow its rapid pace, and to cooperate with it,
> even though in only a small degree. I can testify to its presences, and to the deep faith
> I derive from it in the future of the human race.[21]

In the invocation of "providential law" and elsewhere, he aligns himself with the
rhetoric of natural science being developed by many nineteenth-century writers.
This rhetoric guides Varigny's positivistic account of his fourteen years in
Hawai'i, but proves inadequate when he writes about the volcano. Then the alter-
native Native Hawaiian narrative subverts Varigny's customary invocations of the
Christian God's supposed "natural" laws.

Varigny begins the account of his visit to Kilauea, like many other travel writers, by offering a description of local lore. Pele, he writes, is the "goddess of those subterranean fires that have created the islands, she whose furies have so often deranged and rearranged them" (78). Varigny adds that, while he cannot understand why "the Egyptians deified the onion," the sight of the fires of Kilauea have made it seem reasonable to him why Hawaiians would "choose to deify and worship fire" (78). Later, when Varigny sees his guides praying to Pele, he declares that offering prayers seems a good idea: "I swear I was tempted to follow their example . . . not before the pagan goddess: only before the power of the Almighty" (78). In these opening passages, then, while appearing sympathetic, Varigny carefully distinguishes between pagan Native beliefs and his own.

Varigny next describes the fiery ebb and flow of lava on the caldera floor and concludes, "Pele, so say the natives, is recovering her forces, preparing new manifestations of her power" (79). He was thus beginning to use Pele as an explanation for what he himself was witnessing—though here still he appended a parenthetical "so say the natives" to distance himself from this narrative. Shortly after, Varigny decides to hike down nearer to the caldera floor. His guides object "based on the indignation Pele would feel, with which I was only moderately concerned" (79). His final phrase may be sincere, or, perhaps sardonic, but once Varigny has climbed down into the pit, his references to Pele are no longer equivocal.

A mound of lava forms and Varigny reports that he wondered "if the great mass would head toward us or in the opposite direction. Just as Kanana, my guide, had predicted, it was toward us that Pele was decidedly racing" (80). By including Kanana in the sentence, Varigny invokes Pele as explanation while simultaneously associating it with a Native. In his final words about Kilauea, however, no such distancing occurs. They had to walk some distance before "I was able to catch my breath and savor the blessing of fresh air. Meanwhile, nothing could remove the awful taste of sulphur that seized me by the throat. Pele had avenged herself in her fashion" (80). Varigny's account illustrates the considerable attraction the Pele narrative had even for Euroamericans, like Varigny, who were self-consciously committed to explanations based on natural laws. Few foreigners traveled to Hawai'i's volcanoes in the nineteenth century without enlisting guides, bearers, and cooks. On the long climb, such visitors acquired some understanding of Native Hawaiian Pele beliefs. Appropriating elements of these beliefs provided a coherent narrative to help visitors account for the sights that otherwise might have left them sputtering.

The missionaries, however, were sworn enemies of all mentions of Pele, whether from the pens of Euroamericans or the mouths of Hawaiians. William Ellis's journal, for example, includes this warning in its 1825 preface, addressed "To the Members and Patrons of the Sandwich Island Mission" and seemingly not written by Ellis himself: "Nor must we be surprised, if the former views which the Hawaiian has been accustomed to entertain respecting Pele, the goddess he

supposes to preside over volcanoes, should not at once be eradicated; as he is continually reminded of her power, by almost every object that meets his eyes, from
the rude cliffs of lava, against which the billows of the ocean dash, even to the
lofty craters, her ancient seat amid perpetual snows."[22] In its poetic, concluding
clauses, one detects that even this missionary writer, too, is flirting with his own
idolatrous attraction to Pele.

Ellis's journal itself shows little comparable sympathy for any Natives or
Native beliefs. He describes, for example, an incident that he titles "A
Controversy with a Priestess of Pele." Ellis recounts that he preached one morning to a gathering in Hilo from the text, "Happy is that people whose God is the
Lord." As he was leaving "an old woman . . . all at once exclaimed, 'Powerful are
the gods of Hawaii, and great is Pele, the goddess of Hawaii, she shall save
Maaro'" (215).[23] Ellis continues walking away, thinking to ignore her, until he is
told that this woman is a priest of Pele. This knowledge, he reports, made him feel
it was necessary to return to confront her.

Ellis asks her "if she thought Jehovah was good, and those happy who made
him their God?" The woman, named Oani, replies: "He is your good God, (or
best God), and it is right that you should worship him; but Pele is my deity, and
the great goddess of Hawaii. Kiraurea is the place of her abode. Ohiaotelani (the
northern peak of the volcano) is one corner of her house. From the land beyond
the sky, in former times, she came" (216). Ellis describes his several attempts to
convince Oani that "Pele is a creature of their own invention" (216). Oani continues to reply with a tolerance for many gods that Ellis rebukes. Ellis advises
Oani and "all present" that they must accept Jehovah as the one god "to escape
the everlasting death that would overtake all the idolatrous and wicked" (217).
Ellis also argues that Pele does not deserve to be worshiped, as she is perpetually
destroying the island with lava and earthquakes. Oani counters that not Pele but
Ellis and his countryman are the ones who are destroying Hawai'i. Ellis writes:
"She mentioned the names of several chiefs, and then asked who destroyed
these? Not Pele, but the rum of the foreigners, whose God you are so fond of.
Their diseases and their rum have destroyed more of the king's men, than all the
volcanoes on the island" (217).[24] Oani remains unconvinced by Ellis's further
fulmination, and it is evident in Ellis's attacks on Pele here and elsewhere in his
journal (e.g., 117; 162) that he is projecting a Jehovah-like mean-spiritedness
onto a god whose behavior in the mele and chants that have survived do not warrant such a description.

Regardless of the accuracy of Ellis's views about Pele, it is clear that he believed her to be an important obstacle to the acceptance of his peculiar sect of
Christianity. He seized opportunities to deny and mock her. For example, when
his guides prayed to Pele at Kilauea, Ellis claims, "We answered we were sorry
to see them offering to an imaginary deity the gifts [ohelo berries] of the true
God; but hoped that they would soon know better, and acknowledge Jehovah
alone in all the benefits they received" (163).

Because direct attacks, mocking, and preaching were not enough, Ellis and his fellow missionaries needed as well an alternative narrative of the volcano's behavior to offer to Kanaka Maoli as a replacement. If Pele was claimed to be "supernatural," to repeat one of Ellis's charges, then it was necessary to construct a countering notion of "the natural" to fill Pele's rhetorical place. "As far as their language and mental capability admitted," Ellis would write, missionaries like himself should endeavor "to explain some of the causes of volcanic fire" (175) to Native Hawaiians. Their purpose, Ellis goes on, was not primarily to share the knowledge of natural science. "Our principal solicitude, however, was to lead their minds to God, who created the world, and whose almighty power controls the elements of nature in all their diversified operations; but of whom, though they beheld the wondrous works of his hand, they were lamentably ignorant" (175).

Wright, Takahashi, and Griggs conclude that, in large part because of the work of Ellis and other missionaries, "Probably more was learned in the nineteenth century from direct observation of volcanic activity in Hawaiʻi than anywhere else in the world."[25] By recording and preaching about these observations of God's "wondrous works" as part of a story of "natural forces," the missionaries and their coreligionists created a counter-narrative about the volcano that was as elaborate and complex as Oani's and those who believed like her. It is this same missionary-sponsored, counter-narrative that the U.S. government now preaches to Kilauea's 2.5 million visitors each year.

IN THE OLD AND THE NEW HAWAIIAN CONTACT ZONE

The contestation among travel writing, natural history, and Native Pele narratives occupied a nineteenth-century discursive space much like what Pratt describes as a "contact zone." Such zones, she writes, are "the space of colonial encounters, the space in which people geographically and historically separated come into contact with each other and establish ongoing relations, usually involving conditions of coercion, radical inequality, and intractable conflict."[26] Though the Pele narrative completely dominated the volcano area when the missionaries arrived, it was substantially overwhelmed by a Euroamerican, natural science narrative in the space of one hundred years. Two events signal the spectacular success of the colonizer's rhetoric. The first was in 1912, when the Hawaiian Volcano Observatory (HVO) was established on the rim of Kilauea crater, with funds provided by the Massachusetts Institute of Technology and by a group of island businessmen, most of whom were Euroamerican. According to Wright, Takahashi and Griggs, the most important such local supporter was Lorrin Thurston, owner-publisher of the *Pacific Commercial Advertiser*, Honolulu's largest newspaper. (Thurston had earlier committed treason in leading the overthrow of the Hawaiian constitution, which he had sworn to protect.) Thurston's paper promoted annexation and later the rhetoric of natural science as a part of its effort to denigrate Kanaka Maoli and promote the importation of metropolitan culture.

Then, in 1916, the U.S. Congress established Kilauea and its surroundings as the nation's twelfth national park. Thomas Jaggar, the geologist-promoter responsible for the establishment of HVO, argued for the creation of this park as a place for "the systematic study of volcanology" and of "the earth's primitive processes."[27] The HVO and Hawaii Volcanoes National Park (HVNP) then formed an allied apparatus to advance and disseminate the rhetoric that the missionaries had found so useful in their proselytizing work.

Visitors to Kilauea today are thus repeatedly invited to interpret the place as an important site for science, which is defined as an apparatus for producing universal truth. There is little reference to it also being a place of worship other than as a part of "myths" and "folklore," which are offered as fanciful narratives that have been superseded by more enlightened views. Even most Kanaka Maoli now must pay cash to representatives of the U.S. government in order to enter. Pamphlets supplied by park rangers elaborate on the many official signs offering lay versions of geologic narratives. It is this scientific narrative, too, that is taught in the surrounding Hawaiian schools and is invoked in newspapers and on broadcast news programs when describing volcanic activity. What Pratt calls "the highly asymmetrical relations of domination and subordination" (4) found in contact zones have thus successfully forced Pele to the periphery even at Kilauea, which Oani and others assert is her home.

Despite the power of these well-funded, official, rhetorical apparatuses, the Pele narrative survives. In fact, at the end of the twentieth century, there has been a marked resurgence of interest in traditional Native Hawaiian views, among both Hawaiians and non-Hawaiians. This raises perplexing issues, for the appropriation of a Pele rhetoric by non-Hawaiians often seems more to reaffirm a continuing Euroamerican hegemony than to support autonomous, alternative, Native views.

As Figure 4.1 illustrates, some of the most egregious current appropriations of Pele are being made by practitioners of new-age religions. Non-Hawaiians guided by such beliefs are visiting Hawai'i's volcanoes to leave ersatz offerings. According to HVNP rangers, these offerings have included pigs' heads, new-age crystals, chicken carcasses, incense, candles, bottles of liquor, and, increasingly, piles of rocks resembling lava pyramids.[28] For such people, Hawai'i's volcanoes are like the Egyptian pyramids, Stonehenge and other places—sites of "harmonic convergence" and/or "sites of power." Such a narrative has consequences much like that produced by metropolitan scientific rhetoric, which constructs Kilauea as a site of universal natural processes. Both rhetorics background the sense of a unique Native site to make global connections that displace traditional Kanaka Maoli views.

Observing the increase in occurrence of such new-age offerings "hurts inside," Lyons Kapi'ioho Naone says. Naone, a Kanaka Maoli cultural practitioner, also believes that "people need to be told they can't just make up stuff and say it's

Figure 4.1   "A Journey to the Sacred Sites of Hawaii"

Come & Enjoy the Experience!

Discover:

✦ The history, language, rituals & philosophy of Hawaiian Shamanism
✦ The variety and qualities of many sacred locations around the Big Island .
✦ A powerful connection to your Higher Self
✦ Connecting with the energy of Pele at an active volcano
✦ The scents, tastes & culture of Hawaii
✦ Boost your immune system
✦ Rejuvenation of your life force Regenerate your health
✦ The real "Magic of Hawaii" that most tourists never see

Private sessions of Hawaiian Huna Kane and Time Line Therapy™ are available throughout the week

Stay & Enjoy:
After two days of relaxation following this Sacred Journey, join Nicki Katchur in a certification training in Huna Kane

A JOURNEY TO THE SACRED SITES OF HAWAII

Remembering Ancient Initiations

Presented by:
John Tozeland
&
Nicki Katchur

Swim with the Dolphins

Trance-Action Consultants

134 Wallingford Cresc, Winnipeg, MB. R3P 1L4
888 TRANCE 6 (872-6326)
(204) 488-2055 fax (204) 489-7145
email tozeland@trance-action.com
http://www.trance-action.com

Source: Brochure from Trance-Action Consultants, 134 Wallingford Cresc., Winnipeg, Manitoba, Canada.

Hawaiian."[29] Unfortunately, in a contact zone such as modern Hawai'i, asymmetries of power make it unlikely that pleas like Naone's will change Euroamerican behavior. Metropolitan appropriations are disseminated worldwide, but the voices of Naone and others like him are barely heard.

Even non-Native visitors to Hawaiian volcanoes who do not embrace new-age religions seem prone to embracing Euroamerican fabrications of Pele. In *Powerstones: Letters to a Goddess*, Linda Ching and Robin Stephens detail the history of "Pele's curse," the belief that Pele sends bad luck to anyone who takes rocks from the volcano's area. Many people are aware of this so-called curse but many, nonetheless, continue to take rocks. Enough of these decide later that they made a mistake so that "each year more than 2,000 pounds of rocks are returned to Hawaii Volcanoes National Park."[30] Ching and Stephens reproduce a selection from some of the letters that have accompanied these packages. "Dear Sir," one reads. "Please return this rock to the park. I'm not superstitious but I have no doubt. The Curse Works" (21). Another letter is addressed "To Whom It may Concern (Pele)," and implores: "Please return the contents of this box to the trail going to the ocean and to the black sand beach. HURRY!!!!!!!!!!!" (24).

Pele's curse is probably the fragment of Hawaiian religion known most widely among Euroamericans, except it is not of Kanaka Maoli but of Euroamerican origin. As Ching and Stephens make clear, the notion that Pele sends bad luck to those who take her rocks was invented by park rangers in the 1940s in an effort to discourage visitors from disturbing the natural landscape. Ching and Stephens conclude that "the fanciful little tale gathered moss at every revolution, finally becoming so big and so powerful, so imbued with mana, or psychic power, that today, people around the world know of the modern urban legend and believe that it has affected their lives" (90). Native Hawaiians do not have the connivance to make up nonsense and call it American and then to roll this ball around the world until it becomes widely believed. Powerful representational technologies are required to produce and disseminate such fabrications. Such apparatuses are controlled so overwhelmingly by Euroamericans that the current, renewed, popular interest in Pele seems likely to continue to be constructed more out of Euroamerican than Native Hawaiian beliefs.

Foreign representations overwhelming Native beliefs are well illustrated in Michele Jamal's *Volcanic Visions: Encounters with Other Worlds*. Although nineteenth-century visitors like Isabella Bird and Mark Twain came to the volcano with the attitude of sightseers (much like many who visit HVNP today), Jamal frames the narrative of her visits as a pilgrimage. She travels to Hawai'i not to observe but to experience and be transformed: "I wanted to be near the active volcano, perceiving my mood fluctuations, the effects of living near Pele, the volcano goddess. In her atmosphere and surroundings I wanted to kindle the flames within, and emerge with the awakenings of my own primordial goddess, prophesying and speaking in tongues."[31] Jamal succeeds beyond even these ambitious expectations, for in her six months in the islands she discovers that Pele is her "ally and sister" who awakens her "slumbering power" so Jamal can be freed "from the bonds of exploitation, self-doubt and invalidation delivered by patriarchal minds" (18). Jamal also finds that the Native stories of Pele's migrations through the islands "can be considered analogous to the individual's spiritual quest for enlightenment" (3). Pele and the other Hawaiian gods did truly come from the sky, Jamal finally concludes, for they were placed in the Pacific on the lost islands of Mu by beings from outer space who drive the heavens in UFOs.

Jamal's book is better crafted and nearer to mainstream nature writing than many other recent texts by Euroamericans that similarly reinvent Pele to fit metropolitan, new-age senses of spirituality. Before writing *Volcanic Visions*, Jamal published *Shape Shifters: Shaman Women in Contemporary Society*, a study of dreams and archetypes grounded more in texts than visions.[32] *Volcanic Visions*, too, provides much "factual" information about Pele, Native Hawaiians, volcanoes, and the current eruption of Puʻu ʻO. It does not present itself, then, as a work of fantasy or of fiction but rather embraces the rhetoric of many contemporary books that similarly trace the spiritual quests of their authors, often as they travel to sites sacred to indigenous people whom earlier Euroamericans had displaced.

The worldwide distribution and potential influence of books such as *Volcanic Visions* can be contrasted with the distribution of Pualani Kanakaʻole Kanahele and Duke Kalani Wise's *Ka Honua Ola*, one of the definitive texts by Native Hawaiians on their sense of Pele.[33] This work collects many of the chants and lore of the Kanakaʻole family, for whom Pele is an ancestor, as well as an annotated bibliography of most of the Hawaiian- and English-language literature on Pele and related Hawaiian figures. This extraordinary text exists only as a handbound report and has never been offered for sale even in Hawaiʻi's own commercial bookstores. Worldwide distribution, of course, is inconceivable, as this Native text does not revision Pele in a familiar metropolitan rhetoric like that Jamal employs.

Some people hope that texts like Jamal's and fabrications like Pele's curse will encourage interest in and respect for Native Hawaiians. It seems more likely, however, that such Euroamerican appropriations increase the marginalization of traditional Native Hawaiian beliefs. One further example may make this process of marginalization clearer. The American vocalist Tori Amos invokes Pele in the title of her 1996 compact disc, *Boys for Pele*, and in one of the songs as well. The lyrics to this song, "Muhammad my Friend," include this stanza:

and Moses I know
I know you've seen fire
but you've never seen fire
until you've seen Pele blow
and I've never seen light
but I sure have seen gold
and Gladys save a place for me
on your grapevine
till I get my own TV show[34]

The next stanza includes references to Cracker Jacks, the Pope's rubber robe, and "a girl/back in Bethlehem." Pele's appearance within such a metropolitan pastiche seems unlikely to increase respect for Native Hawaiians or Native places. The title given to a review of the album by Neil Spencer suggests the tone this music evokes. "Goddess Pele lifted Tori out of darkness," the headline claims.[35] The text makes clear what a close listening confirms, that Amos's focus in *Boys for Pele* is primarily on trapping boys for Tori (see Figure 4.2). Worldwide distribution of this music perpetuates the belief that Native places are proper sites for the gratification of Euroamerican desires.

Figure 4.2   *Boys for Pele* CD cover

VOLCANO IN CONTEMPORARY NATURE WRITING

A related appropriation of the Pele narrative grounds the texts of many of the na-ture writers who have visited Hawai'i's volcanoes since the beginning of the cur-rent eruption that started in 1983. These writers accept the mechanistic interpre-tations constructed by the nineteenth-century scientific rhetoric. In large measure, in fact, such writers seem to be seeking to find ways to make this rhetoric more generally available and accepted by metropolitan publics, in this way extending the "interpretive" work of rangers at the HVNP. These nature writers now func-tion rather like public relations or publicists for science. However, when writing about Hawai'i's volcano, today's fashion dictates that dollops of a Native narra-tive be included as well.

James D. Houston's "Fire in the Night" is paradigmatic. Houston describes his excursion with a geologist to gather samples of lava pouring into the ocean. As

Houston tells the story of the drive and hike, he offers descriptions of the history of the ongoing eruption and of the work of the staff of the HVO in studying it. Within this celebration of science and scientists, Houston makes episodic references to Pele, whom he describes as "the goddess of fire, who is said to make her home in a crater about fifteen miles from where we were walking."[36]

The climax of the short piece comes when the geologist shows Houston how to stick a hand ax into moving lava to "bring away a gob of the molten stuff" (115). The geologist remarks to Houston that "Pele is being good to you" (120), as conditions are perfect and Houston successfully scoops a good sample. Houston throws the hardening ball on the ground and, as it cools, presses his heel into it, individualizing his souvenir in the same manner as did the many early travelers to the Americas that Pratt describes.

Travelers distinguish themselves from earlier, less self-conscious colonizers, however, by occasionally voicing second thoughts about their imperial actions. Houston, for example, broods:

> I did not feel right about bringing this trophy back home. I kept thinking about the tug of the lava as I pulled the axe away. Through the handle I had felt its texture, its consistency, and something else that haunted me. A reluctance. A protest. As if live flesh were being torn from a body.
> Maybe this was what the Hawaiians meant when they said all the rocks there belong to Pele and should not leave the island. (121)

Houston's "second thoughts" do not lead him to question either Euroamerican science or its colonialist hegemony. It is these apparatuses, after all, that have smoothed his access to the site of the lava flow and provided him with the tools, guides, and expertise necessary for him to experience that seeming "live flesh . . . being torn from a body." The invocation of Pele and Hawaiian beliefs adds a touch of the exotic for Houston's mostly non-Hawaiian readers, but the text marks these off within a poetic rhetoric that differs from the positivistic rhetoric Houston employs when discussing geology. Houston writes "as if" and "maybe" for things Hawaiian, but his accounts of the geologist's descriptions of the site are presented as facts. Even Houston's reference to Hawaiian beliefs about carrying rocks home is, as mentioned earlier, actually a Euroamerican invention.

Houston offers his conclusion that "maybe Pele was another word for the living stuff of earth, and maybe I had finally understood something, through my hands, something I had heard about and read about and talked about and even tried to write about" (121). All reliable accounts, both Native and non-Native, make evident that Pele is *not* another word for the living stuff of the earth, and yet Houston's mainly metropolitan readers are unlikely to know this. Houston's text thus exemplifies a very clearly defined, Euroamerican genre, one that Gary Nabhan describes as "the combining of the two cultures of humanistic art and technical science into a seamless view of culture and nature interacting."[37] Houston's work accomplishes just such a combining, creating a single narrative out of some mundane, geological fieldwork and his neoromantic, sublime experience with a supposedly living earth. This makes convincing writing for metropolitan audiences, but neither the rhetoric of humanistic art nor of technical science—either separately or combined—represents Native Hawaiian experiences of the volcano or Pele. Such nature writing, to paraphrase Stephen Greenblatt once again, is not about the other but is rather a practice upon the other.

Metropolitan nature writing seems likely to continue to produce and distribute influential representations of Kilauea volcano, as well as other Native sites. As Edward Hoagland says, at its best, such writing can "combine rhapsody with science and connect science with rhapsody."[38] Frank Stewart recommends this genre in *A Natural History of Nature Writing* precisely because nature writers integrate the two cultures of science and art: "They are aware of the limits of both objectivity and subjectivity in giving accurate accounts of nature that will grip our emotional as well as rational understanding. They pursue this understanding with an avidity for fact accessible only through the scientific method and with a passion for metaphors, patterns, feelings, and self-awareness accessible only through poetry and art. In this way they seek to make our minds and our hearts whole again" (xv-xvi). The pursuit of a return to a supposed, preexisting "wholeness" is, of course, a part of the tradition of the romantic sublime we earlier discussed. As Stewart's analysis and Houston's example make clear, however, the commitment of nature writers remains to a rhetoric of "accurate accounts," to what Stewart says is "a literary art as rigorous as natural science, with a similar allegiance to verifiable fact" (xix). A claim that the earth is living, then, is thought compatible with positivist verification, a verification Houston seeks by dipping the hand ax into the flow. Euroamerican science and humanism may be enriched by this integration of narratives, but it is not clear in what ways, if any, Native believers in Pele are enriched as well.[39]

Many of the scientists who have spent years working at HVO have found ways to show respect for Native Hawaiian beliefs without simultaneously offering to represent those beliefs to metropolitan audiences. Though earlier scientists tried to replace the Pele narrative with their own, many current HVO scientists are becoming supportive of the principle that Hawaiians have the right to use the HVNP as a site where alternative traditional rituals and beliefs will be sustained. Some geologists now want the two narratives to coexist. For example, Reggie Okamura, retired Chief of Operations at HVO, has said, "I totally believe in her [Pele]. And that doesn't interfere with my beliefs in science. I can live comfortably with both of these beliefs."[40]

Scientists such as Okamura do not take their dual beliefs as a warrant for integrating traditional Pele narratives into their scientific publications, but nature writers like Houston and others have not been so reticent. These latter invocations of Pele may indeed have the effect that Stewart wishes for nature writing about Hawai'i—that is, they may increase Euroamerican intolerance for "destruction of this irreplaceable island world."[41] Such an effect comes at a great price, however, for the "spirit of the land" that Stewart says nature writing evokes seems much unlike the Pele of Oani, the Hawaiian woman Ellis vowed to silence in 1825.

PELE IN ART

Palikapu Dedman, one of the founders of the Pele Defense Fund, maintains that "Pele is important to all the Hawaiians. Because it is the last identity sort of god per se that we can relate to in its physical form. That is what Pele means to me today. . . . If Pele is the last one to bring that to the surface, then that's how important she is."[42] The "physical form" Dedman refers to has lately been rendered by artists using a variety of representational techniques brought to the islands by non-Hawaiians. These visual renderings have been appearing at the same time that new-age religions and nature writing have been representing Pele in texts. Current trends suggest that visual images will become increasingly common in metropolitan societies, so it seems likely that visual representations of Pele will become even more well known than the one represented in Euroamerican texts.

Recently constructed images of Pele can be found in books and in art galleries, in paintings and photographs, on jewelry, sewn into quilts, rugs, and dolls, glazed on pottery, sculpted in many media, and constructed out of electronic bits by computer software programs. Most of these images are being crafted by Euroamericans who have not had any training in Native Hawaiian beliefs. Most of their art is being bought by and displayed in the houses and on the bodies of Euroamericans. The Pele art industry, then, reflects Euroamerican traditions more than those of Native Hawaiians. Still, much of the pleasure and value consumers experience in possessing such objects stems from their supposing that these visual images express exotic Native spiritual beliefs.

Before the arrival of Euroamericans, Hawaiians seldom constructed images of Pele. Her story was spoken, sung, chanted, and danced. She was often seen in many different bodily forms, but these sightings were not reproduced in commodifiable forms. Even though Euroamericans began constructing representations of the islands as soon as they arrived, they did not turn Pele into a commodity until recently. Instead, the sketches, paintings, and maps made of Kilauea volcano over a century operated as elements in the apparatus of natural science being constructed to displace the Pele narrative. The distribution of so many visual images of the volcano that systematically omitted references to Pele reinforced Euroamerican claims that her narrative was anachronistic. Thus, for example, as David Forbes reports, the most influential congruence of painters Hawai'i has ever seen, the so-called Volcano School, which flourished in the final decades of the nineteenth century, painted many representations of eruptions and lava flows, but few images of Pele.[43] This work served as the fine arts equivalent of the nearly concurrent work of missionaries, travel writers, and scientists who were simultaneously constructing anti-Pele, "naturalistic" views of this traditional Hawaiian site.

The paucity of earlier imaging of Pele suggests that the current flood of pictorial representations requires explanation. For one thing, many more artists now live in the volcano area or are able to travel there frequently. In addition, the east rift zone eruption is over a decade old and has produced many spectacular sights—destroying a village, a subdivision, a famous black sand beach, and several important Native Hawaiian sites. The general, renewed, metropolitan interest in Native peoples and their cultures has no doubt also been a factor, as has the simultaneous resurgence of Kanaka Maoli interest in Pele. Artists have turned to Pele, then, for many of the same reasons that nature writers have started writing about her after a silence of many years.

Pele sits on paper, canvas, clothing, jewelry, and elsewhere, signifying in much the same way as such contemporary metropolitan icons as Elvis, Michael Jordan, and Madonna. As an icon that now travels, Pele loses her identity with her particular, unique place. When Pele hangs on walls in Honolulu and Hong Kong, her home in the craters of Kilauea becomes less essential and is thus one step closer to being turned into an amusement park or being destroyed by bombs or by the Army Corps of Engineers in an effort to save private property. When foreigners use Pele to decorate T-shirts, earrings, and the walls of conference rooms, the Native practice of Pele worship is repressed more than remembered. Each time Pele is reproduced, the belief that Euroamerican apparatuses can master Native places is reinforced. Those Native Hawaiians who know Pele as their ancestor may one day be so inundated by these images that their own visualizations of Pele will be changed.

It has become common for metropolitan critics to disparage attempts to maintain separate Native traditions. These critics argue that there are no "pure" or "authentic" cultures left on the earth. Homi Bhabha offers one influential version of this argument when he maintains that Native social formations typically exist in a Third Space based upon the inscription and articulation of each culture's hybridity. For Bhabha, hybridity is imitation with a difference. It is a creative adaptation by the colonized or subordinate that simultaneously copies and mocks the cultural practices of the dominant. This perspective usefully calls attention to the way Native people resist through creative modification the dominant cultures that are imposed upon them. It is in this way, for example, that Epeli Hau'ofa argues in "Our Sea of Islands" that Pacific peoples are today adapting modern communication and transportation technologies to revitalize their precontact traditions of heroic exploration and transoceanic trade.[44]

Bhabha is most interested in how Native peoples mimic Euroamericans, but it is clear that Euroamericans mimic Natives, too, and that this mimicry by dominant cultures has effects quite different from mimicry by those who have been colonized. The latter are often forced to copy their colonizers in order to survive. Even when such mimicry is in some sense freely chosen, mimicry by Native peoples little alters the colonizer's social formations. When Euroamericans mimic Native peoples, however, their mimicry is often widely distributed in commodities such as compact discs, books, films, and television productions. Such commodities suggest to some that Native beliefs are being preserved and honored by Euroamericans, when in fact this mimicry is more likely constructing distinctively hybrid forms. These hybrid representations then are often broadcast back at Natives and effect an alternation in the way that these people experience themselves. Such productions create pressures among Natives to become more like that which the hybrid representations of Euroamerican commodities depict.[45]

Arguments such as Bhabha's that emphasize reciprocal hybridities can encourage the dominant cultures' continuing mining of Native resources to fulfill foreign desires. Such rhetorics of a universal hybridity, offered mostly by metropolitan critics, can be viewed as the latest variant in a nearly two-centuries-old campaign to replace Pele with Euroamerican narratives. Pele survived the missionary and scientific onslaught by remaining outside the dominant culture, but now she faces a new threat from those who wish not so much to silence her but rather to speak on her behalf, and in Euroamerican rhetorical forms. Once Pele becomes generally associated with pop songs by Tori Amos and with images created by Euroamericans, what Palikapu Dedman calls the last Hawaiian identity may be gone.

PELE AS ANCESTOR

For many Hawaiians, Pele is associated primarily with an oral and not a textual or visual arts tradition. Some Euroamericans have managed to collect and transcribe fragments of the Native oral tradition, but these texts have tended to mistranslate and misidentify Hawaiian beliefs, often by relying on previous Euroamerican texts. A compounding of errors has thus made it likely that Euroamerican experts are becoming with each succeeding generation less and less knowledgeable about Hawaiian beliefs.

One example of a pandemic expert misunderstanding is emblematic. In most Euroamerican texts, Pele is called a "god." According to many Hawaiians, however, Pele could not be a god (or goddess, as an even more recent appellation terms her), for traditional Hawaiians had no gods. Herb Kawainui Kane writes, for example: "One cultural fact is the absence in the Polynesian language of equivalents for such Western religious terms as 'divine,' 'god,' 'adoration,' 'holy,' 'sacrifice,' 'supernatural,' and 'religion.' As used by Cook's men and by some anthropologists today, such terms misinterpret Polynesian thought."[46] Marshal Sahlins's decades-long attempt to represent Hawaiian beliefs fails spectacularly, Kane says, precisely because Sahlins does not understand the fundamental fact that Kanaka Moali prior to 1778 had "no vision of the supernatural as a *separate* sphere from the natural universe." (265).

Kane points out that at least one non-Native understood this. He cites E. S. Craighill Handy, who wrote in 1923: "The native does not distinguish supernatural and natural, as we do. *Atua* were simply beings with powers and qualities of the same kind as those of living men, but greater. Some men and women were *atua* in this life; most became *atua* after death."[47] Many Hawaiians recognized Pele as an atua in her life, many more after her death. Her presence then and now was especially felt among those who descended from her or from other members of her family. Such Pele beliefs are ancient and traditional, and have survived two centuries of Euroamerican colonization. For example, Palikapu Dedman recently observed, "I was brought up that Pele wasn't just a supernatural god as Jesus is, or other religious people may look at their gods. But as family. She was just as much alive today, and still is, in the Hawaiian's mind then as now." Dedman goes on, "I don't think the religion ever died. I think a lot of Hawaiians pulled back and went indoors. A lot of them went underground, kept their religion within their family knowing that it was something you could not throw away because it is too many thousands of years in existence that you just can't cast it away because somebody came with a new idea of religion and a new life for you."[48]

The family of Edith Kanaka'ole also knows itself as a Pele family. In offering for print many chants and meles, Pualani Kanaka'ole Kanahele speaks of them as family stories: "Let us interpret for ourselves, and everyone else must allow us this privilege, about who our ancestors were, how they thought, and why they made certain decisions. We will treat them with honor, dignity, love and respect whether they be Gods, ali'i or kānaka because they are 'ohana."[49]

Haunani-Kay Trask's call for a "moratorium on studying, unearthing, slicing, crushing, and analyzing us" seems especially appropriate when thinking of outsider representations of Pele.[50] Heeding Kanahele's plea to allow Hawaiians "to interpret for themselves" who Pele is and, therefore, what the volcano means, seems an act of respect that would cost outsiders little more than some increased restraint. Still, such a moratorium seems unlikely, for Euroamericans seem as determined today as was Captain Cook to use their metropolitan rhetoric of possession to appropriate even the most personal and sacred Native Hawaiian sites.

Chapter Five

Echo Tourism:
The Narrative of Nostalgia in Waikīkī

The subsistence lifestyle of these Hawaiian people, living in the shadow of
Leʻahi (Diamond Head), was one of leisure and abundance. . . . This prosperity
allowed time for recreation and rest. Surfing, canoeing, and swimming have always been an important part of life in this ancient place and though much has
changed in modern Waikiki, these traditions remain.

Glen Grant[1]

There is no more famous Hawaiian place than Waikīkī, and yet there is no site in
Hawaiʻi where Kanaka Maoli have been more thoroughly displaced. The opening
pages of David Lodge's novel, *Paradise News*, illustrate the degree to which
Natives are now alienated from this once Native place. "What do they see in it,
eh?" Leslie Pearson, an airport receptionist, asks at London's Heathrow Airport,
as he and his colleague load passengers bound for Honolulu. Pearson is incredu-
lous that the people before him have freely paid hundreds of pounds to be cooped
up in "one of those oversized sardine cans" for nearly twenty hours. "What are
they *after*?" Pearson asks when his first question is not answered.

Pearson's colleague finally replies. "The free esses, innit?" he says. "Sun, sand
and sex."[2]

There are no Hawaiians and no allusions to Native places in Lodge's description of the attractions of Hawaiʻi, nor are there many in most contemporary references to the islands. Kanaka Maoli have in fact become so absent from the expected sun, sand, and sex that visitors associate with Waikīkī that some supporters
of the tourist industry have lately begun fretting that this Nativeless image might
be costing them some money. Many recent plans argue for what the *Honolulu
Advertiser* describes as the "Hawaiiannizing" of Waikīkī.[3] George S. Kanahele
explains this perspective as "a growing sense of urgency as more and more people

85

realize that Waikīkī cannot remain competitive in international tourism unless it maintains its uniqueness, the realization being that uniqueness ultimately comes from its being Hawaiian."[4]

Before reviewing some of these plans to restore Hawaiian culture to Waikīkī, it will be useful to review how Kanaka Maoli were eliminated from representations of this area in the first place. Like so much else in the history of rhetoric since Euroamerican settlers immigrated to the islands, constructions of race played a foundational role.

KANAKAS AS NIGGERS

Some central elements of the Euroamerican rhetoric of race were reviewed in the discussion of kama'āina in chapter 3. Not mentioned there, however, was the single most influential passage about Hawaiians ever produced. This famous statement began as a speech that was offered for decades in many cities across America by a writer who represented himself as an expert on what he persisted in calling "The Sandwich Isles." As this writer's fame grew, so, too, did the size of his speaking fees and of his appreciative audiences. Though he had spent but a few months in the islands, he was sometimes introduced as a Native. This writer turned speechmaker induced masses of auditors in both North America and England to laugh at the inferior race he sometimes called niggers but, more often, "kanakas."

Kanakas "will lie for a dollar when they could get a dollar and a half for telling the truth," he told his audiences (7–8). "They will cheat anybody" (8). They love and care for puppies better than they care for their children: "They sleep with them, they don't mind the fleas" (10). "They passionately love and tenderly care for the puppy, and feed it from their own hands until it is a full-grown dog—and then they cook and eat it" (11). The speechmaker further proclaimed: "Kanakas are cruel by nature. They will put a live chicken in the hot embers merely to see it caper about. They used to be cruel to themselves before the missionaries came. They used to tear and burn their flesh, or shave their heads, or pluck out their eyes, or knock out a couple of their front teeth, when a great chief died" (14). This natural cruelty guided the treatment of women, audiences learned, as kanaka women "were the abject slaves of the men; they were degraded to the rank of brutes and beasts and considered to be no better; they were kept at hard labor and were beaten and contemptuously treated by their lords" (17).

This cruel and despicable race has lost its former fierceness, however. "One would as soon expect a rabbit to fight as one of these" (11). In such ways, Mark Twain charmed audiences for thirty years into accepting that Hawai'i is a place where travelers might expect to find safe lodging amid once fierce but now rabbitlike Natives.[5]

Though Twain exploited the rhetoric for comedy, during the same decades researchers were elaborating the rhetoric of race in a more systematic way, creating the classifications necessary for science. As Foucault argues, such classifications facilitate colonialism, as they enable the assigning of positions, regulating of groups, and enforcing of boundaries that imperial administrations require. David Spurr traces the centrality of racial classifications in the work of such nineteenth-century philosophers and scientists as Charles Darwin, Thomas Carlye and John Stuart Mill, each of whom struggled to establish acceptable, universalized schemas for ordering the indigenous peoples of the world.[6] Scientists and philosophers constructed theories of race for specialists, but it was left to journalists, travel writers, novelists and short story writers to provide the general public with examples of how these so-called races behaved. Popular texts like those by Twain illustrated how the abstract categories of science fit "naturally" within the actual experiences of the writers—who, typically, presented themselves as people much like their readers.

The celebrated historian Henry Adams reported on his 1890 visit with King Kalākaua in a letter that illustrates how constructions of race grounded mainstream American thinking:

We went to the little palace at half-past nine in the morning, and Kalakaua received us informally in his ugly drawing-room. His Majesty is half Hawaiian and half Negro; talks quite admirable English in a charming voice; has admirable manners; and—forgive me just this once more—seems to me a somewhat superior Chester A. Arthur; a type surprisingly common among the natives.

To be sure, His Majesty is not wise, and he has—or is said to have—vices, such as whiskey and—others; but is the only interesting figure in the government, and is really . . . [sic] amusing. I have listened by the hour to the accounts of his varied weaknesses and especially to his sympathy with ancient Hawaii and archaic faiths, such as black pigs and necromancy.[7]

Adams's labeling of Kalākaua as a "half Negro" is supposed to help make the supposedly "ugly drawing-room" at Iolani Palace understandable. To be a superior Chester A. Arthur, in Adams's view, is to be a superior buffoon. Even Adams's limp praise—calling Kalākaua "the only interesting figure in government"— mocks simultaneously, for a "half Hawaiian and half Negro" is expectedly a holder of "archaic faiths" and an exhibitor of "varied weaknesses." Adams's representation justifies action to usurp the Native government and replace it with that of a "superior" race.

This letter illustrates a popular view of Hawaiians circulating in North America at the close of the nineteenth century, a view confirmed by the cartoon that appeared on an 1894 cover of the American magazine *Judge* (see Figure 5.1). The overthrow of the Hawaiian monarchy was then a year old. The cartoonist draws Queen Liliʻuokalani, then known to be petitioning the United States for reinstatement, with exaggerated Negroid features and black skin, signifiers to Americans that the Queen was of a race unsuitable to rule.

Figure 5.1   Cartoon of Lili'uokalani in *Judge*
(February 17, 1894). (The poem, "Lili to
Grover," says: "You listened to my DOLE-ful
tale; / You tried your best—'twas no avail. / It's
through no fault of yours or mine / That I can't
be your VALENTINE.")

Reprinted with permission of the Bishop Museum.

Early twentieth-century American ideas about Hawaiians are clearly on view in
Jack London's *The House of Pride*, his first collection of stories with a Hawaiian
setting. This book, published in 1909, contains six stories, of which three focus
on leprosy and three on the mixing of races in Hawai'i. Leprosy and race-mixing
were comparably scandalous topics with American audiences at that time, and the
ambitious London's exploitation of both helped him become the best-selling author in the world. London wrote some of his stories while residing in Waikīkī, and
so was the second writer, following the earlier Robert Louis Stevenson, to produce well-known work there.[8]

London wrote for readers in the United States where it was not only unacceptable but still even illegal to marry a person of another race. Contracting leprosy,

for many Americans, would have seemed a better fate. London relies upon these fears throughout *The House of Pride*.[9] His construction of race in "Aloha Oe" was typical.

"Hawaii has a ripening climate," London writes in this story, "and Dorothy Sambrooke has been exposed to it under exceptionally ripening circumstances" (68). On a four-week visit with her American father, a U.S. senator, sixteen-year-old Dorothy falls in love with twenty-year-old Steve Knight.

> It was he who had given them their first exhibition of surf riding, out at Waikiki Beach, paddling his narrow board seaward until he became a disappearing speck, and then, suddenly reappearing, rising like a sea-god from of the welter of spume and churning white—rising swiftly higher and higher, shoulders and chest and loins and limbs, until he stood poised on the smoking crest of a mighty, mile-long billow, his feet buried in the flying foam, hurling beachward with the speed of an express train and stepping calmly ashore at their astounded feet. That had been her first glimpse of Steve. (70)

This "sea-god," as readers suspect but Dorothy learns too late, is part Hawaiian. Just as the "tropics had entered" Dorothy's "blood" (68), so "a quarter-strain of tropic sunshine streamed in his [Steve's] veins" (73). London explains, Steve "could have dinner with her and her father, dance with her, and be a member of the entertainment committee, but because there was tropic sunshine in his veins he could not marry her" (73). London and his readers assumed this rhetoric of blood had a scientific base.

References to leprosy disappeared from London's second and last volume of stories with a Hawaiian locale, *On the Makaloa Mat*, published posthumously. Plots built on constructions of race, however, still define the Hawaiian experience. In the title story, "On the Makaloa Mat," London seems especially obsessed to show lay audiences how Euroamerican, "scientific" notions of race can be used to explain the behavior of Hawaiians. The first line of the story places the text within this familiar racialized narrative. "Unlike the women of most warm races," London writes, "those of Hawaii age well and nobly" (107).

Two sisters, Martha and Bella, sit under a hau tree at Martha's house on the beach at Waikīkī. Martha is described as sharing "the color of the skin of the grandchildren—the unmistakable Hawaiian color" (108). Color signifies race for London, and his story provides a demonstration that this "unmistakable Hawaiian color" rules the behavior of all who carry even a tiny fraction of Hawaiian blood. "One eighth and one sixteenth Hawaiian were they, which meant that seven eighths and fifteen sixteenths white blood informed that skin, yet failed to obliterate the modicum of golden tawny brown of Polynesia" (108).

This failure "to obliterate" the dangerous, warm race explains most of the important action in the story—even the loving rapport between the two sisters. "But the thorough comprehension [their knowledge of each other] resided in the fact that in each of them one fourth of them was the sun-warm, love-warm heart of

Hawaii" (109). Bella tells her sister about a two-week affair she had had with
Prince Liholiho forty years before. She had been married to a haole at the time,
"a gray frozen demigod" interested in money only. Liholiho appeared and ap-
pealed to something racial within her. Bella justifies herself to Martha: "What
would you, Sister Martha? You know what we Hawaiians are. You know what we
were half a hundred years ago" (127). The trace of Hawaiian blood explains what
London's American audiences understand as sinful behavior.

   This construction of race as an effect of blood that cannot be obliterated also
operates in "On the Makaloa Mat" to explain why foreign settlers in Hawai'i have
gotten rich while Hawaiians have become impoverished. Those like Bella and
Martha with some Hawaiian blood are shown to have prospered because of their
shrewd and calculating non-Hawaiian spouses. For example, Martha's husband
appears for the first time at the end of the story. "Erect, slender, gray-haired, of
graceful military bearing, Roscoe Scandwell was a member of the 'Big Five,'
which, by the interlocking of interests, determined the destinies of all Hawaii.
Himself pure haole" (132).[10]

   London's bluntness in expressing his racial views is out of fashion today. Even
James Michener has written of one of London's Hawai'i-based stories
that London "actually denigrated an entire body of people, largely on racist
grounds."[11] Yet Euroamerican, pseudo-scientific classification systems focused
on blood continue to dominate constructions of the islands. They ground
Michener's own influential fictions representing Hawai'i and the Pacific, as well
as most of the histories and advertising that are associated with Waikīkī. Still
probably the most frequently read book among tourists in the islands, Michener's
Hawaii relies upon a racial rhetoric little different from that Twain and London
employed.[12] The "Golden Man" Michener invokes in his final chapter is instanti-
ated through four characters, one Chinese, one Japanese, one haole, and one
Hawaiian. As Stephen H. Sumida points out, Michener associates each of these
men with a particular stereotypical racial quality. As a result, "Michener's *Hawaii*
is an allegory in which the Polynesian represents Nobility and Aloha; the Chinese
represents Tenacity and Shrewdness in Business; the Japanese represents Loyalty
and Competence; the haole, that is, the Caucasian, represents Technological
Power, Ambition, and, somehow, Godliness."[13] Michener's allegorical, modern
Hawaiian, Kelly Kanakoa, represented as a descendent of the ali'i who first settled Hawai'i, earns his living as a gigolo for rich American widows and divorcees.
As Sumida argues, "The 'flower' in Hawaii's songs, Kelly is himself being
plucked by visitors in their dreams of islands" (81). The Euroamerican rhetoric of
race thus remains for Michener, as it was for Twain and London, a natural hierarchy with Hawaiians as servants, entertainers, and sexual playthings for Caucasians, who are a supposedly superior race that biology places on top.[14]

   In contemporary Waikīkī, it is not only Caucasians but also Asians, and especially the Japanese, who assume the role of racial superiors as they continue to
displace Kanaka Maoli from their homes.

HAWAIIANS AS ANCIENTS

In Michener's *Hawaii*, Hawaiians are represented as a distinct race with certain, blood-determined characteristics. But, just as important, they are also depicted as a race whose time of prospering has passed. In the competition among races that Michener claims characterizes contemporary Hawai'i, those with a predominance of Hawaiian blood are handicapped by inherited characteristics that are supposedly of little use in the modern industrial age. Michener explains that these racial characteristics once led to a flourishing civilization in the islands, but he suggests that in modern economies these inborn traits are now more a hindrance than a help.

The notion that nonliterate peoples represent "man's past" is, of course, a trope that appears in a broad range of Euroamerican texts and as a foundational narrative in the "science" of anthropology. In this academic discipline, people like the Hawaiians were first called "savages," then "primitives." Later the label "preliterate" was adopted in an attempt to mask the moral judgment implied by the earlier concepts. Still "preliterate" perpetuates the assumption that races should be understood within a time sequence leading inexorably toward literacy. The contemporary term "nonliterate" avoids this problem but still assesses the Other by the absence of a metropolitan trait—that is, by the Other's failure to be more like the very ones issuing categories.

The construction of Hawaiians as an atavistic race left over from mankind's past began in the very first representation of the islands, in Cook's and King's 1784 volumes (discussed in chapter 2). The extraordinary rate of death by disease that followed upon Western contact was offered by some Euroamericans as evidence that the primitive Hawaiian race was unfit to "compete" in the modern world. Indeed, by the mid-nineteenth century, the surviving Hawaiians were of interest to many Euroamericans primarily as a living memorial to an edenic, pastoral imaginary past.

Twain's description of a solitary horse ride through Waikīkī in 1866 is paradigmatic. Fewer than one hundred years after Cook's arrival, the ride is already for him a journey of nostalgia through a place defined by loss. Twain's description anticipates the "restoration" projects that have become so common for Waikīkī at the end of the late twentieth century.

> Nearby is an interesting ruin—the meager remains of an ancient heathen temple—a place where human sacrifices were offered up in those old bygone days when the simple child of nature, yielding momentarily to sin when sorely tempted, acknowledged his error when calm reflection had shown it to him, and came forward with noble frankness and offered up his grandmother as an atoning sacrifice—in those old days when the luckless sinner could keep on cleansing his conscience and achieving periodical happiness as long as his relations held out.[15]

Waikīkī interests Twain not so much for what it is, not for the living Hawaiians there or near, but for what its "ruins" suggest about "those old bygone days."

This same longing for what Twain over a hundred years ago called the "historical points" is currently being touted by many as one answer to Waikīkī's economic doldrums. The Waikīkī Master Plan, completed in 1992, for example, proposes a thorough redevelopment of the area in an effort to emphasize its connectedness to Native Hawaiians. As Serge Marek remarks, the Waikīkī Master Plan envisions "a reconstruction of space and place in Waikīkī along the lines of an attractive theme park for tourists. History trails, 'public' spaces, street signs, and entire neighborhoods will be designed to fit the needs of tourists who expect an exotic Hawaiian experience in urban Waikīkī."[16]

These types of projects, Jon Goss argues, place tourists in Hawai'i within a "master narrative of nostalgia," a narrative that tells a story of neglect and then of recovery through restoration. Those who are lured to spend their money in the context of this nostalgia participate in what Spencer Lieneweber calls "echo tourism." This tourism fetishizes echoes of a supposed authenticity now available mostly to those with the ability to pay.[17]

Hotels in Waikīkī aspire to represent themselves as "heroes" in this echo narrative. By restoring what they (but few Kanaka Maoli) define as Hawaiianness, hotels claim that they are providing visitors and, to some extent, even residents with an experience of Waikīkī as a place where the ancient culture that was lost is now being recovered. Such a restoration, like the echo tourism it supports, strangely flourishes without the consent, opinion, or even presence of most of the hundreds of thousands of living Native Hawaiians.[18]

RACE, CULTURE, AND LAND

The continuing representation of a supposed naturalized hierarchy of races and the identification of Kanaka Maoli with the irrevocable past are necessary but not sufficient for the success of echo tourism. This narrative of nostalgia also requires what Marek calls the "dehumanization" of Hawaiian culture (125), which effectively disassociates cultural practices from particular peoples. So-called Hawaiian culture is thus taught, exhibited, and sold even when there are no Hawaiian people involved. Marek observes, "Waikīkī as a social, spiritual, and political place for Native Hawaiians, in all its complexity, is either de-emphasized or ignored completely" (119). Tourists in Waikīkī, for example, pay to learn how to hula, weave mats, string leis, and paddle outrigger canoes. They go to luaus, eat "Hawaiian" foods, served in supposedly "Hawaiian" ways, and are entertained by "Hawaiian" dances and music. Increasing the number of venues and patrons for such pursuits is one goal of hoteliers who wish to restore Hawaiianness to Waikīkī. But because culture has been separated from concrete people, these experiences can be, and often are, produced without the consent or participation of any Hawaiians.

As discussed in chapter 3, kama'āina haoles pioneered this strategy of claiming to "preserve" Hawaiian crafts while simultaneously usurping the Native lands where these cultural practices flourish. The koa bowls, calabashes, feather leis, fine kapa, quilts, and other artifacts so often proudly displayed in wealthy, contemporary, kama'āina homes are the models for the Waikīkī hotel decor. In both kama'āina homes and Waikīkī hotels, Hawaiian artifacts are prized, but the Hawaiian people are not.

George Kanahele's twenty-seven goals for restoring "Hawaiianness" to Waikīkī illustrate what happens when Hawaiian culture is conceived without Hawaiian people.[19] Among them are:

Goal I: Use Hawaiian designs and motifs for interiors (13).

Goal L: Use Hawaiian words, place names, etc., accurately and respectfully (16).

Goal N: Use Hawaiian (not Polynesian) music and dance to entertain and promote Waikīkī (18).

Goal O: Make more judicious use of Hawaiian myths and legends (21).

Goal T: Establish an "Historical Trail" (23).

Goal V: Establish an authentic Hawaiian village (31).

This is baldly proclaimed echo tourism; Kanahele here emphasizes a nostalgia for "bygone days" much like Twain already longed for in 1866. Kanahele's plan would increase the paying visitor's sense of experiencing an exotic past where being Hawaiian was once *but is no longer* important. Notions such as "myths," "legends," a "historical trail," and "authentic village" identify Hawaiians with a time before modernity. Kanahele thus offers a program for restoring Hawaiianness to Waikīkī that does not alter the current subaltern status of Kanaka Maoli. Living Hawaiians are not necessary in Kanahele's plan for making Waikīkī a more Hawaiian place, and they will not necessarily acquire more power or have any of their lands or traditional rights restored as a result.

Echo tourism not only separates Kanaka Maoli from their cultural practices, it also undermines Hawaiian claims that the island's indigenous people possess a special, familial relationship with the land. It is commonplace for settlers in Hawai'i to discuss the myriad, contemporary, social problems of the race of Hawaiians, to lament their bad health, their disproportionate imprisonment, their relatively low rates of educational attainment, their high rates of homelessness and poverty, yet simultaneously ignore the issue of stolen Hawaiian lands. By thus dividing the people from their land, Euroamericans undermine the traditional Native Hawaiian integration of the two.

An often cited passage by Twain once again provides an apposite illustration. According to his biographer Albert Bigelow Paine, in 1889, twenty-three years after his visit to the islands, Twain delivered another version of his "Sandwich Islands" speech, but "at the close the poetry of his memories once more possessed him."[20] Twain's remarks have since been reprinted numerous times, including in a recent Hawai'i Visitor's Bureau promotion whose inserts were placed in magazines throughout North America. After speaking for most of his talk about the stupidity, dishonesty, immorality, and cowardice of the race of Kanakas, Twain concludes:

> No alien land in all the world has any deep strong charm for me but that one, no other land could so longingly and so beseechingly haunt me, sleeping and walking, through half a lifetime, as that one has done. Other things leave me, but it abides; other things change, but it remains the same. For me its balmy airs are always blowing, its summer seas flashing in the sun; the pulsing of its surfbeats is in my ear, I can see its garlanded crags, its leaping cascades, its plumy palms drowsing by the shore, its remote summits floating like islands above the cloud wrack; I can feel the spirit of its woodland solitudes, I can hear the splash of its brooks; in my nostrils still lives the breath of flowers that perished twenty years ago.[21]

The charms and haunting Twain refers to are conspicuously lacking a single reference to Native Hawaiians. The "alien land" does not require them to provoke Twain's reverie in this "prose poem," so christened by A. Grove Day and others. In rhapsodizing about a Hawai'i without Hawaiians, Twain anticipates many later twentieth-century representations of Waikīkī.

Michener's *Hawaii* constructs the division between Hawaiian lands and the Hawaiian race in an especially effective way. There are six sections to the novel, and the first, "From the Boundless Deep," offers a narrative of the islands without including any people whatsoever. The following four chapters treat successive waves of "immigrants"—the Hawaiians first, then the Caucasians, the Chinese, and finally the Japanese. This progression, like the dedication of the book to "All the peoples who came to Hawaii," undermines the claim that any particular group possesses a familial relationship with the land. This novel continues to be a staple for tourists in Hawai'i, in part, I would speculate, because it offers the comforting notion that tourists are not displacing Hawaiians but only participating in a supposedly continuous sequence of traveling that stretches back two thousand years.

Marek points out that the common practice of constructing maps and pictures with Waikīkī prominently separated off from the city and people of Honolulu further encourages the displacement of Hawaiians from Waikīkī. These maps and representations create a "floating" space (97), Marek writes, producing "a more marketable and more controllable space of consumption" (94). The 1992 Waikiki Master Plan that is the focus of Marek's study begins each of its several chapters with the same photograph picturing the coconut grove at Helumoa as it looked in the 1880s. Using this ancient picture as the master image for a development plan for contemporary Waikīkī seems an attempt to associate today's tourist destination with Hawai'i's past. It is a past, however, that focuses on landscapes while eliminating Kanaka Maoli.

Pukui, Elbert, and Mookini explain the Hawaiian meaning of Helumoa as "Old land division near the Royal Hawaiian Hotel at Helu-moa Street, Waikīkī, and site of a *heiau* where Ka-hahana was sacrificed. *Lit.*, chicken scratch. (Chickens scratched to find maggots in the victim's body. The supernatural chicken,

Kaʻau-hele-moa, flew here from Kaʻau Crater in Pālolo.)"[22] The Waikiki Master Plan, of course, is not interested in heiaus or memories of a chicken who ate the maggots from the body of Ka-hahana. The Plan, instead, pictures Helumoa as a site for tourist pleasures, as a site for the sun, sand, and sex that Lodge emphasizes in *Paradise News*. The photograph of Helumoa placed so prominently throughout the Plan carefully omits each time the two (probable) Hawaiians paddling an outrigger canoe that constitute the foreground of the original image (see Figures 5.2 and 5.3). Marek speculates on why the government-financed authors of the Waikiki Master Plan removed these Natives. "Could it be," he writes, "these two Hawaiians point too closely to the fact that not just Hawaiian *aliʻi* lived in Waikiki, but that it was also a place utilized by Native Hawaiians in general, *and not just for leisure purposes?*" (116). Marek's speculations about the intentions of the Plan's authors remain uncertain, but this removal of the paddlers from the photograph repeats a common pattern in contemporary Hawaiʻi, a pattern of representing Native places as sites where Kanaka Maoli do not belong.

Figure 5.2   Helumoa coconut grove

Reprinted with permission of the Bishop Museum.

Figure 5.3   Helumoa as cropped for the Waikīkī Master Plan

Reprinted with permission of the Bishop Museum.

WAIKĪKĪ AS ROYAL PLAYGROUND

The phenomenon of people voluntarily travelling long distances away from their families and communities to visit places defined as sites of pleasure is now so common that it is easy to forget how recent this practice is. Tourism hardly existed two hundred years ago, but today this industry is likely soon to surpass both agriculture and manufacturing to become the largest, single source of employment in the world economy. In *The Tourist Gaze: Leisure and Travel in Contemporary Societies*, John Urry details how modern tourism differs from the pilgrimages, touring and traveling undertaken by Anglo-Europeans in earlier times. In an epigraph to his book, Urry quotes Robert Runcie, the Archbishop of Canterbury, who maintains, "In the middle ages people were tourists because of their religion, whereas now they are tourists because tourism is their religion."[23]

The emergence of the modern industrial state, which created the practice of a regulated, separate sphere of wage labor, simultaneously encouraged the development of tourism as something like a modern religion. Industrialization transformed the Anglo-European home from being the center of all life for centuries, including the life of work, into a site where people rest, prepare and eat meals, and otherwise recuperate from spending the majority of their waking hours laboring for wages. Urry sees tourism then having developed out of a desire to experience a third site unlike the sites of both work and the home. Tourist sites are best understood "not in terms of some intrinsic characteristics, but through the contrasts implied with non-tourist social practices, particularly those based within the home and paid work" (2).

Urry argues that "acting as a tourist is one of the defining characteristics of being 'modern'" (2–3). "Not to 'go away' is like not possessing a car or a nice house. It [vacationing] is a marker of status in modern societies and is also thought to be necessary to health" (4). In the early nineteenth century, missionaries, along with some other Euroamericans, introduced to Hawaiʻi these peculiar notions about designating separate sites for work, home, and leisure. By 1865, Euroamerican notions of social space had changed so rapidly that one Honolulu newspaper reported: "Quite a little community of foreign families are now residing at the beach at Waikiki. The distance from town is so short that a person may be in town at his business all day, and go out that evening when the change of atmosphere is truly refreshing while the surf bathing cannot help but be invigorating."[24]

Mid- and late nineteenth-century Hawaiian royalty were prominent among the first "tourists" in Waikīkī. They began to use the site as an escape from home and work, often in the company of their wealthy Euroamerican employees, visitors, and friends. When Twain visited Waikīkī in 1866, for example, he passed by what he described as "about a dozen cottages, some frame and the others of native grass, nestled sleepily in the shade here and there. . . . At a little distance these cabins have a furry appearance, as if they might be made of bear skins. They are very cool and pleasant inside. The King's flag was flying from the roof of one of the cottages, and His Majesty was probably within. He owns the whole concern thereabouts, and passes his time there frequently, on sultry days 'laying off.' The spot is called 'the King's Grove.'"[25] This representation of royal leisure reflects that which millions of tourists hope to experience in Waikīkī today.

Twain was not of sufficient wealth or fame to call on King Lot, also known as Kamehameha V. A few decades later, however, in 1889, Robert Louis Stevenson, then at the height of his celebrity, was entertained in Waikīkī by King Kalākaua, at the King's vacation residence. The ensuing luau occasioned one of the most frequently reproduced photographs of Waikīkī, a picture of Stevenson, Lili'uokalani, and King Kalākaua seated on the floor together at the head of a lavish display of food, the sort of experience hoteliers would soon be claiming to offer for sale to wealthy travelers (see Figure 5.4).

Stevenson lived in Waikīkī beach houses for almost six months. He befriended one of his neighbors, a fellow Scotsman, Archibald S. Cleghorn, who had married King Kalākaua's sister, Princess Mariam Likelike, then deceased. Cleghorn's daughter, Ka'iulani, would a few years later be declared heir-apparent to the throne by her aunt, Queen Lili'uokalani. Such was the society to be found at the various second residences in Waikīkī at the close of the century. Such was the place that Kalākaua described in his 1881 book *The Legends and Myths of Hawaii* as the "beautiful and dreamy suburb of Waikiki."[26]

Figure 5.4   Robert Louis Stevenson at King Kalākaua's luau

Reprinted with permission of Hawai'i State Archives.

Royal residences disappeared from Waikīkī with the overthrow of the Hawaiian Kingdom in 1893. Kalākaua's dreamy suburb became an exclusive area for rich, mostly American-born, merchants. The subsequent history of Waikīkī is well summarized in Barry S. Nakamura's study of the reclamation project that led to the dredging of the Ala Wai canal by Walter Dillingham's Hawaiian Dredging Company. Nakamura shows this massive, public-works project was falsely sold to the public as a necessity for "health reasons." In fact, Dillingham and his political and business allies pushed through the necessary legislation that destroyed the taro and rice farming that was then flourishing in the area. Dillingham owned the only dredge capable of doing the job, and he was subsequently paid an exorbitant fee by the territorial government for his company's work.[27]

Part of the contract allowed Dillingham to keep and sell the extra fill material. Other legislation required neighboring landowners to fill in their lowlands, so Dillingham profited again by selling the excess fill to those many now suddenly required to buy it. The filled-in lands had been home to much stonework for ponds, heiau (temples), and dwellings that demonstrated the prior presence of Kanaka Maoli. As Don Hibbard and David Franzen write, "In a matter of eight years, the work of countless anonymous Hawaiians, work that had survived for centuries, was undone."[28]

Once the Ala Wai canal project was finished, the Waikīkī area became ripe for intense urban development. The depression of the 1930s and then World War II slowed that growth, but the end of the war and statehood encouraged the eruption that produced contemporary Waikīkī. Dillingham and his heirs continued to benefit from insider deals, as did many other non-Native businessmen with sufficient money to influence local and federal politicians. Then, as now, the largest landowners in Waikīkī were foundations with links to the nineteenth-century Hawaiian royalty. (The Queen Emma Foundation holds title to 18.57 acres, Kamehameha School/Bishop Estate to 16.82 acres, and the Liluokalani Trust to 15.41 acres.) Despite this nominal control by Native Hawaiians, there is today little or nothing on these lands to distinguish them from adjoining Waikīkī properties owned by transnational corporations. All are dominated by efforts to manufacture for non-Natives pleasures associated with echo tourism.

THE CONTEMPORARY MASTER NARRATIVE

George Kanahele's *Waikīkī 100 B.C. to 1900 A.D.: An Untold Story* is an impressive attempt to present the long history of Waikīkī as a Native site. A useful, short summary of Waikīkī's subsequent twentieth-century history can be seen in the video *Taking Waikiki: From Self-Sufficiency to Dependency*, first released in 1994. The script closely follows the argument Nakamura developed in his remarkable MA thesis, "The Story of Waikiki and the 'Reclamation' Project."[29] Unfortunately, neither Kanahele's emphasis on Kanaka Maoli nor Nakamura's narrative of the corruption that fueled the development of Waikīkī is much known by either tourists or residents in the islands today. Visitors are instead encouraged through many cultural productions to envision themselves as participants in a tradition of racial supremacy and royal leisure like that experienced by such famous Anglo-American visitors as Twain, Stevenson, and London. Books by these three, for example, probably appear on more hotel and drugstore book racks in Waikīkī than in any other place in the world. Residents are instructed through government-sponsored curricula in public schools and through annual advertising campaigns to show gratitude to tourists for every dollar they spend.

The narrative of Waikīkī as an ancient Hawaiian site for pleasure is offered to tourists and residents in many forms. For example, Hibbard and Franzen's popular history of the area, titled *The View from Diamond Head*, announces this perspective in its subtitle: *Royal Residence to Urban Resort*. After a brief opening chapter authored by Kanaka Maoli Nathan Nāpōkā, Hibbard and Franzen take over to focus on the years Waikīkī was a "royal residence," thereby de-emphasizing the many centuries of Hawaiian history when Kanaka Maoli leaders were chiefs and not royals, the many centuries when Waikīkī was a site for ways of daily living that few modern tourists would enjoy. This repression of Waikīkī's indigenous history allows Hibbard and Franzen and other contemporary apologists for tourism to identify Waikīkī's past with recreation and royal pleasures, especially as those pleasures were associated with European styles of the late nineteenth and early twentieth centuries. As Marek points out, "This period of time is safe because it is just old enough to connect Waikīkī leisure use by Hawaiian *ali'i* to present resort conditions, but not far enough back to show Waikīkī as a vibrant Native Hawaiian social place, one that had not yet begun to be dominated by foreigners."[30]

Each of the two most prestigious hotels in Waikīkī offers separate, customized, historical narratives that do the same work as the Hibbard and Franzen book, assuring guests that Native Hawaiians, too, envisioned Waikīkī as a site for recreation. The Royal Hawaiian Hotel packages this reassuring narrative in a book celebrating itself, entitled *The Pink Palace*, and the Moana hotel (currently managed by Sheraton) presents its allied narrative of Waikīkī both in a book (*The First Lady of Waikiki*) and in a second-floor gallery with photographs, videos, artifacts, and explanatory texts.[31] Tourists are led to conceive of themselves as people like those earlier elites who experienced Waikīkī in their beach houses, and of the hotels as a place of escape from the realms of work and home. Such an experience, as Urry explains, encourages "a limited breaking with established routines and practices of everyday life . . . , allowing one's senses to engage with a set of stimuli that contrast with the everyday and the mundane."[32]

It is vital that this "breaking" with everyday routines be "limited," for unsettling established routines can be frightening as well as recreational.[33] Placing the Waikīkī experience within a narrative of earlier royal and elite vacationing helps to allay visitor fears they will be confronted with truly strange customs. Though Waikīkī was once a Native Hawaiian place, the narrative acknowledges, these

Hawaiians were mostly kings and queens and their families, "passing their time," as Twain phrased it, "laying off." This narrative, as Marek explains, constructs Kanaka Maoli as if they "have a natural disposition to recreation, i.e. they are a recreation-oriented culture."[34] Contemporary tourists are thus encouraged to believe that most Hawaiians used Waikīkī much like today's Euroamerican and Asian visitors do—for sun, sand and sex.

RESISTANCE

For each element of the Euroamerican rhetoric that grounds contemporary echo tourism in Waikīkī, there are multiple Native alternatives. It is commonplace, for example, for Euroamericans to associate race with blood quantum, but many within the Native Hawaiian community define themselves instead by genealogies that map connections to places, ancestors, and spirits. Though Euroamericans understand genealogies as tables that calculate fractions of blood relationships, Kehaulani Kauanui explains that Hawaiian genealogies are probably better thought of as family stories to be told in different ways at different times for different purposes. To be Hawaiian is to be included in these stories, and not necessarily to possess some biological trait that haole science identifies.[35]

Kanaka Maoli also resist the Euroamerican representation of Hawaiians as a people primarily identified with the past. Contemporary Kanaka Maoli see themselves as much a part of the present and future as are the hotel managers and advertising executives who, in Haunani-Kay Trask's words, attempt to "memorialize" the passing of Native Hawaiians.[36]

And since echo tourism separates people and cultural practices, some Kanaka Maoli insist that making kapa, worshipping Hawaiian ancestors, dancing and singing the hula, as well as many other practices, are skills that cannot be understood by anyone not included in Kanaka Maoli genealogies and/or instructed by Native kūpuna.

Similarly, echo tourism separates land and people, but an increasing number of Kanaka Maoli assert that the two mutually constitute each other. Native places consist of conjunctions of land and people so, in this view, Native identity depends on land as much as or more than on bodies and cultural practices. This perspective understands that present-day Waikīkī sits atop Hawaiians. Restoring Hawaiianness to Waikīkī—to those who reject the Euroamerican rhetoric of race—requires restoring Hawaiian people there, along with their relationships with the ocean and land.

Such a restoration seems unlikely soon. In the interim, it may be helpful to increase the presence of reminders of Kanaka Maoli in Waikīkī, to implement many of the goals that George S. Kanahele, among others, proposes. The multinationals who control Waikīkī view these "improvements" as a way to add value to their investments. As one hotel manager says, "Hawaii has to have its own image and a big component of that will be Hawaiian culture."[37] Such "components" nonetheless have the potential to subvert the echo tourism they are intended to buttress. After all, the more often Hawaiian echoes resound throughout Waikīkī, the more possibilities there may be for Kanaka Maoli to step forward and assert their proprietary rights to these beaches and lands.

Tourist destinations typically have short life cycles, and there are few reasons to believe that Waikīkī will escape the familiar boom-and-bust pattern. Fifty years from now Waikīkī will be much altered, perhaps even be as different from the present as it is different now from what it was in 1945. It may seem likely that Waikīkī in the future will still be controlled by Euroamericans and owners of transnational corporations, but it is possible that all or much of this site could once again become a Native Hawaiian place. Doubts of course immediately arise, but this possibility is little more fantastic than predictions of today's Waikīkī likely would have seemed to readers of a study like this a half century ago. Remember that title to fifty acres in Waikīkī is already held by three nonprofit foundations legally (though perhaps today not much in practice) committed to serving Native Hawaiians. These landlords might in the future become less controlled by non-Native and more informed by Kanaka Maoli visions.

A first step in creating the possibility of Waikīkī as a restored Hawaiian place is in imagining it, in beginning to believe in the possibility. Another step requires mounting effective challenges to the Euroamerican rhetoric of race that sustains echo tourism. Haunani-Kay Trask offers numerous such challenges in her essays and poetry. In "Waikīkī," for example, Trask offers a counter-narrative that begins:

all those 5 gallon
toilets flushing
away tourist waste
into our waters

Waikīkī home
of *ali'i*
sewer center
of Hawai'i

8 billion dollar
beach secret
rendezvous for pimps

Hong Kong hoodlums
Japanese capitalists
haole punkers[38]

Though Trask does accept Waikīkī's modern association with royalty, she manipulates this familiar narrative to challenge the rights of tourists to envision themselves as heirs to this tradition. The tourist waste flushing "into our waters" asserts these waters belong to Hawaiians and not to the pimps, hoodlums, capitalists, and punkers currently polluting this Native place.

In her essays and lectures, Trask accuses those Hawaiians who work in Waikīkī of participating in "cultural prostitution," a process she describes in her poem "Colonization" as "selling identity / for nickels / and dimes / in the whorehouses / of tourism."[39] She explains: "For the sake of our loved ones, our families, our elders, and our relatives, we participate in the wage system because we feel there is no other way."[40] This participation leads some Hawaiians to become complicitous in the production and distribution of representations of Hawaiian history that are aimed at producing pleasure and profit for non-Hawaiians. "What better way to take our culture than to remake our image?" Trask asks.[41]

Trask's counter-narrative intervenes in the echo tourism that continues to construct Hawaiians much as Twain did in his "Sandwich Islands" speeches a century ago. Trask is sometimes accused of being too strident in her opposition to settler representations of Kanaka Maoli, but my review in this chapter of Twain's and many similar texts should clarify why they provoke her vigorous response.

Chapter Six

Safe Savagery: Hollywood's Hawai'i

On this point stands a pritty large Village, the inhabitants of which thronged off the Ship with hogs and women. It was not possible to keep the latter out of the Ship and no women I ever met with were more ready to bestow their favours, indeed it appeared to me that they came with no other view.

Captain James Cook[1]

This entry in Cook's journal, penned as he lay anchored off the island of Hawai'i, presages one image that would come to dominate cinematic representations of Hawai'i.

Cook conceived of the inhabitants of the village as exclusively male, and so categorized the women with the hogs. These animal-like women, he concluded, "came with no other view" than to have sex with his men.

Similar reductions of Native Hawaiians' motivation to a single, sexualized dimension became a staple of popular films more than a century later. The impact of this cinematic simplification is difficult to overestimate, for most of what Euroamericans today know about Hawai'i they have learned from movies and television. Moving pictures make an especially strong impact in what Martin Heidegger describes as "the age of the world picture."[2] Some of the implications of this unusual, contemporary association of the visual with reality will concern us in chapters 7 and 8 of this study, bur for now it is sufficient simply to note that films and videos constitute what Laura Mulvey calls "an advanced representational system."[3] Films produce multilayered representations that seem to most members of the metropole to mirror reality with an immediacy and verisimilitude that written texts lack. The great power of this advanced representational system derives in part from its ability to include viewers within its frame, to offer an engaged position to its spectators.

I want to examine here how filmic conventions construct for spectators a Native Hawaiian wantonness that elaborates the sexualized representation Cook describes in his journal. I begin with the earliest silents and end with films produced in the early sixties, when Gidget and Elvis made their initial island visits. By that time, the image of Native Hawaiians that would appear on television and in later films had become so firmly established that it would change little in the succeeding thirty years.[4]

My exclusive focus on films with Hawaiian locales is arbitrary, as these films are often conflated with representations of other imaginary Pacific places. As Floyd Matson points out, "The blurring of Hawai'i in these South Seas epics was aggravated by the widespread use (of imitation) of Hawaiian settings, the appropriation of Hawaiian language and artifacts, and the casting of Hawaiian actors (or actors given Hawaiian names)."[5] In choosing films to examine here, I nonetheless restrict myself to those that explicitly claim a Hawaiian locale (e.g., *Waikiki Wedding*) or those that prominently use the Hawaiian language or refer to Native Hawaiian places or culture (e.g., the 1932 *Bird of Paradise*). The influence on images of Hawai'i of such films as *South Pacific*, shot in Hawai'i but claiming to picture other tropical islands, has probably been great, as Rob Wilson argues. Still, this short study focuses on those many films that have unequivocally offered the Hawaiian islands for view.[6]

PRIMITIVE SEXUALITY

As Glenn Man writes, South Seas films typically offer their audiences "a two-hour glimpse of an edenic paradise where the natives were simple, childlike, and innocent, where everyday activities consisted of fishing, gathering coconuts and bananas, feasting, dancing, and, of course, lovemaking and then more lovemaking."[7] In *The Rhetoric of Empire*, David Spurr calls this a rhetorical mode of idealization and traces its genealogy to Montaigne and before.[8] Early silents offering Hawaiian locales relied prominently upon an idealizing trope by prominently associating all Native Hawaiians, but especially Kanaka Maoli women, with a supposedly "uncivilized" and unrestrained sexuality.

The two-reel comedy *Hula Honeymoon* (circa 1927), for example, follows the hijinks of an American couple who, riding in their car, are unloaded off a ship onto the streets of 1920s Honolulu. The first "natives" they see are two women in grass skirts dancing and singing along the beach at Waikīkī. The husband soon begins chasing one of these women in and around the trunks of trees in a coconut grove. The Native woman turns on him, rubs her nose against his, and, a panel tells the audience, she thus proclaims her desire to wed. Similarly, the silent film *Hula* (1927), featuring superstar Clara Bow, builds its plot on the premise that, since Bow has been raised not by her American parents but by a Hawaiian cowboy, she will act "instinctively."[9] The poster for the film gushed, "Sensational Story of an Unconquered Island Girl." The film shows "unconquered" to mean, among other things, that Bow will ride a horse inside a living room, eat voraciously and lustily with her fingers, dance wildly and lasciviously, and, most

Figure 6.1   Clara Bow as Hula

Source: Made in Paradise, Honolulu: Mutual Publishing. Photo
courtesy of Luis I. Reyes and Mutual Publishing.

important, be repeatedly sexually aggressive toward the men she desires. These
films suggests that such are the primitive behaviors of those whose ancestors
Cook described as ever "ready to bestow their favours."

A more multilayered idealization of the sexualized Native appears in the series
of movie musicals produced in the 1930s and early 1940s. The very first of these,
Flirtation Walk (1934), illustrates most of the strategies to be found in such succeeding musicals as *Waikiki Wedding* (1937), *Hawaii Calls* (1938), *Honolulu*
(1939), *Hawaiian Nights* (1939), and *Song of the Islands* (1942). Only the first
third of *Flirtation Walk* is set in the islands (the remainder is at West Point), but
this first portion shows the stars, Dick Powell and Ruby Keeler, unexpectedly
walking in upon a luau. We are shown here what Man writes about South Seas
films in general, "a paradise where Anglo-Saxon customs and inhibitions could
be shed along with Western clothes" (17). Powell explains to newcomer Keeler
that a luau is a feast "in honor of love." He further suggests, in the highly cen-
sored language of the time, it is a place for ravenous lovemaking. Keeler there-

after eagerly leads Powell toward what she calls "a love feast," where, as Robert S. Schmitt succinctly describes it, audiences see "Powell singing two songs in Hawaiian, a chorus line of 100 island dancers, and Sol Hoopii and his orchestra."[10] This idealized setting has its idealized effect on Keeler: Though she is the daughter of the commandant, her edenic experience at the luau causes her to fall hopelessly in love with Private Powell.

When, twenty-five years later, Gidget and Elvis star in musicals with Hawaiian locales, Hawaiians are still represented as idealized sexual primitives. Natives form a background in front of which Deborah Walley (Gidget) and Elvis Presley act out their separate, seemingly more complex Euroamerican dramas. Hawaiians smile, swim, surf, fish, sing, play instruments, and serve delicious and exotic foods in small, supporting roles in these films. They remain childlike, simple, and innocent, continuing a model of representation that began in the silents of the 1920s and persists into the 1990s in television productions such as *The Byrds of Paradise* and *Marker*.

The portrayal of Hawaiians as idealized sexual primitives has the effect of suggesting that Native Hawaiians are a people on the margins of history. In every film mentioned here, Hawaiians are seen as people of the past and Euroamericans are a people of the present and the future. These representations of Kanaka Maoli are much like those that Catherine Belsey has described typifying early modern Anglo-European representations of women and children. Hawaiians in films, like those early modern women and children, are constructed as people who lack "access to the language which defines, delimits and locates power."[11]

To adopt Belsey's terminology further, Hawaiians as idealized primitives are depicted as a people who are subject to the manipulations of others, but who are not themselves the authors of important meanings and actions. Hawaiians exist as agents in these films only within their idealized separate, peripheral, and subordinate spheres. *Flirtation Walk*, for example, constructs a Hawai'i dominated by the American military. Hawaiians in this film, as in so many others, fill a role much like children and dogs occupy in other Hollywood productions of the time. They lack developed subjectivities and appear mostly as interludes within a central story being told about the agency and complex subjectivities of haoles. This recurrent idealization of Hawaiians, common to dozens of films and hundreds of television shows, helps to convince American audiences that Hawaiians exist for the pleasure of non-Hawaiians, and without an independent subjectivity or culture that needs to be either the military's, the government's, or a visitor's concern.

THE MALE GAZE

It is not only Hawaiian people who are sexualized in Hollywood films. As Phyllis Turnbull and Kathy E. Ferguson point out, Euroamericans represent the islands on the whole "as a soft, feminine, welcoming place, waiting and receptive."[12] Films feminize Kanaka Maoli and the islands in part by constructing their narratives through an assumed male gaze, forcing both women and men to look on through this presumedly heterosexual male perspective.

Mulvey explains the elements of this technique: "There are three different looks associated with cinema: that of the camera as it records the profilmic event, that of the audience as it watches the final product, and that of the characters as they look at each other within the film illusion. The conventions of the narrative film deny the first two and subordinate them to the third, the conscious aim being always to eliminate intrusive camera presence and prevent a distancing awareness in the audience."[13] The very first panel in *Hula*, for example, establishes the camera's heterosexist male perspective. The panel announces: "A Hawaiian Isle—a land of singing seas and swinging hips—where Volcanoes are often active and maidens always are." Hula Calhoun, like the anonymous hula dancers in *Hula Honeymoon*, "always" is sexually active, just as Gidget is later suspected of becoming because she has "gone Hawaiian all the way." Films centered on Hawai'i use the camera to force viewers to ogle Native women or supposedly Nativized women such as Hula Calhoun. The camera further associates these female bodies with a feminized land, claiming both are eager for Euroamerican, masculinist taking. The threefold view Mulvey names inscribes a male-centered perspective again and again: The camera watches Native women, men in the films watch Native women, and men and women in theaters are expected to watch Native women as well.

Many of these films work like stripteases in inviting the audience to identify with a male protagonist in looking at and desiring women, who can be expected in the course of the films to disrobe. Native Hawaiian women are presented as bodies eager to bestow their favors, or at least a glance at their favors, within a narrative that presents such gestures as commonplace. Women in the films and in theaters are expected to gaze on these sexualized cinematic Native women as well.[14] A pivotal scene featuring John Wayne and Nancy Olson in *Big Jim McLain*, released in 1952, illustrates how this masculinist perspective is manipulated to include women, both those on the screen and those sitting in the audience.

Wayne has recently arrived in Honolulu with his partner, James Arness, pursuing their job of "hunting commies" for the House Committee on Un-American Activities. On the first day of the investigation, Wayne meets Olson and asks her for a date. After touring a little, permitting the camera to show Diamond Head and the view from Tantalus, Wayne and Olson end up poolside at a hotel watching and listening to Natives singing love songs in Hawaiian. The Native female soloist is shown being given a lei by a Native man, then the audience is offered a shot of Wayne gazing lovingly across the table, quickly followed by a parallel shot of Olson gazing back at him. The camera returns to Wayne, who moves his gaze from Olson to stare off toward the female Hawaiian singer. We are shown Olson again, but she continues to look at Wayne, now no longer looking at her. The camera focuses on Wayne once more, as he first looks at the Hawaiian, then turns to face Olson. She gazes romantically at him. Wayne is pictured again, eyeing Olson, before looking off once more toward the Native singer. Olson has steadfastly gazed at Wayne, but Wayne twice has broken his returning gaze to enjoy a view of the Hawaiian woman crooning a love song.

This musical gazing ends abruptly to thrust viewers into the next scene, in which Olson is in Wayne's hotel room, speaking her love for Wayne. We understand as they hold hands that as Wayne's gaze shifted back and forth between Olson and the Native singer, and as Olson's gaze remained fixed on Wayne, the two have attached themselves to each other. They speak of marriage. They seem thereafter to be living together. The primitive sexuality of the Native woman has stimulated Wayne just as Cook and earlier filmmakers have led audiences to expect.

It is nearly impossible to imagine a Hollywood film reversing the gender roles in a bonding scene like this one in *Big Jim McLain*. There is little precedent in the sexualizing rhetoric that would allow a female character such as Olson to shift her gaze alternatively from Wayne to a sexualized Native man, thereby increasing her ardor for Wayne. In most of these films, Native men pair up only with those Native women that the Euroamerican men choose to reject. Similarly, Native men are rarely brought forward to dance or sing solos, or to have their bodies lovingly examined by the camera for the eyes of audiences or foreign female characters on screen. When there are small speaking roles for Hawaiian men, they are for family members of the desired Native woman, as in *Hula* and *Hula Honeymoon*, or they are mocked as failed rivals for the Native woman's love, as in the original *Bird of Paradise* (1932).

One partial exception to this trend is found in Elvis Presley's first film with a Hawaiian locale, *Blue Hawaii* (1961; see Figure 6.2). Elvis here acts a role much like that pioneered by Clara Bow in *Hula* almost four decades earlier. That Elvis is a non-Native local is made clear through his frequent visits to his very Caucasian parents, Angela Lansbury and Roland Winters. However, like Bow, Elvis is shown to be under the spell of the primitive Native customs more than of his rich haole parents. In the film's rhetoric, Elvis's singing and dancing construct the familiar, idealized, Hawaiian freedom and sexuality. He is often surrounded by beachboy musicians and backup singers who appear to be Natives and with his familiar ambiguously dark skin, Elvis easily fits into these scenes. In being associated with another racial minority in *Blue Hawaii*, Elvis was but expanding the role he was already playing in sanitizing African American rhythm and blues to make it acceptable for a wider, racist, white American audience.

Even though Elvis is associated with a sexualized Hawaiian culture to an extent unprecedented for males of any race, *Blue Hawaii* reinscribes the filmic rhetoric of the male gaze. Just as the 1927 *Hula* opens with shots of Clara Bow swimming nude, *Blue Hawaii*—a film that one might think would focus on Elvis's body—offers its obligatory nude swimming shot by pointing the camera at Joan Blackman, the actress playing Elvis's faithful hapa-haole girlfriend, Maile Duval. Elvis does strut around in swimming trunks and offer a few moments of his famous dancing, which Howard Thompson, the arch *New York Times* reviewer, in

Figure 6.2   Elvis Presley and Joan Blackman in publicity photograph for *Blue Hawaii*

Source: Made in Paradise, Honolulu: Mutual Publishing. Reprinted with permission of Luis I. Reyes and Mutual Publishing.

his 1962 review of the film called "rhythmical spasms." It is, however, primarily women's gyrations and women's bodies in bathing suits that *Blue Hawaii* offers its audience. The sexualizing of Hawai'i remains written principally on the bodies of women ("a flock of pretty girls," the *Times* reviewer writes), even in this film featuring America's premier male sex star.[15]

DEBASEMENT AND DANGER

Paradoxically, although Hawaiians are repeatedly idealized in American films, they are often simultaneously represented as a threat to Euroamericans. Spurr names this common colonialist trope the rhetoric of debasement.[16] The example of Joseph Conrad's Kurtz, in *Heart of Darkness*, is similar to a host of other instances in Euroamerican writing that Spurr examines. In Conrad's novella, Kurtz is a powerful, civilized man whose psyche is threatened and then, finally, defeated by the "wild" African Natives.[17] Spurr concludes "that the obsessive debasement of the Other in colonial discourse arises not simply from fear and the recognition of difference but also, on another level, from a desire for and identification with the Other which must be resisted" (80). This twin movement of fear and desire has been and remains a prominent component in films with a Hawaiian locale.

The two silents mentioned earlier, *Hula* and *Hula Honeymoon*, each suggest that Euroamerican men are likely to be tempted in Hawai'i to abandon their civilized marriages and "go native" to satisfy their "primitive" desires. The early talkie *Bird of Paradise* similarly explores the many supposed dangers Euroamericans are likely to face should they yield to the alluring debasements of Polynesian cultures. Joel McCrea, playing the Kurtz-like, civilized man, is shown experiencing for a time the idealized sexual life with a Native woman (see Figure 6.3). Still, it is the fearful consequences of yielding to such plea-

Figure 6.3   Dolores Del Rio and Joel McCrea in publicity photograph for *Bird of Paradise*

Source: Made in Paradise, Honolulu: Mutual Publishing. Photo courtesy of Luis I. Reyes and Mutual Publishing.

sures that dominates the filmic narrative. McCrea is several times threatened by the Natives of an unnamed island—who speak Hawaiian and worship a volcano god called Pele. Near the climax, McCrea is captured and tied to a post beside his Native girlfriend, Luana (played by the Hispanic Dolores Del Rio). They are both to die by being thrown as sacrifices into the volcano's fires. McCrea's Euroamerican friends save Luana and him at the last minute but, later, Luana decides to sacrifice her own life to Pele to remove a curse that she believes threatens McCrea's life.

Bird of Paradise was such a successful movie that it was remade in 1951, with Louis Jourdan playing the Euroamerican male lead and Debra Paget cast as the ersatz Native. The *New York Times* reviewer Bosley Crowther wrote of this remake that "there is nothing at all surprising—or even clever—about the way in which the young lady finally has to high-dive into the volcano to propitiate the gods. They've been high-diving into volcanoes or otherwise bribing the angry gods ever since Laurett Taylor did it in [the stage play] 'Bird of Paradise' back in 1912."[18] Crowther's disdain, an almost de rigueur feature of movie reviews in the *Times* in this era, should not deflect notice from his recognition that "high-diving" or "otherwise bribing" the gods had become a familiar trope. It was, of course, Natives and, especially, Native women who tended to die in these films. The threat of death usually confronted the Euroamerican male lead as well, the consequence of his yielding to the temptation to "go native" and debase himself. Eventually, however, Euroamerican "reason" or "morality" prevails and the hero (and audience) exit chastened but alive.

The dangers associated with visiting Hawai'i remain the focus of a later film such as *Gidget Goes Hawaiian* (1961). James Darren sings the title song, which includes the words, "When Gidget goes Hawaiian, she goes Hawaiian all the way." At one level, going Native here relies upon the idealization trope, for Gidget is shown feasting, sunbathing, surfing, and dancing hula on the beach by the Royal Hawaiian Hotel—representations of an edenic Hawai'i. But when Darren sings that Gidget is going "Hawaiian all the way" in this film, it implies she is "going all the way" sexually. Gidget faces the same temptation in the Native Hawaiian land that Conrad described Kurtz facing in Africa: Both consider abandoning "restraint in the gratification of . . . various lusts."[19]

Elvis Presley also confronts this danger in his films with Hawaiian locales. In *Blue Hawaii*, the Elvis character flirts with the danger of going Native and gratifying his various "primitive" lusts. He refuses to embrace the conventional life of his Euroamerican parents. His mother, played by Angela Lansbury with an exaggerated southern accent, repeatedly chides her Chadwick (Elvis), "I don't want you wasting your time with those beachboys . . . or that Native girl." We see Elvis tempted by the "dangerous" Native Hawaiian culture to abandon his father's Great Hawaiian Fruit Company (successor to Kurtz's Trading Concern) to dally with a succession of willing women, and to surf, sing, dance, and feast. In *Paradise, Hawaiian Style*, made five years later, much less plot interrupts the string of songs, but once again Elvis is caught between the demands of conventional business practices and his desire to yield to the temptations that the islands are offering him.

The *New York Times* reviewer Vincent Canby wrote of *Paradise, Hawaiian Style*, "It's all harmless and forgettable, though one disturbing question does arise: Is it statehood that is making Hawaii look like a tropical Disneyland, or is it simply Mr. Presley's presence?"[20] Canby is correct, I believe, to find it "disturbing" that Hawai'i is represented as "a tropical Disneyland" and as a place where an independent Native culture threatens the smooth working of Euroamerican businesses. Kurtz notoriously concludes from his experience that because of the threat to business that Africans pose, Europeans should "exterminate the brutes." Similar genocidal rhetoric often accompanies colonial representations of Native peoples as dangerous and debased. Spurr cites a passage from Winston Churchill's 1897 report to a London newspaper concerning his thoughts about the tribes of the Indian Northwest Frontier, where Churchill was for a time a correspondent: "I find it impossible to come to any other conclusion than that, in proportion as these valleys are purged from the pernicious vermin that infest them, so will the happiness of humanity be increased, and the progress of mankind accelerated."[21] The rhetoric of films with a Hawaiian locale is not often so direct, and yet the dangers that "going Hawaiian all the way" present do seem regularly to encourage genocidal-like solutions. Again and again throughout four decades in Hollywood's imagination, Natives die to eliminate the temptation they present to American characters.

Spurr concludes from his study of colonialist writing that "the abjection of the savage has always served as a pretext for imperial conquest and domination" (80). Because colonizing outsiders like Gidget and Elvis feel a desire to go Native and become like those they are colonizing, their films help justify policies that encourage the domestication of the Hawaiian culture, which is blamed for tempting them to make their grievous errors. These movies display the effect that Spurr finds recurring in Euroamerican representations of Native people throughout the world: "The supposed danger of the European's degeneration in the presence of the primitive becomes both the source and the pretext for an obsessive reprehension of the Other" (81–82). Though Gidget and Elvis toy with embracing the supposed debasement of going Native, both resolve their conflicts by concluding their films with a reaffirmation of the superiority of the dominant Euroamerican cultures within which they were born.

THE PLACE OF RACE

As is true for so many of the foreign representations of Kanaka Maoli discussed in this book, Hollywood films have frequently constructed elaborately negative images of a so-called Hawaiian race. The earliest films with Hawaiian locales were, perhaps surprisingly, noticeably more egalitarian in their racial narratives than were those that followed. In both the silents *Aloha Oe* (1915) and *A Fallen Idol* (1919), Native women and American men overcome obstacles to end in each other's arms. Significantly, both of the Native women leads in these films are represented as royalty; Kalaniweo in *Aloha Oe* is the chief's daughter, and Laone in *A Fallen Idol* is a "princess." The films suggest that Hawaiian women of such esteemed blood are worthy of the average American Davids and Keiths who pursue them. The dangers inherent in racial mixing are at the heart of these films, but they include acknowledgment of the possibility that these dangers can be surmounted if the Native is royal.[22]

By the 1930s, however, racial mixing had become unequivocally unacceptable. When the racially tolerant *Aloha Oe* was remade as *Aloha* in 1931, the notion of a successful racial intermarriage was no longer offered in the final reel. In *Aloha Oe*, David saves Kalaniweo from being sacrificed, and this marks the beginning of their successful love. In *Aloha*, the Native woman, Ilanu, commits suicide by jumping into a volcano because she has become convinced her marriage with the white Jimmy can never work. The viewer, it seems, is expected to agree with her. As the *American Film Institute Catalog* describes the plot, Old Ben—a longtime non-Native Hawaiian resident—early in the film warns "Jimmy not to get involved with a native girl by pointing to his half-caste children and quoting Kipling."[23] Ilanu is also warned by her people, including her grandfather, who explains that her own mother had been driven to die in the volcano because she had married a white man. Jimmy and Ilanu defy the warnings, choose each other over their families, experience many difficulties, and, in Ilanu's suicide, prove the danger of mixing the Hawaiian and the Caucasian races.

Hollywood's construction of Hawaiians reiterates many of the characteristics previously reviewed in the discussion of the role of race in the creation of contemporary Waikīkī (see chapter 5). Hawaiians are repeatedly presented as people whose lives are less complex and less valuable than the lives of Euroamericans. For example their diminished value makes it easier for them to be sacrificed to volcanoes, as they have been in many films, because dead Hawaiians are seen as losing not much more than their sexualized bodies. (Native women jump into volcanoes, for example, in *Aloha Oe*, *The White Flower*, *Aloha*, and in both the 1931 and the 1952 remake of *Bird of Paradise*.) *White Heat* (1934) is an exception to the usual racial construction of Hawaiians, and so deserves a deeper look.

In *White Heat*, according to the summary in the *American Film Institute Catalog*, viewers are once more offered the familiar sight of a non-Native male protagonist, William, falling in love with a Native Hawaiian, Leilani. Other films of this decade featured Hawaiians of royal blood, but Leilani is not so distinguished. Still, the couple are shown living happily together in a common-law marriage before Johnny is called away from the islands to return to San Francisco. There he marries a rich socialite, the daughter of the owner of the sugar company that employs Johnny. When Johnny and his new wife return to the islands, the wife grows bored and invites the romantic interest of a Native man. She rejects him, then yields to the attentions of her newly arrived, former fiancé. Later the wife starts a cane fire that threatens to burn the crop and the entire plantation. Johnny falls from his horse while fighting the blaze and Leilani, his earlier and still faithful lover, saves his life. The wife flees in a yacht with her former fiancé, but Johnny and Leilani remain in the islands, presumably to live reunited and happy in their extramarital, interracial love.

The film was shot on Kaua'i at Waimea Mill and, unlike most so-called Hawaiian films, had a cast that included many Hawaiians. In addition to Leilani being a commoner, the film breaks unprecedented ground in showing an American woman—Johnny's mainland wife—being attracted to a Native man. She rejects him, but this remains the only instance I have discovered from these first four decades of films wherein a Euroamerican woman might desire a Hawaiian man. I am inclined to speculate that this and the other unique approaches to race in *White Heat* can be attributed in part to Lois Weber, the writer and director of this film. Weber was a well-known silent film director, but *White Heat* was the only talkie she ever made. Few other women seem to have been prominently connected with any of the films made with Hawaiian locales, and it may be that Weber's gender influenced some of the ways she made *White Heat* to challenge Hollywood's masculinist conventions about race.[24]

There are many conventions, however, that Weber's film does not challenge. Here once again Hawaiians mirror Cook's description—that is, they are a race with more primitive sexual habits than their foreign counterparts. Leilani lives with William early in the film as William's housekeeper and mistress because, it seems, as a Native she is thought to be beneath him, both economically and morally. Her "immorality" is more acceptable than it would be in a Caucasian female protagonist. *White Heat* can end with Leilani and William reuniting outside of matrimony because, again, the racially Othered Hawaiians in these films are not supposed to be restrained by the same "civilized" self as are Euroamerican antagonists and protagonists.

Hawaiians in Hollywood films are occasionally depicted as constructing marriages among themselves. Ilanu in *Aloha* and Luana in *Bird of Paradise*, for example, almost marry Native men—before they rush off to be with the "superior," non-Native men who captivate them. Marriage among Hawaiians, however, is not shown to be honored as much as non-Native marriages.

Racialized constructions of Hawaiians with their titillating hints of immorality were also prominent elements within the narratives of two new cinematic genres of the 1930s: the series featuring Charlie Chan, and the diverse films now known as classical Hollywood musicals.

The popular Charlie Chan films reconceptualized Hawai'i as a site of danger and debasement. This new type of film de-emphasized the island's supposed sexuality to focus instead on what Floyd Matson describes as "the motif of a vaguely sinister Hawaii, a crossroads of international crime." Matson adds, "It is likely that this darkening of Hawaii was made more plausible to national audiences by the melodramatic Massie trial of the early thirties in Honolulu, involving Clarence Darrow, murder, and intimations of interracial rape."[25] The alleged Massie rape was supposed to have been perpetrated by nonwhites on a white woman. Such an allegation would not have been given much publicity in the islands or on the continent if a Kanaka Maoli woman had been the victim. In *A Fallen Idol* (1919), for example, the Hawaiian princess Lanoe is raped without much apparent devaluation of her worth, because such an act is reputed to mean little to Native women, even if they are of royal blood.

In addition to adding excitement to crime films, racialized Hawaiians were also staples in the 1930s in that period's best known new genre, the musical. In *Waikiki Wedding* (1937), *Hawaii Calls* (1938), *Honolulu* (1939) and *Song of the Islands* (1944), stars such as Bing Crosby, Bobby Breen, Eleanor Powell, Robert Young, and Betty Grable visited the islands (or at least seemed to) and contributed significantly to America's sense of the biological traits of the supposed Hawaiian race. There are many Native-like faces in *Flirtation Walk* (1934), the earliest of these musical extravaganzas (filmed in Hollywood), but the Natives exist for Keeler, as they do presumably for the audience, as titillatingly immoral others. They provide pleasure for those who, like Gidget and the millions of tourists who would follow, "see" at the luau that they are among a throng of less sexually constrained, racialized others. Powell and Keeler are at the love feast but not of it. They enjoy this site of safe savagery for a time (Powell is even asked to sing), but then they withdraw to be by themselves on a nearby cliff overlooking the ocean. The glow of the Native site remains within them, the camera convinces us, so that when Powell and Keeler embrace for the first time it is, in part, because they have acquired some of the ardor and romance they found in their visit to the debaucheries of racialized and sexualized others.

Interracial pairings disappear from cinematic narratives in the 1930s and do not resurface for thirty years. The lone exception, the 1948 comedy *Miss Tatlock's Millions*, illustrates how virulently racist Hollywood films had become. This screenplay centers on a character that the *New York Times* reviewer Bosley Crowther describes as "a giggling, gawking halfwit." He is the heir to millions but disappears early in the film to reappear at the denouement accompanied by, shockingly, a Hawaiian wife and, in Crowther's words, "a couple of cross-bred tots." These mixed-race children lead the reviewer to suggest the "comic pretensions" in the film are "questionable" and "cruel." Only a man with "a pitiful affliction" would marry a Hawaiian in the Hollywood world of the 1940s and 1950s.[26] Such was the immense distance in sensibility that had been traveled since the American protagonist of Lois Weber's 1934 *White Heat* chose a Hawaiian mistress over his lawful American wife.

ADMINISTRATION AND MANAGEMENT

The trope of idealization and the trope of danger and debasement are prominent throughout films with a Hawaiian locale. A third trope Spurr identifies in colonialist rhetoric, the trope of administration and management, did not emerge until later, although it evolved to dominate most Hollywood films depicting Hawai'i. This rhetoric acknowledges both the idealized attractiveness and the supposed danger of the Hawaiian race and culture, but provides strategies for managing the Natives without resorting to such crude methods as directly "exterminating the brutes." The trope of administration and management structures one of the most influential films ever made about Hawai'i, the Bing Crosby musical, *Waikiki Wedding* (1937).

Crosby plays the part of a publicity agent for Imperial Pineapple (see Figure 6.4). He selects Shirley Ross from Birch Falls, Iowa, as the winner of a "Pineapple Girl" contest. As the film begins, Ross is in the islands beginning her free vacation, but she is so unhappy that she is threatening to return home. She had been promised a "three-week romantic adventure," she says, but so far Hawai'i has seemed to be "just like Birch Falls but with palm trees." Crosby's job is now in jeopardy precisely because Ross is not experiencing what earlier Hollywood films had led her (and audiences) to expect. As Ross heads toward the boat to sail back to Iowa, a series of "romantic adventures" divert her, and it is these adventures that constitute the bulk of the nonsinging moments of the film.

Figure 6.4   Bing Crosby in *Waikiki Wedding*

Reprinted with permission of DeSoto Brown Collection.

Ross is given a pearl, which leads her taxi driver to kidnap and deliver her to a gang of Hawaiian men. Crosby rescues her, but, with the gang, they all head to another island to offer the pearl as a palliative to a threatening volcano. After much dancing and singing, Ross is told she alone can carry the pearl in the sacred Native ceremony for which masses are assembling. As she solemnly performs this task, the Hawaiian priest discovers the pearl is a fake and so orders Ross to be held captive. The volcano erupts angrily as, under cover of night, Crosby leads Ross in her escape. They sail toward freedom, with the fiery volcano forming a background for their declarations of love.

Ross thus receives the romantic adventure promised when she won the Pineapple Girl contest, a romantic adventure that reenacts many of the moments previous films about Hawai'i had transformed into cliches. (Native ceremonies to propitiate an angry volcano had been used, for example, prominently in the first *Bird of Paradise* released but five years before. Valuable pearls had been a part of South Sea films since such silents as *Hidden Pearls* [1918] and *Vengeance of the Deep* [1923], and were a theme famously and successfully used in F. W. Murnau's *Tabu* [1931], shot with an all-Native cast in Tahiti.) Ross's experiences thus reinforce both the tropes of idealization and of danger and debasement previously discussed. Halfway through Ross's adventures in *Waikiki Wedding*, however, it is revealed to the audience that Crosby is stage-managing every Native Hawaiian act. Those Hawaiian behaviors, which in previous films had been represented as existing autonomously, appear again in *Waikiki Wedding* only because Crosby, the businessman foreigner, is paying Natives to dance, sing, feast, worship their volcanic god, and capture Ross to serve his interests. What had previously been "authentic" has now become a commercial performance directed by and for non-Natives.

Crosby produces an entire island as the simulacrum of a foreign-imagined Hawaiian culture that by 1937, Hollywood was suggesting could not exist without foreign administration. In several musicals that rapidly followed *Waikiki Wedding*, *Hawaii Calls* (1938), *Honolulu* (1939) and *Song of the Islands* (1942), Native Hawaiian culture becomes even less autonomous than it was made to seem under Crosby's manipulative hands. Hollywood versions of even a simulated volcano worship or of an authentic, separate, Native village life all but disappear, a tropological development that reaches its contemporary form in the Elvis films of the 1960s.

In the first of these, *Blue Hawaii*, Elvis sings the title song—introduced by Crosby in *Waikiki Wedding*—and concludes the film by embracing an occupation as a tourist agent, a role also pioneered by Crosby. In *Blue Hawaii*, however, Elvis does little managing of Hawaiian culture and Hawaiians still seem to exist independently in this first Elvis film. Although they are often found at Euroamerican-managed hotels, they are also shown living at the beach and attending their own functions, like, for example, when Elvis sings at the birthday party for his hapa haole girlfriend's Hawaiian grandmother. The film ends with a choreographed but nonetheless "authentic" local wedding.

By the time of Elvis's second Hawaiian film, Native Hawaiians no longer possess their own, independent lives. They have become much what they remain for
most tourists today—a people to be found exclusively at hotels and in Polynesian
shows. *Paradise, Hawaiian Style* (1966) seems like a long commercial for a series of hotels and especially for the Polynesian Cultural Center. The once idealized and dangerous Hawaiians seem in this film to be safely administered, rather
like the once-wild animals one views at a zoo. Elvis, as a tourist-oriented heli-
copter pilot, guides the audience as they island hop, much as Crosby guided Ross
thirty years before. Crosby's Natives, however, submitted to management within
their own residual, private Native places. By 1966, all Hawaiians are depicted as
having submitted so thoroughly to Euroamerican management that visitors buy
tickets for versions of the tour pioneered by Crosby's Pineapple Girl. Her jungle
ride in a real Hawaiian forest with real Hawaiian villages has become a walk
through the tourist shows in Lāʻie and Waikīkī.

The impact of these cinematic representations of Hawaiians as a race manipulated
and managed by Euroamericans is likely to have been very great. When *Waikiki
Wedding* was produced, the musical as a genre was peaking and Crosby was establishing himself as one of its elite male stars. Both "Blue Hawaii" and "Sweet
Leilani," two of the five "Hawaiian" songs presented in the film, broke into the top-
ten charts on the American mainland, the first and last time Hawaiian-influenced
music would have such a large commercial success. DeSoto Brown argues that
Waikiki Wedding should be considered one of the important cultural productions that
incited the Hawaiian fad of the 1930s and after. This fad manifested, among other
phenomena, "Polynesian" and "Tiki" bars and restaurants in hotels across America.[27]

The Elvis films thirty years later seem likely to have had a comparable if not
quite as great an impact. Their focus on a Euroamerican star acting against a
background of local people, who are represented as less intelligent, powerful, and
charismatic, would be repeated in weekly episodes for twelve years in such television productions as *Hawaii Five-O* (1968–1980), and in most of the more than
ninety other television series and programs later produced in the islands. To my
knowledge, there has never been a single, major film or television production that
reversed this trope and showed Kanaka Maoli as superior to non-Natives. Even
the locally produced feature film *Goodbye Paradise* (1992) stars a Caucasian (Joe
Moore), who confronts various dilemmas in his job as the manager of Hawaiians
and other subordinates. A second, recently produced, local feature film, *Picture
Bride* (1995), presents the Hawaiʻi of Japanese immigrants early in the twentieth
century. In this isolated plantation world, the film teaches, people from several
races flourished by aiding the ongoing displacement of Kanaka Maoli.

FUTURE FILMS WITH HAWAIIAN LOCALES

Christopher Paul Lee of TriStar Pictures is developing a screenplay based on the life
of Princess Victoria Kaʻiulani (1875–1899).[28] Were such a film to be made, it would

likely be the first Hollywood production to feature a Hawaiian protagonist and this might change how Hawaiians are represented, but it is my guess that a commercial film about Ka'iulani would likely repeat the familiar tropes I have reviewed here.

Ka'iulani has already been the subject of much Euroamerican idealization. Biographies, principally by non-Hawaiians, emphasize Ka'iulani's metropolitan-style beauty, the tragedy of her loss of a chance to rule, and her subsequent premature death.[29] Much of Ka'iulani's brief adult life was spent in England, where she was taught several languages and the manners one was expected to possess to rule in the fashion of fin-de-siècle European royalty. Ka'iulani's known love interests were all Euroamericans (though her aunt, Queen Lili'uokalani, wrote her once to encourage a marriage to a Japanese prince, in hopes of saving Hawai'i from annexation by the United States). Ka'iulani's few political activities, including a meeting with President Cleveland to protest annexation, were mostly orchestrated by her Scottish father (appointed governor of O'ahu by his sister-in-law, Queen Lili'uokalani) and by her guardian, the haole businessman, Theo Davies. A film about Ka'iulani, thus, is likely to present Hawaiians as a people much like her: physically attractive, nostalgically tragic, pawns in the story of their country's bitter defeat.

The possibility that films could be produced that represent Hawaiians while avoiding tropes of idealization, debasement, and management has been demonstrated by *Once Were Warriors* (1994), a film made by and about contemporary Maoris. Some of the impact of this film upon non-Polynesians derives from its rhetorical absences, from the way it confounds Hollywood-derived expectations. The opening shot shows a bucolic New Zealand landscape, the expected postcard view of vibrantly verdant rolling hillsides, the Eden of the many idealized representations of the Pacific that Euroamericans are accustomed to consuming. Slowly, however, the camera pulls back to show the audience that it has been gazing at a billboard beside a freeway that runs through a Maori slum. The film that follows deconstructs the billboard New Zealand that has dominated metropolitan representations of Polynesians for so long.

Neither landscape nor Natives are idealized in *Once Were Warriors*. Maori culture is not made to appear simple, nor are the Maori themselves presented as childlike. *Once Were Warriors* also subverts the customary trope of debasement and danger. There is degradation in the film, but it is presented as but one element of Maori life and as an element that is not indigenous but instead derives, primarily, as a response to Maori colonization by Anglo-Europeans. Some Maori in the film are indeed dangerous, but mostly to themselves and not to outsiders, as the trope of debasement would lead Euroamerican audiences to suspect. Finally, and most importantly, there is no trope of a managed resolution to the tensions the film displays. Beth decides to return to her family's marae (village) at the end, but Jake remains unrepentantly defiant. He will not be administered by anyone, it seems, neither by Euroamericans nor by Maori elders.

Once Were Warriors seems an especially important film to focus on in closing this discussion because it is said to be the first and only commercial feature film ever made by Polynesians. Its emotional impact throughout the Pacific has been immense. While Euroamericans have tended to see *Once Were Warriors* as a film about alcoholism, many Polynesians have viewed the film with exhilaration, as the first time they have seen people like themselves represented on screen. Such differences in audience responses can remind us that the analysis of Hollywood films I have offered here represents but one perspective. The tropes I have found are not "in the films" so much as in the experience of these films when watched by a Eurocentric viewer like myself. Other types of viewers no doubt experience *Waikiki Wedding, Blue Hawaii, Once Were Warriors,* and the others differently.

Such differences among viewers will become more and more important, I believe, as more films are made by and for Polynesians and then released into the American-film-dominated marketplace. American films rely upon the master trope of the liberal, humanist subject, part of a shift in rhetoric that Foucault traces back to the Renaissance.[30] Belsey places the rise of this Eurocentric trope as a part of the emergence of the bourgeoisie in the second half of the seventeenth century. This subject, Belsey argues, is claimed to be "the free, unconstrained author of meaning and action, the origin of history."[31] Hollywood films in general, and Hollywood films with Hawaiian locales in particular, utilize this view of history as they present supposedly autonomous selves acting within the "free markets" of commerce and romantic love.

One can imagine films made by and for Polynesians that do not offer the liberal humanist subject as the origin of history but that, instead, see the origin of history in the continuing presence of spirits and ancestors. *Once Were Warriors* has been interpreted by Eurocentric audiences, for example, as if it were like other movies they have seen, and so to be understood as presenting the story of particular individuals, of Beth, Jake, and Grace. It can be viewed alternatively as a narrative without interest in or commitment to the Western bourgeois self— viewed as a story, that is, about how the Maori past, present, and future are irrevocably intertwined. Rather than a film about separate individual subjectivities, one can see *Once Were Warriors* as presenting the narrative of a family possessing a single subjectivity, speaking the Maori future through the Maori past.

In creating and screening films with Hawaiian locales, it may be useful to imagine three overlapping categories that loosely parallel the three rhetorical situations outlined in chapter 1. One category collects those movies that continue the genre as it has been, a type we can call *Hollywood films.* These productions exhibit the tropes of idealization, of danger and debasement, and of administration and management. A second type is *alternative films.* These utilize some of the same Hollywood tropes while attempting to subvert them. A film featuring the life of Ka'iulani might fall in such a category, if it were to aim to reverse some of the expected tropes, by presenting Hawaiians as the agents of history and Euroamericans as pawns, for example, or by emphasizing Ka'iulani's subjectivity while representing Euroamericans as simple character types. Such alternative films would have the effect of encouraging alterations in which groups wield power, but would leave the dominant monorhetoric and its attendant structures of power little changed.[32]

A third category I would label *indigenous film*, though with an immediate declaration that "indigenous" must not be misunderstood to suggest a quest for some lost state of Native cultural purity. Films, obviously, could have no place in any purist notions of "traditional culture." Indigenous films offer non-Eurocentric tropes and narratives rather than attempt to revise or reverse those established in Hollywood films. Indigenous films have the effect of encouraging not so much a shift in which groups are in power as a shift in our understandings of what power and reality are. Both Hollywood and alternative films leave Euroamerican social formations unaltered. Indigenous films present other, non-Eurocentric realities, where, for example, the 'āina (earth) itself might speak, or where, as in Vilsoni Hereniko's play *Fine Dancing*, Hina, a Polynesian spirit, drives the action as much as any of the more conventional characters. Indigenous film invokes indigenous realities without nostalgia, without depicting Natives as relics from a linearly historical past, without placing indigenous characters on the periphery of modernity.[33]

Few films produced in the near future are likely to be entirely indigenous, as reacting to and reversing Hollywood's tropes will likely occupy Native filmmakers for many years. Even when indigenous realities are presented, it should be expected that Euroamerican audiences will misunderstand them. Metropolitan audiences will need to be educated to comprehend the conventions of indigenous films, much as indigenous audiences throughout Polynesia and the world have already learned—perhaps too well—the conventions of Hollywood's grammar of representation.

Reorientation:
New Histories, New Hopes

It is a mistake, I believe, to think about the colonizing of Hawai'i without making connections to the related upheavals that were occurring simultaneously in the homelands from which the colonists came. In thinking about these Euroamerican events, moreover, it is important to avoid assuming that Euroamericans share a common experience or single point of view for, of course, the experiences and values of different groups of Euroamericans both at home and in the Pacific have always been varied. Far fewer Euroamericans, for example, benefit from colonialism than most analysts allow. Writers tend to assume the perspective of managers and owners, but the experience of this minority is much different from that of the majority who provide the muscle and the armed force upon which colonialism relies.

There has been a wide gulf between Euroamerican elites and their laborers' experiences in the Pacific since Cook's first visits. In chapter 2, I described how Cook frequently whipped Pacific Islanders, but in fact this was abuse Cook applied even more often to his own crew. Cook and his officers were forbidden by the rules of the British Admiralty from physically punishing each other, since officers, as gentlemen or gentlemen-in-training, were deemed to be too civilized to be hit. Seamen and marines, however, were considered by these officers to be like animals who, since they lacked reason, had to be controlled by force. Natives were assumed to require even more physical force to ensure their compliance, but the officers lived with the crew, so it was the crew they beat more often.

Not much has changed in the attitude of today's elite toward the majority. Beaglehole's perspective, for example, is typical of twentieth-century scholars who write Eurocentric histories. Cook's crew, Beaglehole asserts, were a nearly anonymous, undifferentiated mass, an "almost chance assemblage of men who carried out the orders."[1] Of these one hundred fifty or so sailors and marines:

They were, the majority of them, English, with a scattering of Irish, Welsh, Scotch, Americans, and even Germans. Like their officers, they were nearly all young. We know something of the character in the mass. We can see them ignorant, illiterate, irresponsible, conservative—blockish, even, prone to complaint when faced by novelty—"my mutinous turbulent crew"; drunken when opportunity offered, lecherous; capable of tears, capable of cruelty. Occasionally a head rises above the wave of oblivion; someone falls overboard, and is rescued, or not; another is punished for "insolence and contempt", or drunkenness, or theft, or neglect of duty, or striking a native chief, or—faint hope—attempted desertion; and that unlucky and dishonourable head sinks again. (clxxxiii–clxxxiv)

Only Beaglehole's phrase "my mutinous turbulent crew" is a direct quote from Cook, but Beaglehole's tone closely resembles that used by Cook and his officers. In two hundred years, then, the elite attitude toward the laboring majority has little changed. History remains for Beaglehole and for the majority of twentieth-century historians much like what it was for readers of the first volumes about Hawai'i published in 1784—events associated with the experience of only one class. The perspective of the sailors and marines who were on Cook's voyage, the perspective of those who did the challenging physical work, is not considered worthy of mention, or is mocked as uninformed and unimportant. The presence of this majority in most Euroamerican and almost all Hawaiian histories is noted mostly when these people disturb the more leisured lives of their "betters," whom the majority is supposed to serve uncomplainingly. Scholars assume officers possess skills like those the scholars themselves claim, skills that make them capable of producing universal narratives different in kind and value from the morass of superstition, prejudice, and ignorance attributed to those below deck.

   This common perspective on the relative worth of "educated" and "uneducated" opinion will have to be discredited if those in the working majority—today's descendants of Cook's crew—are to begin to understand that their interests were not then and are not now much like the interests of those who whip them or who, in other ways, determine the majority's life choices. Despite Beaglehole's claim, for example, one could easily show that Cook's crew was no more "a chance assemblage" than were Cook's officers. Both groups of men were chosen for the voyage because of politics, serendipity, and on the basis of their presumed skills and ability to work. The list of derogatory adjectives Beaglehole invokes to discredit Cook's crew could be applied equally well to Cook's officers, whose various journals and logs reveal to be irresponsible, lecherous, drunken, and, most certainly, cruel. Their cruelty and Cook's were responsible for the creation of more pain and many more deaths than was that of the supposed cruelty of "the mass" of the working crew that Beaglehole condemns. Still, although many of the officers returned to England to receive advancement, honors, and opportunities to increase their wealth, the crew, who endured at least equal and usually many more risks, returned to be offered at best the "opportunity" to ship out again on another arduous voyage, to labor below deck, and to be whipped by their "betters" once again.

   "Drunken when opportunity offered," Beaglehole writes of Cook's crew, and "lecherous; capable of tears, capable of cruelty." These are complaints that captains, bosses, employers, and historians make against laborers and against Pacific Natives, in the eighteenth century and in the twentieth. The "problems" Cook claims to have encountered in manipulating Natives and his crew repeat complaints that the aristocracy and rising mercantilist class in England were making at the same time about the mass of workers there. These similarities remind us that Cook's exploration and the subsequent colonization of Hawai'i were elements in a single process, a process that Raymond Williams describes as the "exploitation of the country as a whole by the city as a whole."[2] Agrarian capitalism, an early stage of industrialization, transformed traditional rural life in countrysides not only in England and Europe but also in countrysides occupied by Native peoples around the world.

> The "metropolitan" states, through a system of trade, but also through a complex of economic and political controls, draw food and, more critically, raw materials from these areas of supply, this effective hinterland, that is also the greater part of the earth's surface and that contains the great majority of its people. Thus a model of city and country, in economic and political relationships, has gone beyond the boundaries of the nation-state, and is seen but also challenged as a model of the world. (279)

Propertied elites, through coercion, laws, terrorism, war, and the manipulation of symbolic technologies, created enclosure, credit, and vagrancy laws. These changes disrupted the lives of millions and produced a large, landless, mostly powerless labor force that shifted from place to place as market conditions required. Many former agricultural workers and tenant farmers were forced into vagrancy. Some of these avoided going hungry by agreeing to the form of enslavement provided for those who enlisted and went to sea.

The entire world became England's hinterland such that, by the time Cook sailed on his third voyage to the Pacific, one-third of English trading was done outside of Europe. This trade was transacted with an increasingly important array of colonies where wealth was extracted and produced by Natives and slaves, and by prisoners, peasants, and other poor people who immigrated from the colonizing countries in hopes of finding tolerable living conditions no longer available to them at home. The fruits of this joint labor by Natives and by Euroamericans created empires and immense wealth for a few. For the majority of Natives and Euroamericans, however, many years of hard labor usually produced only the opportunity to continue laboring more.

Cook and his successors introduced to Hawai'i the same agrarian capitalist system that was disrupting the lives of English men and women. Only a few decades after Cook's death, this transformation had so penetrated Hawai'i that the nineteenth-century Hawaiian historian Samuel Kamakau complained that Native chiefs had become cruel in an effort to imitate European rulers and managers. "The lesser chiefs and landlords," he writes, "were likely to oppress the common people and the humble farmers and the squatters on the land."[3] Many Hawaiians began enlisting as seamen to produce wealth for Euroamerican shipowners they never saw. As Noel Kent describes this system, early nineteenth-century Hawaiians at home decimated sandalwood forests in what amounted to an inchoate wage-labor system, a system through which Natives paid taxes to their own elites, who had begun to imitate the consumption patterns of European royalty.[4] After sandalwood and whaling came sugar and tourism, accelerating the process whereby in Hawai'i, as elsewhere, a minority associated with metropolitan areas supervised the labor of an increasingly impoverished majority. Lilikalā Kame'eleihiwa examines how the Euroamerican-encouraged disfigurement of traditional Hawaiian metaphors helped institutionalize this harsh economic system. Much of what Kame'eleihiwa complains of on behalf of the Native majority was suffered as well in their homelands by the European and American majority, and certainly by African Americans, who endured similar dislocations because of nineteenth-century industrialization, though without the Great Dying by disease which Hawaiians endured.[5]

Because most writers in Hawai'i and elsewhere still think like Beaglehole and share the perspective of owners and managers, representations of Hawai'i's past generally minimize the suffering of the world majority within the global capitalist system. Writers instead typically rely on narratives of nationalism that pit Euroamericans against Natives, the first versus the third world, in a competition that workers in neither place ever win. As a result, ever since Cook's day, the displaced rural poor of England, along with what Williams characterizes as "the expropriated Irish and Scots and Welsh," have been led out by their supposed superiors to fight and die on ships and in colonial wars. These wars increased the influence of the few while leaving the world majority in both Euroamerican and colonized countries without significant political or economic power. "It is a strange fate," Williams comments. "The unemployed man from the slums of the cities, the superfluous landless worker, the dispossessed peasant: each of these found employment in killing and disciplining the rural poor of the subordinated countries" (283).

Important alliances will be forged in Hawai'i, I believe, when more people understand that colonialism is not exclusively an evil that Euroamericans do to Hawaiians and other indigenous people. Colonialism is the overseas manifestation of an economic system whereby a minority shapes the lives of the majority of Euroamericans as well.

Part Three

Polyrhetoric as
Critical Traditionalism

Chapter Seven

Kahoʻolawe in Polyrhetoric and Monorhetoric

Just being on Kahoʻolawe is actually a religious ceremony for a lot of people. Hawaiian religion is also a sovereign claim.

Noa Emmet Aluli and Davianna Pōmaikaʻi McGregor[1]

Most representations of Hawaiʻi identify the islands with a linear, irreversible history and with visible phenomena. Most of these representations maintain that the world they construct exists independently, and further that this reality can best be described not by Kanaka Maoli but by Euroamerican, symbolic technologies. Because singularity is so central to this type of representation, I call its discursive strategies *monorhetoric*.

Monorhetoric generally positions Native societies into what Johannes Fabian describes as an "allochronic" present.[2] As a result, as Elizabeth Buck argues, the Hawaiian past is often reduced "to the dubious (for historians) categories of folklore and myth."[3] It is clear, however, that Hawaiians themselves have never lived in the mythic stasis that monorhetoric claims. Their culture has experienced continued development like all other societies. George Kanahele sketches some of the significant transformations in Kanaka Maoli history that impacted one particular place in his book *Waikīkī 100 B.C. to 1900 A.D.: An Untold Story*.[4] Kanahele demonstrates for Waikīkī what anthropologist Marshall Sahlins says was true for Hawaiian culture as a whole, that "from family to state, the arrangements of society were in constant flux."[5]

Sahlins argues this "constant flux" is a consequence of Hawaiians building their relationships "on the shifting sands of love."[6] Although Sahlins offers more nuanced explanations elsewhere, this formulation repeats the extraordinarily persistent, Eurocentric fetishizing of Polynesians' sexuality. I want to explore an alternative explanation that better incorporates how Kanaka Maoli explain themselves. I will examine a number of Kanaka Maoli texts and point to commonalities within them that form what I call a *polyrhetoric*, which emphasizes the multiple, shifting, and context-specific meanings this discourse constructs. While monorhetoric builds a single, linear, visible reality, polyrhetoric forms overlapping, elastic realities that prominently include invisible forces monorhetoric cannot "see" or accept as real.

Much of the history of postcontact Hawai'i can be interpreted as a clash between poly- and monorhetoric. Recent disputes that have focused on the island of Kaho'olawe illustrate the continuing importance of this struggle.

REPRESENTING KAHO'OLAWE

Kaho'olawe, a small island south of Maui, was inhabited by Hawaiians for over a thousand years before it was seized by the U.S. Navy in 1941, the day after the Japanese attack on Pu'uloa (Pearl Harbor). For nearly fifty years thereafter, the island was used as a target range for ships and planes. Kaho'olawe was bombarded with "100- to 3,000-pound bombs, rockets, anti-tank missiles, and ship-to-surface missiles, 60mm to 155mm artillery rounds, anti-personal bomblets and granades."[7] This mass destruction, combined with overgrazing by feral sheep and goats, devastated the plant life on the island and precipitated severe erosion. Following a twenty-year struggle led by Native Hawaiians calling themselves the Protect Kaho'olawe 'Ohana (PKO), the island was finally deeded back to the people of Hawai'i in 1994 to be held in trust by the Kaho'olawe Island Reserve Commission until a sovereign, Native Hawaiian entity is established to assume control.

Monorhetoric and polyrhetoric conceive the past and future of Kaho'olawe in radically different ways. The monorhetorical view began taking shape two hundred years ago when Captain Cook initiated the first charting done in Hawaiian waters. This approach, emphasizing visible data, is today updated hourly by government-supported satellite imagining. Monorhetoric's Kaho'olawe is thus identified with and through photographs, maps, and charts. It is a place knowable through science, scholarship, and reason.

How differently Kaho'olawe is experienced within polyrhetoric is illustrated by an essay and by a recently composed chant, both by Pualani Kanaka'ole Kanahele. In one English-language version of her essay, "Ke Au Lono i Kaho'olawe, Ho'i (The Era of Lono at Kaho'olawe, Returned)," Kanahele emphasizes the copresence of both a physical and a nonphysical world throughout the Hawaiian islands. When members of the PKO visited Kaho'olawe in the 1970s, the monorhetorical view described them as trespassing on federal property whose borders were established by official maps. However, as Kanahele writes about these "trespassers" polyrhetorically, she conceives of the island not as a visible place but rather as a site where "Native Hawaiians were able to reach out from the physical world to the world of the invisible and to their ancestors, who might reach back in return. The contact did not always have a visual manifestation."[8]

Polyrhetoric intertwines the visible and invisible worlds. Thus, as Kanahele maintains, "those Hawaiians who made the first landing on Kahoʻolawe in 1976 were urged to return there by the ʻaumākua of the island" (155). Kanahele describes ceremonies that were enacted to summon the help of the ʻaumākua and of the akua Lono to assist in the revitalization of Kahoʻolawe. These acts constitute, she says, "a modern recovery of native gods" (152).[9] In seeking to win the island back from the military, many realized that "the struggle would have to include those spirits of our ancestors who were familiar with this moku (island) of Kahoʻolawe and its stories. And so, as the political battles ensued, the care of the island was placed under the god Lono. This deity, who is the spiritual manifestation of the island, would aid in the regeneration of the land" (154).

Kanahele believes the Lono ceremonies held on Kahoʻolawe were the first since "the religious battle fought in 1819," when some of the aliʻi turned against worship of the old akua. Kanahele argues, as do many members of the PKO, that the recovery of Kahoʻolawe thus marks a crucial moment in the movement to reclaim both a traditional Hawaiian place and the ʻaumākua and akua who interact there with people experiencing Kanaka Maoli places. This recovery, I am suggesting, requires that polyrhetoric be accepted as a rhetoric that subsumes within it the monorhetoric that has dominated representations of Kahoʻolawe and other islands for so long.

Kanahele's essay illustrates what I earlier described as the second rhetorical situation in contemporary Hawaiʻi: She generally adopts monorhetorical forms in this essay to point toward (but not practice) the polyrhetoric that Kanaka Maoli have used in their reclamation of Kahoʻolawe. Kanahele's monorhetorical prose thus provides a useful guide for examining other Native Hawaiian cultural productions that display polyrhetoric more directly. One such polyrhetorical production is Kanahele's own oli (chant), "He Koihonua No Kanaloa, He Moku (History for Kanaloa, An Island)," a composition that its inaugural publisher calls "an epic genealogical chant for the island" of Kahoʻolawe.[10]

An oli is a chant written to be sung but not to be danced to. While not as prominent in Hawaiʻi today as are hulas (chants that accompany dancing), oli are, according to Kanahele's mother and teacher, Edith Kanakaʻole, "the foundation of all aspects of Hawaiian cultural history."[11] Pualani Kanahele's oli was first chanted by Kaipo Farias and Kekuhi Kanahele at ceremonies on Kahoʻolawe on August 22, 1992, and has recently been republished in *Kahoʻolawe: Nā Leo Kanaloa.*[12]

Kanahele's oli uses the Hawaiian word "koihonua" in its title, a term that is usually translated as "genealogical chant." In her own English translation, however, Kanahele chooses the word "history" instead. This signals, I believe, Kanahele's resolve to reject the monorhetorical perspective that would dismiss her oli's representation of the island as being mythological or less than concretely real. As her essay emphatically explains, for Kanahele the invisible is as palpable as the visible. When she writes that, for example, Kahoʻolawe is "the physical manifestation of Pele's great brother" (23), she offers simultaneously both a literal and a figurative claim. In her essay, she states that part of what she hopes to do is to convince modern people, including Native Hawaiians, that such conceptions are "not playacting" (158). The polylogic of both/and seems central to this project.[13]

The history Kanahele tells in "He Koihonua No Kanaloa, He Moku" combines references to greater and lesser akua with accounts of postcontact and thus, metropolitan, monorhetorically acknowledged events. The second stanza describes Pele's visit, for example, and the fifth stanza recounts a time when "The nativeborn chiefs are replaced by outsiders / Ships of war are brought" (23). Distinctions between the mythological and the historical collapse. "The island is eroded, its fertile land washed out to sea" speaks of visible events acknowledged as real by geologists and other monorhetoricians, just as "Papa is weak with the island Kanaloa, / who is born small, a porpoise" describes equally actual events for Kanahele—the birth of an island as a porpoise through the womb of Papa, an akua.

It is not only the visible and invisible that intertwine in Kanahele's history. The oli relies on a polylogic of both/and for the present and for the past as well. Born of Wākea and Papa, Kahoʻolawe remains their child yet today. Those sites on the island that Pele visited retain her mana (power) for those people who recognize her presence there. Places on the island manifest as vibrant, multilayered sites speaking their stories to those who listen, assisting those who know how to ask. Kanahele's chant makes clear that neither the island itself nor any particular place on the island can be accurately rendered by any single story or myth. Names for the island are as multiple as the stories, for islands exist in polyrhetoric as a collection of shifting relationships—of the past with the present and future, and of people with their ancestors, descendants, and innumerable ʻaumākua and akua. The visible representations that monorhetoric identifies as "the real" Kahoʻolawe appear among the many stories that Kanahele's polyrhetoric includes. "He Koihonua No Kanaloa, He Moku" demonstrates how easily polyrhetoric subsumes within its broad frame the narrow reality that monorhetoric accepts as totality.

COMPETING VERSIONS OF KAHOʻOLAWE

Monorhetoric clashed with polyrhetoric during the 1977 trial of five members of the PKO who were charged with criminal trespass on the island. The prosecution constructed its case monorhetorically so that, for example, it asked defendant Walter Ritte at one point, "Is it not true that you were politically, as well as spiritually, motivated to go to the island?"[14] Establishing distinctions between such supposedly separate realms of politics and spirit was central to the prosecution, as it had to prove that the defendants had visited Kahoʻolawe for a political and not religious purpose. Ritte answered the prosecutor by saying, "I was motivated because I am Hawaiian," thereby resisting the monorhetorical bifurcation of visible and invisible realms.[15] As Jeffrey Tobin points out in his analysis of the trial, when the prosecution later similarly tried to assign the PKO to the category of a "political organization," the defendants replied that the PKO was an ʻohana, a name for a collection of people that Kanaka Maoli define polyrhetorically—that is, in a manner much more loosely and openly conceived than is the biologically based "family" described in Euroamerican law.[16]

The PKO defendants were convicted; the dominant monorhetoric once again asserted its hegemony. Still, this 1977 trial with its rhetorical conflicts marked a significant moment in the resurgence of interest in Kanaka Maoli rights and lifeways. As Tobin details, the trial also has had a lingering, souring effect on the relations between haole scholars of Hawaiʻi and Native Hawaiian activists—a conflict that illustrates also the clash between mono- and polyrhetoric. The prosecution introduced testimony by an anthropologist who argued that Kahoʻolawe traditionally had had but a single monorhetorical meaning for Hawaiians, a meaning unlike that which the PKO was ascribing to it in 1977. As Haunani-Kay Trask summarizes, this anthropologist and others thus argue that the culture practiced by modern Kanaka Maoli is not "authentic."[17]

Tobin analyzes the disagreements between these experts as being a clash between exemplars of Euroamerican and Nativist perspectives. He focuses on one of the leading Euroamerican authorities on Kanaka Maoli, anthropologist Jocelyn Linnekin, and demonstrates that Linnekin's commitment to a social constructivist view of culture commits her to relying heavily upon a distinction between cultural *processes* and cultural *products*. Linnekin valorizes the former over the latter. Writes Tobin, who studied with both Trask and Linnekin, "Linnekin sees Trask's definitions of Hawaiian culture as false in that they are references to culture-as-product—a fixed, obligatory thing. Conversely, Trask see Linnekin's categorization as false, because it involves a non-Hawaiian's determination of 'Hawaiianness'"(158). Tobin suggests that Trask is most outraged not at the particulars of Linnekin's and other scholars' representations of Hawaiians but at the very fact that, at the close of the twentieth century, Native Hawaiians still find themselves in courtrooms and classrooms where they are expected to listen to and sometimes even hire haole "experts" to testify as to what is and is not truly Hawaiian.[18]

Linnekin writes in a social science discourse that, even in its most poststructuralist and humanistic forms, remains thoroughly monorhetorical. For example, Linnekin argues against static structures and for dynamic processes, building her theory on a careful contrasting of these two concepts. Social phenomena, she asserts in an article with Richard Handler, "never exist apart from our interpretations of them."[19] This is monorhetoric in its most explicitly materialist form. There is no room in such a rhetoric for honoring the akua of Kahoʻolawe or of any other island, or for worshipping island sites as the kino lau (multiembodiments) of ancestors and as ʻaumākua who exist separately from human practices.

Past and present Pacific scholars rely similarly on monorhetorical strategies to produce analyses of some Native practices as authentic and others as inauthentic. Roger Keesing, for example, contends in the 1989 inaugural edition of *Contemporary Pacific* that "specialists on the Pacific" have an obligation to identify "*the real pasts*" of Pacific people against the "*mythic pasts* evoked in cultural nationalist rhetoric."[20] Such efforts to expose the supposed current mythmaking of Natives is, as Tobin remarks, difficult to distinguish "from the missionary critique of Native religion" (168). Both rely upon the monorhetorical construction of realities as single, visible, and easily represented by Euroamerican symbolic technologies.

Earlier humanist scholars viewed the past as prologue to the present, but social constructionists such as Linnekin are in a sense reversing this to claim that the present is prologue ("constructor") to the past. Though an innovative theoretical move within the context of Euroamerican culture, constructivist monorhetoric retains the familiar either/or logic, pitting separate categories of past and present, myth and reality, against each other in a scholarly agon. While such an approach may invigorate academic discussions, it does little to weaken the currently hegemonic monorhetoric or to empower alternatives.

If the past is past, as monorhetoric in both its structuralist and constructivist guises assumes, then it makes sense to do as many today propose and turn Kaho'olawe into a cultural park, a memorial to a lost way of life. The island would become a larger and (perhaps) more tastefully done version of the Polynesian Cultural Center. Visitors would go to Kaho'olawe to watch and maybe even themselves for a while play at enacting traditional Hawaiian customs. As Walter Ritte says of people proposing such uses of Kaho'olawe, "They're thinking human needs. They're not thinking of the island's needs."[21] Thinking instead of the island's needs would include thinking polyrhetorically, thinking that on Kaho'olawe, akua, ancestors and 'aumākua live with a vitality and independence much as humans do. In the Kanaka Maoli view, as Davianna McGregor declares, "For a lot of us in the [Protect Kaho'olawe] Ohana, there's a feeling in our gut that the island is calling to help it heal."[22] McGregor explains elsewhere, "Our obligation is to help it heal as it helps us heal."[23] This complex notion of an evolving reciprocity among the past, places, spirits, and people is absent from Euroamerican monorhetoric. This absence, perhaps it is not too great a leap to suggest, incapacitates most metropolitan scholars from valuing Native places as many Natives themselves do.

POLYRHETORIC AS NATIVE HAWAIIAN PRACTICE

Polyrhetoric is by no means restricted to discussions of Kaho'olawe. Rather, this mode of discourse characterizes many Kanaka Maoli cultural productions in Hawai'i today. Many Kanaka Maoli, for example, proclaim that many of the characteristics I here collect under the name polyrhetoric are central to what distinguishes Native Hawaiians from the Euroamericans and Asians who now constitute the majority population in the islands. Pualani Kanahele's essay and oli provide one clear demonstration of the contemporary nature of these characteristics. Also useful is George Kanahele's *Ku Kanaka: Stand Tall*, a mostly monorhetorical prose work I want to now examine in some detail.[24]

Kanahele offers, among much else, a clear explanation of why I thought it appropriate to focus these chapters on various Hawaiian places: "The Hawaiians of old probably were among the most place-conscious peoples in the Pacific" (195). Kanahele points to the preface to *Place Names of Hawaiʻi*, where Samuel H. Elbert maintains, "Hawaiians named taro patches, rocks and trees that represented deities and ancestors, sites of houses and heiau (places of worship), canoe landings, fishing stations in the sea, resting places in the forests, and the tiniest spots where miraculous or interesting events are believed to have taken place."[25] These places often overlap so that, like the island of Kahoʻolawe, they receive different names at different times, and each new naming thickens those layers of meaning established before.

Naming and defining places served a vital function in traditional Hawaiian life, according to Kanahele, because "almost every significant activity . . . was fixed to a place" (175). Kanahele summarizes this significance for a Hawaiian man: "All the important events of his life, from birth to growing up in the love and caring of the women of his ʻohana, his initiation into the hale mua and the rights of manhood, his learning and practicing a trade, his sexual encounters, marriage, and raising of a family, his labor, sacrifices and achievements—occurred in one place, one kuleana, in one ahupuaʻa" (181).

One's place was the home for the spirits of one's ancestors, for the special akua of that place, as well as for one's family. Place names were tied to the history of these ancestors, akua, and families, so "if you knew the names of places, you knew, in effect, your history. Ignorance of places meant ignorance of your past and origins" (184).[26]

Most if not all places were alive with the spirits and akua that inhabited them. Natural phenomena and seasonal processes were "manifestations of the gods or possess mana in their own right" (188). The ʻāina was sacred, says Kanahele, but not the land or the sea. The degree of sanctity different places possessed varied from occasion to occasion. "Hence, sacred places will appear or disappear as people, influenced by the gods and circumstances and time, decide what is sacred and what is profane" (188). Such dynamism, I believe, suggests that the multitude of place names that Elbert remarks on are manifestations of polyrhetoric's tendency to discover new places again and again.

Just as places appear and disappear, Kanahele writes, so, too, did Hawaiian akua. Kanahele emphasizes Martha Beckwith's conclusion that "nothing is more characteristic of Hawaiian religion than the constantly increasing multiplication of gods and the diversity of forms which their worship took."[27] The early Hawaiian historian Kapelino had claimed the Hawaiians had "millions upon millions" of akua, an exaggeration, perhaps, but suggestive of the profusion that

Kanahele, among others, details. "When Hawaiians of old prayed," Kanehele writes, "in order not to omit or offend any of the akua they added to the prayer the words, 'Invoke we now the 40,000 gods, the 400,000 gods, the 4,000 gods— *E ho'oulu ana i kini o ke akua, ka lehu o ke akua, ka mano o ke akua*" (70, italics in original).

Kanahele reasons that the Hawaiians were accustomed to creating new akua as new needs arose, and that this explains the proliferation of so many. Hawaiian akua are not omnipotent or omniscient, Kanehele points out, and neither are they immortal. When an akua no longer fulfills her or his reciprocal obligations, Hawaiians abandon the akua and turn to other akua or to discovering an entirely new, more effective one. When in the early 1800s so many of the akua did not seem to be fulfilling their responsibilities, says Kanahele, it was not a particularly unusual notion for Hawaiians to decide to abandon them: "Casting off, smashing, burning, disowning—whatever the method used to get rid of gods—may strike the Christian mind as incredible, if not a bit frivolous, but obviously it was neither unbelievable nor capricious to our kūpuna. In the first place, getting rid of gods is a logical extension of the idea that they are 'man-made.' What a man gives, he can also take away, because not the gods but men are the form-givers" (79). When the first missionaries appeared a year after so many of the old akua had been disowned, Kanahele speculates that most Hawaiians probably believed they could experiment with the fierce American god much like they had been accustomed to with their own. The Hawaiians were thus unprepared for the monorhetorical Jehovah, an akua who denied the reality of all other akua, and who accepted but one version of reality—his own.

The contrast between the multiplying and shifting Hawaiian akua and the single, steadfast, Euroamerican God enacts the difference between poly- and monorhetoric. The "one God" of Euroamericans is associated with one story, one text, and one very momentous earthly appearance. This association continues in contemporary academic monorhetoric, which constructs reality as one story with one truth, known best by text-educated experts. Hawaiian akua, on the other hand, manifest in mischievous kino lau, which are multiple and unpredictable forms. As Michael Keoni Dudley summarizes, "Among the kino lau an akua could assume were human, animal, plant, or mineral forms, the forms of meteorological phenomena, and even action forms."[28] For example, in the Maui section of the fifteenth wa of the Kumulipo, Hina takes human form to bear a child, Maui, but later in the story takes the forms of fire, of a mudhen, and of a scoop for bailing water out of a canoe. Elsewhere in the Kumulipo, Haumea is said to be another form of Hina, and, "He lau kino o ia wahine 'o Haumea" ("The woman Haumea has many bodies").[29]

Such polyrhetorical akua contrast with a comparable Euroamerican figure such as Jesus, a being declared important precisely because of his singularity. "God's only begotten son" came but once and died but once, on a particular date in a very linearly conceived chronology. European Christianity eventually metamorphosed into a monorhetorical, scientific metaphysics making similar claims: that the universe is of a single origin, for example, and that all phenomena have evolved according to one set of unchanging laws. But Kanaka Maoli offer alternative multiple, evolving, and equivocal names and accounts for these phenomena. Kanaloa appears as the island Kahoʻolawe, but also, according to Rowland Reeve, as a palaoa (sperm whale), naiʻa (a dolphin), heʻe (an octopus), honu (a green sea turtle), hāhālua (manta ray), hīhīmanu (sting ray), niuhi (tiger or great white shark), maiʻa (banana), and ʻalaʻalapūloa (a small weed). The recently published *Kahoʻolawe, Nā Leo o Kanaloa* suggests Kanaloa's kino lau include ūnua (a young bird) and koa (a human warrior) as well.[30] ("Nā Leo" also refers to "the voices"—multiple, like the bodies of this akua.)

Just as polyrhetorical dynamism shapes Kanaka Maoli places and the kino lau of akua, Kanahele demonstrates it characterizes Native Hawaiian myths, as well. Myths are not fictions to be contrasted with the "real" events that Euroamerican rhetoric describes. Instead, as did Pualani Kanahele in the texts discussed above, George Kanahele explains that myths are "the most real" (49) of the Hawaiian's creations, "the fountainhead of our ideals" (50). These polyrhetorical fountainheads, as should be expected, exist in many contrasting versions. Even one of the earliest Hawaiian historians, David Malo, remarked, "It is very surprising to hear how contradictory are the accounts given by the ancients of the origin of the land here in Hawaiʻi. It is in their genealogies that we shall see the disagreement of their ideas in this regard."[31] Malo ascribed the disagreement among the traditions to the lack of writing in precontact Hawaiʻi, and indeed it seems likely that writing, or at least print, is a technology that discourages variation and polyrhetoric. (Possible changes that electronic hypertexts might precipitate in mono- and polyrhetoric will concern us in chapter 8.) Malo's surprise at the "contradictions" could be due in part to him being educated to accept Euroamerican monotheism and to expect single, best versions.

Kanehele explains the profusion of versions in much the way that he explains the overthrow of the akua. Revisions of old myths were composed as new occasions and new needs arose, he surmises. These compositions reflected personal interests, as they were composed by those people "who represented the elite of Hawaiian society, who, because well endowed, well born, well trained, enjoyed priestly authority and the protection of the nobility" (64). These people revised myths to serve dual purposes: to please the aliʻi they served, and also to satisfy the always shifting general requirements of the genre. In such an environment, Kanahele says, "we can safely assume that myth making went on continuously, involving many myth makers and resulting in many competing products" (55).[32]

The Kumulipo, Hawaii's best known sacred text, illustrates the profound differences between Native and Euroamerican texts, and between the two rhetorics as well. Monorhetorical scholars treat the first published edition, Kalākaua's Hawaiian-language version printed in 1889, as if it were comparable to what Euroamericans understand as a sacred text.[33] Kalākaua's version of the Kumulipo, however, is probably better understood as one more instance of polyrhetoric, for one of Kalākaua's purposes was to use the Kumulipo to establish legitimacy for himself against those who were maintaining that only descendants of Kamehameha had the right to rule. Kanehele points out that Kupihea declared Kalākaua put his version together "to jeer at rival factions among the chiefs of his day and laud his own family rank" (55). Kumulipo translator Martha Beckwith agrees, explaining that Kalākaua's "first division of the chant is a reworking from old material"[34] (311), whereas later divisions, after the dawn of light, were "clearly designed to give the genealogical history of the family of Keawe" (312), from whom Kalākaua claimed descent. As Kimo Campbell explains, "Kalakaua, interested in providing a more substantial and dignified presence than the election afforded him, used the Kumulipo genealogy to establish himself as a descendant of the ancient chiefs of Hawaii."[35] Even the subsequent English translation of Kalākaua's version made by Kalākaua's sister, Lili'uokalani, in 1897, was the creation of a particular moment, composed for a specific audience. The translation, Lili'uokalani explained in her "Introduction," "pleasantly employed me while imprisoned by the present rulers of Hawaii."[36] Lili'uokalani hoped her translation would help focus attention on the illegal overthrow of the monarchy by making available on the continent (through a Boston publisher) a document that emphasized the legitimacy of her particular royal line.

POLYRHETORIC AS CRITICAL TRADITIONALISM

The cultural practices I collect here under the label polyrhetoric can enhance, I believe, the flourishing of a critical traditionalism in the islands.[37] In *After the Revolution: Waking to Global Capitalism* and a subsequent series of articles, Arif Dirlik explains why critical traditionalism (which he calls critical localism) is essential in the struggle against global localism, now a prominent element of contemporary capitalism. The success of today's transnational corporations, Dirlik points out, is in part produced by their "unprecedented penetration of local society."[38] Through the practice of global localism, corporations adapt their products and advertising to fit local market conditions yet maintain their global aims of creating profits for owners who usually live at a great distance from the targeted localities. Dirlik points out that "the radical slogan of an earlier day, 'Think globally, act locally,' has been assimilated by transnational corporations with far greater success than in any radical strategy" (34). The strategy of global localism enables products like Coca-Cola, Marlboro cigarettes, and Nike shoes to invade diverse localities worldwide. Rob Wilson points out in Hawai'i, for example, it is through global localism that the well-known Local Motion surfshops and brands, once owned by Hawai'i residents, have become subsidiaries of a transnational corporation that exploits the stores' supposed "localness" to produce profit for owners who live far away.[39]

Dirlik argues that effective oppositional local movements must self-consciously pit themselves against this global trend. In general, he argues, the very invocation of the idea of a Native or "local" practice or people arises only through invoking an "extra-local" realm of outsiders. Dirlik maintains that "it is counter-productive and epistemological misleading to assert the priority of the local over the global as if the local may be comprehended in isolation from the global."[40]

Dirlik insists that awareness of the dialectic between the local and the nonlocal does not disturb the integrity of the local but, on the contrary, is necessary to enable the local to oppose effectively current global trends. A local movement that does not understand global capital's own effective promotion of local Kanaka Maoli practices is susceptible to having its practices appropriated. Illustrative battles over appropriation of the hula by Kodak and other transnationals are reviewed in Elizabeth Buck's *Paradise Remade*,[41] and earlier chapters in this book examined similar appropriations of entire Native sites such as Waikīkī and Kilauea volcano, and the appropriation of Kanaka Maoli akua such as Pele. Those who practice traditional Native polyrhetoric without simultaneously actively resisting metropolitan appropriations may find themselves acting as manufacturers of exotic products that transnationals advertise and sell.

Dirlik celebrates local awareness of global forces because he believes, like Ashis Nandy, that it is only in the diverse and heterogeneous collection of local alternatives that one can find effective resistances to the current global homogenization. Each distinct locality must oppose the same global trend in its individual way, Dirlik argues, for each locality contains traditions unlike those in other localities. Much metropolitan theorizing, Dirlik complains, has tended to view indigenous resistances as if they were homogenous. Dirlik concludes: "Ironically, the insistence on heterogeneity understood without reference to structural contexts, as in postcolonial criticism, leads also to homogenization of differences, as if all differences were equally different, in terms both of location and the distribution of power."[42] Dirlik points out that it would be counterproductive to replace the current transnational hegemony with any single alternative even if the postcolonial local were everywhere the same. Such a monolithic replacement would simply substitute a new global hegemony for the present one.

In sum, then, there can be no general global theory of the local, and no unified global alternative to capitalism. The current claims and search among monorhetorical thinkers for such a general theory should cease.

Dirlik's analysis of critical localism provides a useful context for thinking about Kanaka Maoli polyrhetoric. Dirlik adapts the work of Ward Churchill to point out that each indigenous practice can be viewed as "both a legacy and a project."[43] Polyrhetoric is an important *legacy* in Hawaiʻi, predating colonialism, and should be valorized for this reason alone. But it is also a central element in the Native *project* of maintaining and strengthening a viable, alternative Hawaiian, way of life. Certainly many of the Hawaiians I have referred to in these pages argue for the importance of this way of life for themselves and for their fellow Hawaiians.

Polyrhetoric and similar local alternatives also suggest a project for Euroamericans and other nonindigenous people, for they provide complex alternatives at a time when few of these can be found within metropolitan thought. Dirlik, like others, points out that the recent transformation of socialisms in Europe, China, and elsewhere leave many with no alternative to free-market capitalism, a form of life that perhaps not even all its apologists believe should become the earth's sole cultural form. The impulse to nourish alternatives to this global culture has been anesthetized, if not lost, along with a faith among many that life could possibly be lived much differently. As many critics have argued, postmodernism itself seems to be little more than an expression of one more stage of capitalism, and so postmodernism supports the continuance of much the same trajectory that has guided Europe and America for centuries. Those Euroamericans who seek radical alternatives must look outside their own cultures for possibilities. When an alternative such as polyrhetoric is found, non-Natives should do what they can to nourish it.

The rest of this chapter examines some of the uses and problems in employing polyrhetoric as a critical localism to interrogate contemporary metropolitan thought.

RESISTING THE CONQUEST OF THE WORLD AS PICTURE

Polyrhetoric forms a much different project of resistance for Hawaiians—for whom it is not only a project but also a legacy—than it does for non-Hawaiians. When used by non-Hawaiians such as myself, polyrhetoric is in danger of becoming but one more appropriated Native form. To avoid this, non-Natives can use polyrhetoric as a tool in interrogating non-Native dominant forms. Such a use does not claim to be itself polyrhetorical but rather a project working toward some hybrid form—to use Pratt's term, some transculturated rhetoric that is neither mono- nor polyrhetoric.[44]

The danger of metropolitan appropriations of polyrhetoric is especially great, as there seems to be significant resonance between polyrhetoric and certain strains of Euroamerican postmodernism.[45] The latter, in fact, often seems to be straining to escape from the dominant monorhetoric with its logic of either/or to reach toward a more polyrhetorical logic of both/and. There are, I think, especially deep affinities between polyrhetoric and the deterritorializing rhizomatics developed by Deleuze and Guattari, and I will discuss some of these commonalities further in chapter 8. Such searches for affinities can, however, too easily metamorphose into suggestions that the Euroamerican tradition understands and can represent polyrhetoric or similarly that polyrhetoric can be absorbed within monorhetoric in such a way as to leave monorhetoric undisturbed.

I hope here to avoid both these tendencies toward appropriation by employing polyrhetoric monorhetorically in an interrogation of monorhetoric itself. For purposes of illustration of the power of this approach, I will focus on a single example: on how polyrhetoric interrogates the contemporary metropolitan emphasis on the visible and on pictures.

Monorhetoric's prejudice for the visible is not new, as evidenced by both the textual and pictorial representations of Hawai'i that appeared in Cook's and King's first volumes and in many early volumes describing the islands (see chapter 2). This enlightenment emphasis on the visible is explored in *The Order of Things*, in which Foucault argues that the new disciplines of natural history were developed in the eighteenth century as an apparatus to reduce "the whole area of the visible to a system of variables all of whose values can be designated, if not by a quantity, at least by a perfectly clear and always definite description."[46] According to Foucault, this apparatus did not describe a preexisting world but created one, so that there was "a new field of visibility being constituted in all its density" (132). Chapter 4 detailed how natural science practices were used to displace Pele and to reconstruct the nature of various Hawaiian places. The apparatus of anthropology later adopted a similar method of what Fabian calls "visualism" to construct its objects as phenomena identical to what could be depicted in maps, diagrams, trees, and tables.[47]

Emphases on picturing reality have lately begun to dominate metropolitan thought even more. Martin Heidegger notoriously called ours "the age of the world picture,"[48] a general argument that W.J.T. Mitchell has recently exhaustively supported in two monographs, *Iconology: Image, Text, Ideology* and *Picture Theory*.[49] Mitchell presents ample evidence in the latter book that metropolitan cultures have indeed taken a "pictorial turn" (11), with the consequence that "modern thought has re-oriented itself about visual paradigms" (9). Mitchell points out that people live now in environments saturated with visual representations—live, that is, "in a culture dominated by pictures, visual simulations, stereotypes, illusion, copies, reproductions, imitations, and fantasies" (2) that together "are altering the very structure of human experience" (3). This culture, which Heidegger called "the conquest of the world as picture" (134), constructs the visual as the bedrock of what is real.

Nineteenth-century photography seems to have been especially influential in precipitating a transformation in Euroamerican rhetoric that moving pictures, then video, and now computer imaging have accelerated at an ever increasing rate. Though humans have been making pictures for at least fourteen thousand years, they have been making photographs for fewer than two hundred. Photographs seem to be associated with changes as deep and wide ranging as the transformations precipitated by such earlier innovations as writing and printing. The proliferation of picture technologies easily dwarfs the rate of adoption of either writing or printing. Only fifty years ago, for example, pictures formed but a small part of an American newspaper. Now pictures sometimes constitute over half of each page. Fifty years ago, *Life* magazine stood almost alone in its American market niche as a photographic newsmagazine. Now there are thousands of magazines filled with pictures, and these represent but a small portion of the deluge of images that people in monorhetorically dominated societies see daily. Television, a medium that is fundamentally picture based, has replaced newspapers, magazines, and movie-house newsreels as the prime source of "information." CD-ROMs and the Internet are transforming computers into yet another vehicle for delivering seas of pictures. The World Wide Web will soon be available over television cable, giving the masses access to a hybrid of movies, interactive video games, and hypertext magazines; three-dimensional pictures for the Web are already in development. Frank Tillman estimates that there are now around 200 million photographs taken worldwide every day. In addition to these images, there are uncountable millions of feet of frames recorded daily on film and video. And within another decade, digitalized computer imaging likely will be producing many more pictures than all these other methods combined.[50]

The older representational technologies (e.g., writing and painting) were said to require human intervention in creating representations, but photography and its related technologies claim to capture *traces* of the phenomena themselves, mechanically, without human, creative effort. As Roland Barthes explains, "Every photograph is a certificate of presence."[51] He elaborates: "Painting can feign reality without having seen it. Discourse combines signs which have referents, of course, but these referents can be and are most often 'chimeras.' Contrary to these imitations, in Photography I can never deny that *the thing has been there*. There is a superimposition here: of reality and the past. And since this constraint exists only for Photography, we must consider it, by reduction, as the very essence, the *noeme* of Photography" (76–77). Barthes's claims for photography display the bias of a culture conquered by pictures. Statements like his in fact have been a part of the rhetoric surrounding photography since its invention. In the notice he circulated in 1838 in an attempt to attract investors for his revolutionary invention, Louis Daguerre wrote, "The daguerreotype is not merely an instrument which serves to draw nature . . . [it] gives her the power to reproduce herself."[52] Barthes maintained similarly, well over one hundred years later, that reference "is the founding order of Photography" (77).

Today, photographs are accepted as proof of the existence of objects, people, and events. As Sontag summarizes, photographs "now provide most of the knowledge people have about the look of the past and the reach of the present. What is written about a person or an event is frankly an interpretation, as are handmade visual statements, like paintings and drawings. Photographic images do not seem to be statements about the world so much as pieces of it, miniatures of reality that anyone can make or acquire" (4).

Photographs are claimed to collect physical traces from a distant reality and to construct reality itself as a "place" constituted by material traces that can be "caught" by cameras. Reality and even private experiences are thus transformed into a supposed temporal series, happening in a visible physical space. In metropolitan rhetoric, cameras suggest, as Susan Sontag writes, that "time consists of interesting events, events worth photographing" (17). Because of the camera, contemporary monorhetorical culture tends to experience time as a secondary characteristic of space, for time is daily "captured" as a series of distinct spaces, a series of viewable "moments" that have left "traces" on film. The resulting changes in metropolitan representations have been massive. Although earlier writers such as Mark Twain and Isabella Bird had to offer lengthy paragraphs to describe the volcano and other sites in Hawaiʻi to their audience, for most people today the islands are the sum of its pictures, "miniatures of reality" that are visible everywhere. Millions of people visit annually who have never before been in the islands but who have seen "pieces" of it for years and years in photographic images. Contemporary writers thus assume their readers have already so often seen Hawaiʻi represented that its appearance can be assumed. Hawaiʻi has become an object much like any frequently reproduced famous painting. As William Gaddis points out in his novel, *The Recognitions*, the *Mona Lisa* itself can no longer be seen. What happens in front of her is a recollection of encounters with hundreds of previous viewings of the painting's simulacra.[53] In the same way, Hawaiʻi exists for most people as the occasion for recalling the thousands of images that have been seen on postcards and posters, and in books, films, and television productions.

The conquest of the world as picture has created what Michael Keith and Steve Pile label "the contemporary vogue for a spatialized vocabulary" among cultural critics and social scientists.[54] "Early work on the spatialization of cultural politics," Edward Soja and Barbara Hooper point out, "can be found in the writings of Siegfried Kracauer and Walter Benjamin, Franz Fanon and Simone de Beauvoir, Michel Foucault and Henri Lefebvre."[55] Influential later theorists such as Fredric Jameson and Edward Said solidified the trend. Jameson claims, for example, that "space and spatial logic"[56] now so dominate metropolitan cultures that every new theory will "necessarily have to raise spatial issues as its fundamental organizing concern" (89). In *Culture and Imperialism*, Said adapts spatial rhetoric to ground his sweeping study of colonialism, which he calls "the struggle over geography."[57] Even Dirlik's analysis of critical regionalism, discussed above, adopts the language of geography to picture the role of local resistances in global systems.

Smith and Katz provide a suggestive list of some of the many spatial terms that have come into recent prominence. They write: "'Theoretical spaces' have been 'explored', 'mapped', 'charted', 'contested', 'colonized', 'decolonized', and everyone seems to be 'traveling'."[58] They point, as well, to such prevalent terms as positionality, locality, marginality, grounding, displacement, territory, and nomadism.

The vogue for a spatialized vocabulary seems to be spreading into wider and wider circles of metropolitan thought. David Bell and Gill Valentine, for example, point to the explosion of writing of what they call "the geographical literature of sexualities"[59] and point to such recent work as Gillian Rose's *Feminism and Geography*, Doreen Massey's *Space, Place and Gender*, Paul Rodaway's *Sensuous Geographies* (1994), as well as the new journal, *Gender, Place and*

Culture, which first appeared in 1994, to support their claim that gender and identity studies have now been captured by rhetorics of space.[60]

Since, as Mary Pukui, George Kanahele, and others claim, Native Hawaiians constitute one of the most place-conscious peoples in the world, it might seem to some that this spatial turn has moved metropolitan representations closer to Kanaka Maoli rhetoric. It has not, however, for Hawai'i's indigenous places are not spaces identifiable with what can be pictured or seen. On the contrary, it may not be too much of an oversimplification to say that in Native Hawaiian polyrhetoric the invisible plays the foundational role that the pictorial now plays in metropolitan monorhetoric. From the perspective of polyrhetoric, then, contemporary monorhetoric seems to be a very primitive, limited, one might even say, infantile, point of view.

INTERROGATING PICTURES

The explanations monorhetoricians offer for the pictorial turn tend toward self-congratulations and arrogance. Foucault, for example, offers one especially influential reasoning for the contemporary emphasis on the spatial and pictorial. He claims that in the nineteenth century space "was treated as the dead, the fixed, the undialectical, the immobile. . . . Time, on the contrary, was richness, fecundity, life, dialectic."[61] To correct this, Foucault says he self-consciously adopted a rhetoric that valorized space over time. Foucault could thus declare at the end of his life: "The present epoch will perhaps be above all the epoch of space. We are in the epoch of simultaneity: we are in the epoch of juxtaposition, the epoch of the near and far, of the side-by-side, of the dispersed. We are at a moment, I believe, when our experience of the world is less that of a long life developing through time than that of a network that connects points and intersects with its own skein."[62]

An "epoch of space" may solve some metropolitan theoretical problems, but it is not helpful in representing Kanaka Maoli or, probably, most other places. The very notion of historicism that Foucault and others wished to correct is almost incomprehensible in the Hawaiian language. For Hawaiians, as Kame'eleihiwa writes, the past is called *ka wā mahope*, that is, "the time in front or before."[63] The past is more the shape of the future than a pattern of events no longer present. Space, for Native Hawaiians, was never fixed or dead, as Foucault complains it was for nineteenth-century Europeans. Still, many writers have eagerly applied Foucauldian and allied notions to Native cultures, assuming these Euroamerican concepts to be universal.

It is especially important not to be dazzled by Foucault's celebration of simultaneity, juxtaposition, networks, and skeins. Though these notions may be moving a little in the direction of the polyrhetoric of Native Hawaiians, they remain firmly rooted within a materialist epistemology that is incompatible with Native places teeming with multiple, dynamic versions of akua, 'aumākua and ancestors. The consequences of such a materialism can be seen in the separate work of Edward Soja and David Harvey, influential theorists in the creation of what Soja calls "postmodern geography."[64] Despite their many differences, as Gillian Rose points out, Soja and Harvey share a rhetoric that claims "both society and social theory are a result of mainly economic impulses."[65] In Native Hawaiian polyrhetoric, however, as illustrated by Pualani Kanahele's oli discussed above, economics operates as just one among many forces in creating a place. Rose concludes her critique of Soja and Harvey by calling for a rhetoric that no longer embodies "the characteristics of western masculinity: hard, logical, certain, oppressive" (120). Hawaiian polyrhetoric, I am suggesting, constitutes a well-established, complex alternative of the sort that metropolitan critics such as Rose crave.

In addition to Foucault's explanation that spatial rhetorics correct an earlier overemphasis on the temporal, some others have argued that the recent vogue for space among cultural critics reflects psychological needs. Michael Keith and Steve Pile claim, for example, that in the "contemporary vogue for a spatialized vocabulary" one can see that "there is a sense in which the geographic is being used to provide a securer grounding in the increasingly uncertain world of social and cultural theory. . . . [T]here is a seductive desire to return to some vestige of certainty via an aesthetisized vocabulary of *tying down* elusive concepts, *mapping* uncertainties, and looking *for common ground*" (emphases in original).[66] Neil Smith and Cindi Katz argue, similarly, that spatial metaphors are in use "to provide some semblance of order for an otherwise floating world of ideas." This explanation implies that metropolitan theorists are persons who seek "a radical questioning of all else, a decentering destabilization of previously fixed realities and assumptions."[67] Such self-aggrandizing claims recall those earlier, halcyon days in the late 1970s and early 1980s when theory swaggered into the humanities promising to deconstruct the old regime and to reconfigure something radical and new. These claims now seem to have been both self-serving and self-deluding. They romanticized metropolitan academics, exaggerating mightily the degree to which such people would be willing to depart from the "fixed realities and assumptions" of the cultures in which they lived. It is clear that the theorizing of most of these thinkers remains within the bounds of the monorhetorical hegemony within which they were trained.

Metropolitan rhetoric, then, most likely became more spatial and pictorial in an effort to resonate better with the proliferation of visual images now choking metropolitan societies. The vogue for geographical concepts is best understood as being but one more manifestation of the conquest of the world as picture. It is not a change brought about due to courageous theorists finding a way to undermine metropolitan thought and valorize non-Eurocentric truths, nor is it a rhetoric that much encourages these theorists to oppose a continuing Euroamerican expansionism. For deeper and effective interrogations, we must look outside of metropolitan societies toward existing, complex alternatives such as those provided by polyrhetoric.

ON POLYRHETORICALLY INFLECTED MONORHETORIC

Trask argues, "Without doubt, Hawaiians were transformed drastically and ir-reparably after contact, but remnants of earlier lifeways, including values and sym-bols, have persisted."[68] Polyrhetoric is one prominent remnant, what Churchill and Dirlik call a "legacy," that has persisted from precontact times.[69] The notion of rem-nants and legacies, however, raises some further issues that need to be addressed.

There is, first, the question of whether polyrhetoric is an "authentic" legacy from the Native Hawaiian past. As mentioned in our discussion of Kahoʻolawe, some anthropologists and Pacific specialists argue that much of what Native Hawaiians today claim as traditional is in fact of modern invention, concocted for modern rea-sons. Such experts might claim that the practices I label polyrhetoric are more of recent than precontact origin. They could point out, correctly, that I have empha-sized contemporary Native texts and contemporary interpretations of older Native texts rather than directly examining the traditional and archeological record.

I have emphasized contemporary polyrhetoric because current practices are what most interest me. (This is what Churchill and Dirlik call the "project," as op-posed to the legacy aspect of contemporary indigenous practices. The difference is much like that which I specified in chapter 1 as a difference between the sec-ond and third rhetorical situations currently existing in Hawaiʻi.) Whether any practices are "really" traditional seems a question best left for Hawaiians to de-cide, or to ignore. The latter course seems more likely; the very prejudice that there is but a single past with a single history that can be represented more or less accurately in the present is more common to monorhetorical than to polyrhetori-cal thinking. What can be said is that the project of contemporary, Hawaiian polyrhetoric challenges the currently dominant rhetoric in Hawaiʻi. Whether non-Native Pacific experts claim this challenger to be twenty or two thousand years old little changes the present power of this project to interrogate monorhetoric.

A more consequential issue, I believe, concerns the difficulties that arise when an outsider like myself attempts to represent either the legacy or project of poly-rhetoric within a monorhetorical text such as the present study. My monorhetori-cal analysis has often made it seem as if I was claiming that polyrhetoric exists not as a result of my analysis but independently within the Native Hawaiian texts and practices I describe. Such a claim inheres in most monorhetoric, but I want now to emphasize that my representations of Hawaiian practices should be un-derstood as further instances of monorhetoric and not as a representation of polyrhetoric itself. Polyrhetoric is a concept that monorhetoric derives from a study of contemporary Kanaka Maoli, but this need not be associated with a claim that polyrhetoric exists apart from monorhetorical analysis. I conceive of polyrhetoric not as an accurate representation of Kanaka Maoli but as a concep-tual tool to use in encouraging monorhetoric's transformation.

I am stewing here, of course, trying to finesse the important quarrel associated with the question Gayatri Spivak poses as, "Can the subaltern speak?" Linnekin and Trask, as I mentioned earlier, have furiously debated this question.[70] Gananath Obeyesekere and Marshall Sahlins have more recently and notoriously joined this quarrel. Obeyesekere initiated the dispute by claiming in *The Apotheosis of Captain Cook* that Natives possess a privileged knowledge somewhat like that Trask also claims for Hawaiians. Obeyesekere, however, expands Trask's claim to suggest that all colonized Natives share a common experience and so a common insight. Obeyesekere believes this common perspective provides Natives with a privileged understanding not only of colonization but also of each other. Therefore he maintains that his experiences as a native Sri Lankan give him insights into the Native Hawaiian experience that Euroamericans necessarily lack. This belief leads Obeyesekere to make arguments such as this: "When Cook arrived in Hawaii, some anthropologists thought that for Hawaiians he was the god Lono arrived in person. . . . But real-life natives, I think, make a variety of discriminations about the nature of divinity. In South Asia, the king is considered an embodiment of Shiva; yet, as a native, I know that this form of Shiva is different from someone like Sai Baba."[71] In seeking to defend Natives against anthropologists and comparable metropolitan scholars, then, Obeyesekere ignores differences among once-colonized cultures to assert that all cultures that were invaded by Euroamericans experience reality in fundamentally identical ways.[72]

Perhaps something is gained when Sri Lankan anthropologists at Princeton begin to speak on behalf of Native Hawaiians against haole anthropologists at Chicago, but one is left wondering in both cases why Native Hawaiians are not instead being allowed to speak for themselves. One answer to this question, of course, is that there are not many Kanaka Maoli who are interested in speaking and writing within the discourses of social science and cultural studies. These discourses are, after all, not aimed toward serving the interests of Natives. Sahlins, for example, makes a repeated effort in his book to make sure his readers understand that he is not writing "simply" about Native Hawaiians but is instead investigating "vital issues for the human sciences."[73] Sahlins subtitles his monograph, "About Captain Cook, For Example," to emphasize his thinking engages not simply the disputed apotheosis of Cook but rather with, as he writes, "vital issues for the human sciences" (ix). The concrete and particular event of Cook's arrival and reception in Hawaiʻi, like the contemporary fate of an island such as Kahoʻolawe, is not important enough to justify high-ranking monorhetorical professorial positions at either Chicago or Princeton. Prestigious monorhetoricians must instead appear to be contributing to the construction of universalistic hierarchies of knowledge. Both Sahlins and Obeyesekere labor to place the concrete events of Cook's death within a discourse of theoretically "broader issues." It is important to their cultural capital that they not appear to do what Natives do, that is, appear to be telling stories, making myths, or engaging in mere traditional cultural practices. Scholars like Sahlins and Obeyesekere instead present themselves as participating in something much more grandiose: They fashion themselves as constructors of transcultural knowledge and truth, much as Captain Cook also aimed to do in his carefully crafted journals.

My own prose in these pages has probably too often reenacted a similar self-fashioning. I have sometimes made it seem as though it would not be sufficient here only to report or to reprint what Native Hawaiians say and write. I have thus attempted, like Obeyesekere and Sahlins, to connect Kanaka Maoli phenomena to "interesting theoretical issues" in metropolitan thought. Though Native Hawaiians do not seem to have a tradition of rhetoric as understood by Euroamericans, I have nonetheless labeled several of their practices polyrhetoric to help me connect them with a contrastive Euroamerican tradition I call monorhetoric.

Now I would like to state unequivocally (monorhetorically) that polyrhetoric is not something that Hawaiians possess but only a representation that monorhetoricians can construct after encountering Native Hawaiians. This monorhetorical construction may be thought of as being something like the manifestation of Lono that both Obeyesekere and Sahlins argue *some* Native Hawaiians created after their first encounters with Captain Cook. The constructions of both polyrhetoric and Cook-as-Lono reveal more about the preexisting traditions of Euroamericans and of Native Hawaiians, respectively, than they do about the Other.[74]

Distinguishing between preexisting cultural categories and new phenomena provides a strategy for avoiding a problem common in both Obeyesekere and Sahlins. Each claims to know what Native Hawaiians think better than the Natives themselves, though they build their claims on different foundations. Obeyesekere bases his arguments on his own Nativeness and on what Sahlins devastatingly exposes as Obeyesekere's assumption of a naive realist epistemology. As Sahlins writes, "In the final analysis, Obeyesekere's anti-ethnocentrism turns into a symmetrical and inverse ethnocentrism, the Hawaiians consistently practicing a bourgeois rationality, and the Europeans for over two hundred years unable to do anything but produce the myth that 'natives' take them for gods" (8). Sahlins argues against Obeyesekere the alternative thesis that Hawaiians, like people everywhere, do not see an unmediated sense world but rather organize the experience of their senses according to the categories provided them by their culture. People generally apply these categories based on careful observation and empirical inquiry and then they act rationally on the basis of these acts. Because people everywhere undertake their inquiries using different categories, however, Sahlins argues, what is objective and rational for one culture will often not be so for another.

Sahlins concludes that "things are known by their relationships to a system of local knowledge, not simply as objective intuitions" (169). He maintains that Obeyesekere is wrong to believe that Sahlins slanders the intelligence of eighteenth-century Hawaiians when Sahlins persists in maintaining that a powerful faction of them (mostly priests) saw Cook as a manifestation of the akua Lono. These Hawaiians were acting on empirical evidence and drawing rational conclusions, based on their previously established local knowledge. Sahlins maintains he is not suggesting that these Natives acted stupidly by not behaving like the bourgeois rationalists Obeyesekere would have them be. This faction of Hawaiians, instead, writes Sahlins, apotheosized Cook "as a form of their ancestral god—which is to say that Cook was culturally appropriated by them on their own terms" (194). The Hawaiians used their local knowledge creatively, he reasons, just as all people must when they encounter novel phenomena.

Sahlins's argument is a version of the "structure of conjuncture" theory he has been developing in various texts for twenty years. Sahlins writes in *Islands of History*, for example, that "cultural schemes are historically ordered, since to a greater or lesser extent the meanings are revalued as they are practically enacted."[75] Though he uses this theory often in analyzing others, Sahlins exempts himself from his theory's implications. It seems to me, however, that just as Cook was, in Sahlins's view, "culturally appropriated" by Hawaiians "on their own terms," so too should Sahlins—like Obeyesekere—be viewed as understanding Hawaiians through the categories provided by his own "local knowledge." This knowledge, principally derived from a humanistic anthropology, is embedded within Euroamerican monorhetoric. Sahlins's writing is more nuanced and complex, more open to the power of metaphor and alternative logics than most traditional anthropology, but it remains nonetheless proudly within the scholarly tradition that believes in and searches for a single best explanation of an unchanging, linear, and visible reality. A rhetoric so wedded to such a static system cannot accurately conceive of or represent what Natives think within a polyrhetoric that celebrates the multiple, changing, recursive and, often, invisible.[76]

It is monorhetoric itself, I think, and not Sahlins's personal arrogance that leads him to argue that the Hawaiians were only able to know Cook "on their own terms" whereas Sahlins is able to see beyond his own "own terms" to know what Natives think—about Captain Cook, for instance, and about so much else besides. Arrogance is intrinsic to monorhetoric and controls all those who use it. When one's rhetoric asserts that one understands the Native better than she understands herself, it is an easy next step to hiring oneself out as an expert to the governments and corporations who manage and develop Native bodies and lands. Such is the work most expert monorhetoricians have been doing in Hawaiʻi for over one hundred years.

Polyrhetoric, with its mutability and multiplicity, seems less likely to mistake any one representation for the whole of reality. One is less likely, within polyrhetoric, to seek to establish a single correct version of what Natives think about Captain Cook, or about Marshall Sahlins, or about anything at all. Polyrhetoric produces compelling versions, but within a context where additional, equally compelling and contradictory versions are expected, even welcomed.[77]

Native Hawaiians may decide if and how often they want to claim polyrhetoric as their own. I claim only that these pages have established polyrhetoric as a concept that now exists within monorhetoric. I also claim that polyrhetoric is a monorhetorical concept that has emerged from my encounters with Native Hawaiian texts. As Sahlins's theory explains, I have adapted the familiar cultural categories I know to make sense of a new phenomenon. I hope this monorhetorical construction of polyrhetoric will be useful in metamorphosing monorhetoric itself.

"KANALOA IS AGAIN KOHEMĀLAMALAMA"

Polyrhetoric constructs multiple forms, rather like the kino lau, the shifting bodies, of Hawaiian akua. I suggest in the next chapter that this characteristic, among others, may help polyrhetoric thrive in cyberspace even as monorhetoric faces challenges there it will have difficulty overcoming. This is not to suggest that monorhetorical forms will soon disappear, in cyberspace or anywhere else. They may, instead, remain while being transformed. Polyrhetoric may come to contain monorhetoric as one of its many possibilities. There are already those today, as was made clear in chapter 4, who do science while worshipping Pele at the same time.

Many polyrhetorical voices, both human and invisible, are being heard today, on Kahoʻolawe and on other Hawaiian islands. Pualani Kanahele's penultimate stanza in "History for Kanaloa, An Island" speaks of this renewal:

> For this new era, Lono's presence is prayed for,
> Lono's presence at Hale Mua is prayed for
> Kanaloa is again Kohemālamalama
> Kanaloa's power is released once more
> The voice of the drums is sounding
> in the care of Hoku, booming in Laka's breast.[78]

An increasing number of mele, oli, and pule are being composed throughout the islands speaking a comparable message. These voices can be ignored or misrepresented by metropolitan monorhetoric, or these voices can be used as interrogators to guide a revisioning of the dominant monorhetoric in ways like, and in ways probably much unlike, the work this chapter recommends.

Chapter Eight

Hawai'i in Cyberspace

Like the logging road, the information superhighways are being built not because we in the village need them, nor because we asked for them. They are being built because they are needed by the equivalent of logging concessionaires, who have staked huge prior claims over wide tracts of forests they want to harvest.

Roberto Verzola[1]

A transformation in symbolic technologies is under way within the few dozen or so richest countries in the world, a change that seems likely to end or at least to alter significantly the five hundred–year era of print. Since writing in general and books in particular have been central tools in producing the foreign conquest of Hawai'i, it is likely the present technological transformation will alter the apparatuses of colonization in the islands, as well as the possibilities for resistance to this colonization.

As might be expected, the explosion of speculation within metropolitan countries about the so-called emerging cyberculture seldom considers what impact the new technologies may have on the majority of the world's people. Most metropolitan writers instead make the familiar Eurocentric assumption that technological transformations affect those outside dominant cultures much the way they do those within. Technopessimist Sven Birkerts, for example, author of the widely read *The Gutenberg Elegies*, writes in a recent essay that he fears the new technologies will make for a world less "hospitable to old-style individualism." He laments the deterioration of solitary subjects and of the private self. To emphasize the loss he dreads, Birkerts declares, "Think about life in the 1950s in terms of these fundamentals and then project forward to the millennium." Life on earth is becoming worse, he concludes, as the new technologies, "the rush to interconnectivity," steals the material "here and now" of the 1950s rugged individualistic self.[2]

Birkerts's nostalgia for earlier decades when Euroamerican misogyny, racism, and colonialism operated unrestrainedly against Native peoples both abroad and within metropolitan borders is repeated by many conservatives who today be-

151

moan the anticipated end of the era of the book. These scholars seem unaware that print has usually been associated with an elite class and their employees. People who spend significant time writing and reading have always constituted a minority, even in the metropole. If Birkerts is correct that the new technologies will single-handedly produce the destruction of the old culture that encouraged elite print readers unapologetically to colonize nations worldwide, then the majority of the world's people may find this reason to welcome the new age of electronic texts that Birkerts wishes to stall.

Of course, Birkerts's oft-expressed fears about new technologies destroying Euroamerican civilization seem to have little basis in fact. Within metropolitan societies, the electronic "revolution" he opposes has so far little changed the lives of most people except, as Nicholas Baran points out, to increase "economic and educational disparities."[3] Some rhythms in the daily routines of hourly and salaried employees within the metropole may be changing, but little is happening to alter how much power these people have in controlling the conditions of their employment or in how much they share in the profits their efforts help create. The new technologies have also little transformed how most metropolitan people spend their leisure or in how they relate to others outside of the workplace. Though the personal computer and Internet "revolutions" have received much hype, as Baran notes, these technologies remain today primarily "the bailiwick of multimillion-dollar corporations and the mainstream business world" (46). This "revolution" has so far had its deepest cultural impact mostly through quickly enriching a hundred thousand or so high-tech entrepreneurs, software engineers, and lucky middle managers, providing them with annual personal incomes many times larger than the combined incomes of most villages in the third and fourth worlds.

This present, however, is not a reliable guide to the future. A future of borderless banks and nationless currencies enabled by electronic communications is likely to make capitalism even less responsible to the majority. Birkerts is correct, then, in warning that the new technologies are creating new cultural possibilities, and it seems likely the pace of introduction of these new possibilities will accelerate for some time. There has been no revolution, financial or cultural, in metropoles in the final decades of the twentieth century, but one may soon come.

Print seems likely to be one important cultural area especially likely to experience a radical change. Print technologies were essential tools in the rise of capitalism and in European colonization.[4] There is nothing inherent in printing technologies, however, that requires them to act as such tools. Print production, it is now apparent, can also be used to assist in anticolonialism and even to act as transculturated elements among peoples who have been little influenced by metropolitan cultures. Similarly, cybertechnologies, though until now mostly used as tools of a continuing colonial globalization, create a myriad of possibilities as well.

No one at present can answer the question of whether cybertechnologies will finally be tools producing good or evil for Native peoples. They may operate mostly as have most logging roads—as technological innovations that at first seem helpful to indigenous peoples but that ultimately assist the expansion of metropolitan cultures into previously inaccessible areas. Or cybertechnologies may aid some or perhaps many indigenous people to form coalitions so together they can produce increasingly effective resistances to globalization. (Some initiatives in this direction will be discussed below.) Or it is possible that cybertechnologies may even help some indigenous people find new ways to perpetuate their alternative cultures. Some teachers at Hawaiian-language immersion schools, for example, believe networked computers have many more benefits than liabilities "for students in a language recovery program" like theirs.[5] Additional possible benefits for Kanaka Maoli traditions are the focus of the final sections of this chapter.

Some of the possibilities for resistance and cultural invigoration that cybertechnologies offer arise in part, as Mark Poster argues, because this technology has the potential to put "cultural acts, symbolization in all forms, in the hands of all participants; it radically decentralizes the positions of speech, publishing, filmmaking, radio and television broadcasting, in short, the apparatuses of cultural production."[6] Poster's cyberoptimism stands in neat opposition to Birkerts's cyberanxiety, but I suspect that people in both the metropole and the rest of the world will end up using the new technology in such a range of ways that neither Poster's nor Birkerts's perspectives will prove prescient. Nonetheless, in the following pages, I explore reasons for optimism like those Poster discusses. I focus on the oppositional and alternative cultural uses that Native Hawaiians have begun to make of cyberspace. That these technologies can be used to increase the profits and influence of multinationals in Hawai'i and elsewhere seems obvious. What requires more demonstration is how these technologies might be used as well by Native people for Native purposes.

THE NATION OF HAWAI'I

In Hawai'i today, as in most metropolitan locales, information is channeled through a small number of media outlets owned and supervised by a homogenous minority. In *Democracy Upside Down*, Calvin Exoo demonstrates how the mass media in the United States supports an ethos of capitalist individualism and a belief in a fantasized "American Way" that rationalizes the existing cultural hegemony. Exoo illustrates ways the mass media trivializes what it labels "the news" principally by emphasizing personalities and by sensationalizing events, thereby deflecting attention from history, social trends, and systemic injustices.[7]

Such trivializing and sensationalizing were clearly evident in Hawai'i in 1995, when the commercial Hawaiian media focused on the murder trial of a California celebrity but mostly ignored the incarceration and trial of the head of state of the Nation of Hawai'i, Dennis Bumpy Kanahele. The O.J. Simpson trial was front-page news for many months, though none of the principals in the case had any ties to the islands. Meanwhile, on most days Kanahele's trial was not reported in the local news at all, or was relegated either to a small space on the inner pages of the major newspapers or to very short segments on television news shows. The little that was written or presented on local television stations trivialized Kanahele's trial by focusing on the head of state's personality or alleged past history of violence. Kanahele and his lawyers repeatedly insisted that the trial could best be understood within the context of the history of American colonialism in the Pacific. They pointed to earlier, similar trials, such as that of Hawai'i's Queen Lili'uokalani held in 1893. The media, however, like the federal judge trying the case, refused to review Hawai'i's history or to accept that the trial could be seen as reflecting the continuing violence a settler culture produces by imposing its will on an indigenous people. The media instead represented Kanahele as an isolated individual, denying voice to his insistence that he was the representative of an organized Kanaka Maoli resistance movement.

Before, during, and after the trial, it was possible to find Kanahele's own representation of himself and of the trial on the Nation of Hawai'i's site on the World Wide Web. Here the events leading to Kanahele's incarceration were examined employing a rhetoric that did not assume an ethos of capitalist individualism or a belief in the fundamental fairness of the American conquest of Hawai'i. Here, daily, the Nation of Hawai'i operated independently of the sound bites or short quotes that the mass media used in representing the American federal government's narrative. Ed Rampell, for example, began his news story at the Nation of Hawai'i's site with: "Dennis 'Bumpy' Kanahele was kidnapped by federal authorities at Honolulu International Airport on August 2." Rampell further placed events in a historical context by claiming that "keeping a dark-skinned person who has not been found guilty of a crime behind bars is in keeping with another old American tradition called slavery. And the plight of brown political prisoners, like Robert Wilcox and Queen Lili'uokalani, is a century-old repressive tradition in Hawai'i."[8]

The Nation of Hawai'i site added a further elaboration of its historical perspective on the trial a year later when it added James Podgers's *American Bar Association Journal* article, which begins: "In 1993, Congress apologized to the Native Hawaiians for the political funny business of a century ago when the pineapple and sugar interests overthrew the Kingdom of Hawaii with tactical help from U.S. officials. Another apology will be in order for an unconscionable political trial now underway in the islands to punish one of the sovereignty leaders, Dennis 'Bumpy' Kanahele, for a variety of imagined offenses that amount to the infliction of embarrassment on the U.S."[9]

The Nation of Hawai'i received about six hundred visits to its site each week in 1995 during Kanahele's trial. These numbers suggest the site was already exerting some influence, but what is interesting is the potential this beginning suggests for the future of alternative representations of Native Hawaiians. The increase in access to and use of the World Wide Web since 1995 has been astonishing. Future use in metropolitan countries seems likely to increase even more as costs tumble for computers manufactured without disks and hard drives, computers made for Web access only. User interfaces are also likely to become increasingly less dependent on keystrokes and specialized knowledge, as new machines are designed to operate with remote-control devices like those currently used for choosing video channels. Negroponte predicts: "Television will become more and more digital. . . . So it makes no sense to think of the TV and the PC as anything but one and the same." Negroponte, founder of the MIT hypermedia lab, further speculates that "television sets will grow to resemble keyboardless computers, installed more like sheetrock than furniture."[10] In such a future environment, it may be as easy to click on a Native Hawaiian's version of events as it is now to turn on a television and watch "news" sponsored by the advertisements of multinational corporations.[11]

The Nation of Hawai'i's initial presence on the Internet was constructed by Kekula Crawford, then acting deputy head of state for the Nation of Hawai'i, and by Scott Crawford. In "Self-Determination in the Information Age," the Crawfords explain: "It is our premise that the swiftly evolving information and communication technologies and networking infrastructures are playing an expanding role in supporting the self-determination of peoples and emergent nations." According to the Crawfords, increased connectivity counters the debilitating consequences of the geographical diaspora that is such a frequent accompaniment of colonialism. They contend, "Self-determination struggles may benefit from the ability to form 'virtual communities.' The situation of peoples who are involved with these struggles is often one of dispersion, having been forced from their homelands for military, political or economic reasons." The Crawfords point to the effective use of virtual communities by members of the exiled citizens of Tibet and by the Inuit in colonized Alaska. They intend their own work with the Nation of Hawai'i to be looked to as yet a third example.[12]

Representations in cyberspace may change how outsiders view Native Hawaiians, but perhaps more importantly these representations may also change how Native Hawaiians conceive of themselves. People displaced from their communities in a book and film culture become in large measure dependent upon information about themselves that is shaped by the colonizers' representations. Dispersed into isolated pockets in the islands and, in even greater numbers, across thousands of miles on the continent of North America, Hawaiians today are often dependent on mass market books, films and newspapers to remind themselves of what it means to be Hawaiian. The representations of Hawaiians and of other Native peoples within these broadband, mass-media apparatuses actively encourage complicity with Euroamerican views.

Now, however, it is possible for anyone with a camcorder and/or microphone to send both live and recorded images and/or sounds onto the World Wide Web to be available for all who click on the proper hyperlink. The mass-produced, hegemonic representations that originated at about the same time the Cook and King volumes were printed in London and Europe may then be superseded by multiple representations of places, peoples, and events. Sites such as that maintained by the Nation of Hawai'i are already offering video along with texts, photographs, and audio. Hawaiians dispersed over many islands and continents can access these productions as easily as they tune into broadband commercial newscasting, possibly altering how Native Hawaiians conceive of themselves. The degree of this alteration will not be determined by any technological inevitability but by how many people join with the Crawfords and others to create these alternative sites.[13]

In addition to the Internet's potential for altering how Native Hawaiians are represented, the Crawfords point to the potential for the Internet to increase what they call the "external" political power of indigenous groups worldwide. Cybercasting, they write, provides Native peoples with a powerful means for "sharing experiences, resources, and insights so that those who have learned in one way or another can share their knowledge, and by coordinating actions for solidarity and enhanced effectiveness." If, as metropolitan scholars believe, information will become increasingly more valuable in the coming century, then displaced colonized indigenous people, by working together, may be able to forge alliances to create and control their own informational base, thereby increasing the political power of each Native group.

Already, as the Crawfords point out, indigenous peoples have begun forming alliances that allow them to share resources in cyberspace. Two such Web sites, for example, Native Web <http://www.nativeweb.org> and the Center for World Indigenous Studies <http://www.halcyon.com/fwdp.html>, provide places where indigenous people from around the world can share information and forge coalitions for joint action. At the Nation of Hawai'i, the Crawfords are building a similar site to serve as a hub for indigenous people in the Pacific region. They believe Hawai'i has the potential "to play a distinctly important role in the transition to the information age, including serving as an initial example of a launch point or hub of networks, links, and resources to model and facilitate this development process and to serve as the host to a new virtual gathering of self-determined nations and peoples allied for a secure and sustainable future." Such a possibility is demonstrated by the Nation of Hawai'i site, which collects links to various Pacific groups, including Native Hawaiian groups with other models for Hawaiian sovereignty. How much of this potential for "a new virtual gathering" will be realized is not clear, but it is clear that the transformation from a print to electronic technology presents opportunities for Native Hawaiians that were not conceivable in the age of books, radio, and the Hollywood film. For the first time since the Cook and King volumes inaugurated the rhetoric of possession, Native Hawaiians now have the opportunity to produce and widely distribute alternative representations of themselves.[14]

Few dramatic changes are likely soon, as cyberspace will probably in the short term be dominated by heavily advertised representations. NBC, Time-Warner, Gannett, and of course Microsoft itself, have already established loud presences in the entertainment and news sectors of the Internet. It is possible, then, that the majority of non-Native and even Native peoples will expose themselves primarily to Euroamerican representations even when indigenous and other minority alternatives are available. There are a number of forces, however, that also suggest that transnational corporations may not dominate future consumption of representations of Native peoples in cyberspace to nearly the degree they have in the past. First, as the Crawfords point out, the new technologies enable millions of dispersed people to begin to recognize their common experience of colonization. For the first time, the world majority is beginning to form transnational coalitional resistances to oppose the global economic system vying to displace their noncapitalist societies. The Crawfords quote Richard Griggs's explanation of what he refers to as the "Fourth World": "A convenient shorthand for the Fourth World would be internationally unrecognized nations. These are the 5000 to 6000 nations representing a third of the world's population whose descendants maintain a distinct political culture within the states which claim their territories. In all cases the Fourth World nation is engaged in a struggle to maintain or gain some degree of sovereignty over their national homeland."[15] In the print, film and broadcast television culture that Euroamerican companies brought to Fourth World people, there was little chance for these diverse peoples to learn about their shared experiences, histories, and interests. In the new cyberculture, these people may have the opportunity to discover and define themselves as the world majority. The many who have been colonized may be able to communicate with each other and to build a shared sense that they, and not their minority colonizers, numerically dominate the planet.[16]

Indigenous people may flock to sites made by people like themselves rather than those constructed by outsiders because they can find at their own sites counter-representations that affirm their self-worth and that reward them with an increased access to power. The Native Americans from several tribes currently collaborating to build Native-Net, a site to link the First Peoples of the Americas and, eventually, First Peoples from around the world, argue: "If we don't define who we are on the Net, other people will do it for us. . . . And when that happens, part of who we are disappears."[17] Such pride and determination may help build resistance and encourage indigenous people to avoid frequenting competing commercial sites. Alternative, indigenous sites will have to be effectively constructed, however, to make them as attractive in their way as the sites sponsored by transnationals with deep pockets. Such an aesthetic competition between indigenous people and the corporations was impossible in the ages of books, television and movies, when Native Hawaiians could not begin to create representations of themselves to compete with the level of production of films such as *Waikiki Wedding* or *Blue Hawaii*. In the digital age, however, the Web pages of the Nation of Hawai'i may continue to be as attractive and as satisfying to Web visitors as the pages constructed by the Web giants whose aim is to offer entertainment or services as a vehicle for hawking commercial products.

Current usage patterns provide yet another reason for suspecting that cyber-space may not finally end up dominated by transnational corporations. Decentralization has been and remains a fundamental building block of the Internet, which was created, in part, by the U.S. Defense Department to be a network so amorphously defined that it would survive a thermonuclear war. The exponential growth of the Internet over the past few years has increased this structural fragmentation many times over. The further daily explosion of Internet growth has not seen increased corporate domination and organization but, instead, a proliferation of more and more local area networks (LANs), most of which are owned by small companies and nonprofit organizations. The older components of the Internet, listservs and newsgroups, continue to proliferate as they resist attempts by for-profit Internet servers such as America On-Line and Compu-Serve to organize them into coherent, corporate sites. The Web, the newest and now largest component of the Internet, mirrors the earlier pattern of fragmentation and specialization.

Negroponte summarizes the shift from the older print to the newer electronic media as a shift from an economy of atoms to an economy of digital bits. Bits now "commingle" in multimedia, Negroponte points out, so that textual, audio, pictorial, and video information flows simultaneously in the same electronic stream. Bits are weightless and in infinite supply. They permit new economic and social arrangements, for they cost nothing to reproduce and can be disseminated worldwide instantaneously.

Bits produce words, pictures, audio and video with equal ease. "When information is embodied in atoms, there is need for all sorts of industrial-age means and huge corporations of delivery. But, suddenly, when the focus shifts to bits, the traditional big guys are no longer needed. Do-it-yourself publishing on the Internet makes sense. It does not for paper copy."[18] In a future era where most representations of Kanaka Maoli are made of bits, some of the hegemonic advantages of the currently dominant culture may be weakened. So, too, may some of the rhetorical advantages that have supported Euroamerican representations of Native Hawaiians for two hundred years.

POLYRHETORIC IN CYBERSPACE

Some Hawaiians may discover that electronic media resonate better with Native Hawaiian cultural practices than do the older print and broadcast media that have dominated the symbolic production of Hawai'i for so long.

There continues to be much speculation about the cultural characteristics that the new technologies seem likely to most enable. George P. Landow, one of the pioneer critics of hypertexts, provides what has become a fairly predictable list when he argues these new media encourage "multivocality, open-endedness, multilinear organization, greater inclusion of nontextual information, and fundamental reconfiguration of authorship."[19] These characteristics clearly overlap with what in these pages I have been describing as Kanaka Maoli polyrhetoric. It seems possible, then, that the new electronic media may provide a way for Native Hawaiians to represent themselves without introducing many of the distortions that print, film or video have required.

I want to focus here on just three of the many rhetorical possibilities the new media enable. These three—open-endedness, a preference for rhizomes, and an emphasis on invisibilities—seem to resonate with particular depth with many of the characteristics of polyrhetoric discussed in chapter 7.

Open-endedness

Traditional print texts are fixed, imprisoned in the immobility of the atoms required for their manufacturing. As Eric A. Havelock has shown, such texts require an alphabet that is stable and simple enough to be easily learned in childhood. The shape of words in these texts must be unobtrusive so that people will read them without being distracted by an aesthetic interest in their colors or shapes. As a result of this need for an unobtrusive orthography, scribes before the printing press were continually exhorted to resist their desire to alter texts to increase their visual attractiveness. Handwriting in those eras was judged by how nearly it imitated the appearance of a master's hand or some manuscript standard. As Richard Lanham argues, after Gutenberg and moveable type, this problem with innovative scribes disappeared and it became easier for readers to take writing for granted, to look "through" texts rather than "at" them. Lanham maintains that the standardization of print made possible by the printing press led Euroamerican scholars to de-emphasize the effect of textual surfaces, their "rhetorical force," in Lanham's terms. Discussion focused instead on the supposedly fixed "meanings" imagined to exist in some ethereal realm that could be "seen" by looking through texts to "what texts were about." Texts were assumed to offer access to fixed meanings, and scholars were, and still are, trained to look through the taken-for-granted printed lines toward a hypostatized site of meaning "beyond." People viewing texts this way seek definitive editions and definite readings, as cultural productions are assumed to possess a determinate meaning that can be correctly understood in only one way.[20]

Electronic texts have the potential to undermine this ideological commitment to a fixed realm of meaning. Readers in the new media may thus increasingly experience texts as dynamic systems that resist stability at every turn. There can be neither definitive editions nor authoritative interpretations in pixilated print. Electronic texts encourage such frequent changes that, for example, the Modern Language Association in its new guidelines recommends that citations to sources on the Internet include not only the Universal Resource Locator (URL) address but also the date on which the site was accessed by the researcher.[21] Most scholarly electronic sites include a record of the last date and time that they were altered. New search engines can be instructed to check sites daily to notify users when Web pages of particular interest have been revised. It is becoming expected that texts will undergo frequent alterations.

The stable alphabet that Havelock found so important to the development of the Western tradition is now being played around with to encourage readers to become aware that individual letters and words can be looked at as well as through. As Lanham remarks, any person with a word processor can create fabulously elaborate texts "in ways that would make a medieval scribe weep."[22] The explosive growth in both atom- and bit-based personal magazines—"'zines"—demonstrates the growing fascination of readers with the graphical pleasures of letters, words, and fonts. Fast-growing mass-market magazines such as *Wired* and its imitators emphasize their extravagant orthographies, expecting readers to look at them as well as through.

Hypertexts, an increasingly popular type of electronic writing, further destabilize traditional texts by disrupting their linearity. Just as pixilated print encourages alterations in the look of letters and words, hypertextual constructions encourage variations in the sequence of what is read. For decades many Euroamerican artists and philosophers have strained without much success to lead their audiences to escape the assumption of linearity. Hypertexts consummate this project spectacularly, for readers of hyperlinked texts must strain as hard in the opposite way to try to maintain a linear sense. Hypertexts have no clear beginning, and no clear end. They do not build coherent arguments toward a single denouement. Once one spends some time exploring such texts, what Lanham writes becomes apparent: "Western poetics and philosophy are transformed, for a start. The Aristotelian categories of beginning, middle, and end, it turns out, are based on fixed texts" (125). In place of seeking single conclusions and best versions, electronic texts, along with the pictures, audio, and video that will soon accompany them, encourage a multivocal sensibility.

Kanaka Maoli may find this multivocality and open-endedness match well with their polyrhetorical tradition of multiple versions. Contrasting versions of the "same" events have been difficult to represent in Euroamerican print forms, with their thirst for authoritative texts. For example, the Kumulipo, a traditional oral chant, is said by George Kanahele to have once existed in many forms and to have been continually reshaped according to the circumstances of its performance. King Kalākaua had one version of the chant transcribed and it is this version that has since usually been accepted as "the authentic" Kumulipo. Martha Beckwith, however, recalls Kupihea as saying that Kalākaua "changed and adapted the original source material in order to jeer at rival factions among the chiefs of his day and laud his own family rank."[23] Hypermedia will make it easier to record and distribute multiple versions of chants such as Kumulipo and all other Native cultural productions. If such apparatuses of cultural production had been available in Kalākaua's day, for example, it seems likely that the King's rivals would have countered his version with many of their own. Euroamerican print traditions, instead, encouraged even Native Hawaiians to accept Kalākaua's Kumulipo as if it were a sacred text like the Bible, for which single, authoritative editions were to be expected and preferred. The narrow ideology of print thus encouraged the further displacement of the complex multivocality of Kanaka Maoli traditions. In hypertextual cyberspace, perhaps, this tradition of displacement may begin to be reversed.

Rhizomatics

Hawaiian polyrhetoric is multilayered and evolving, often emphasizing not separate elements but elements sharing a related complexity. Lilikalā Kameʻeleihiwa writes that "the genealogy of the Land, the Gods, Chiefs, and people intertwine with one another, and *with all the myriad aspects of the universe.*"[24] By contrast, most acclaimed monorhetorical ideas are not intertwined with "myriad aspects of the universe" but are more often claimed to be articulated exactly (in words, numbers, or formulae), once and forever. Esteemed models for such static statements include formulations like the ten commandments, the United States Constitution, $e = mc^2$, $pi = 22/7$, and theories such as the one that claims "the material base grounds a cultural superstructure." Kanaka Maoli polyrhetoric more often celebrates interconnections without definite boundaries or solitary authors. Polyrhetorical concepts alter their meanings as they are added to by successive, interconnected parts. This characteristic may enable polyrhetorical concepts to fit more easily into hypermedia than do static monorhetorical productions.

Numerous metropolitan writers have for decades been issuing manifestos proclaiming the need for Euroamericans to reject their rigid, monorhetorical perspective. Gilles Deleuze and Felix Guattari, for example, have argued for an end to rhetoric that relies on an assumption of stable territories and roots, calling instead for a rhizomatic model that would oppose Western models derived from plants such as trees. Such a rhetoric, they maintain, should replace Euroamerican hierarchies and linearity.[25] Unfortunately, like most of the poststructuralist theorizing with which it resonates, Deleuze and Guattari's ideas seem to have little altered Euroamerican thinking. Metropolitan scholarship continues to be generally agonistic and hierarchical, creating structures of argument more closely resembling trees than rhizomes. If scholars wish to move beyond merely reading and writing programmatic statements, to begin instead to try to forge an alternative, rhizomatic culture, the example of Kanaka Maoli polyrhetoric may be helpful. The demands of electronic hypertext may also increasingly encourage this study.

Kameʻeleihiwa's history of the mahele, *Native Lands and Foreign Desires*, provides one useful place to begin learning more about the rhizomatic perspective. Kameʻeleihiwa explains why Kanaka Maoli history must be grounded in the understanding that the Hawaiian people were born as the second child of the union of Wākea and Hoʻohōkūkalani. The first child and older sibling of this union was the kalo plant, known among English speakers as taro. Drawing upon nineteenth-century documents and older oral traditions, Kameʻeleihiwa maintains that "the *kalo* plant, which was the main staple of the people of old, is also the elder brother of the Hawaiian race."[26] The Hawaiian people's relationship with kalo is, Kameʻeleihiwa concludes, one of the "traditional patterns from which all of Hawaiian society flows and the metaphor around which it is organized" (25).

Kalo, of course, is a rhizome, and, like other rhizomes, grows by sending out shoots and roots, often under or across the surface of the ground. Cultivation of kalo offers continual reminders of the connectedness of present plants to earlier plants, and of those earlier plants to the first kalo plant, elder brother to the Hawaiian people themselves. People, akua, spirits, and daily life are intertwined rhizomatically and this plant-illustrated interconnectedness is, according to Kameʻeleihiwa and many others, a foundational notion upon which Hawaiian thinking rests.[27]

As Deleuze and Guattari suggest, rhizome cultivation differs fundamentally from cultivation by seeds. The latter suggest stages of discontinuity and separateness, and also cycles of birth, death, planting, and rebirth. When a seed-bearing plant reproduces, it creates pods and packets that have forms different from itself. These seeds may be and often are stored, so that the time of new planting can take place after the parent plant has been harvested and destroyed. Perhaps many Euroamerican thought forms reflect in some measure the millennia of cultivation by seeds that sustained Euroamericans. Hawaiians, on the other hand, as Kameʻeleihiwa remarks, recognize a continuous, intertwined, rhizomatic structure sustaining their lives.

One further example, pointed to in almost every text about Hawaiians, may be helpful. Mary Kawena Pukui states that the ʻohana is a basic organizing principle of Hawaiian life, and that this concept resonates with the word ʻohā, a synonym for kalo that refers as well to the plant's origins in the original stalk. To be a member of an ʻohana is then to be a node on the open-ended, rhizomatic growth that both gives birth to and feeds each person. The ʻohana's rhizomatic network, says Pukui, includes connections to spirits, akua, ancestors, and future generations, as well as to those people that Euroamericans might recognize as living family members. To be Hawaiian, Pukui maintains, is to be a person configured within a particular ʻohana in an ever-evolving, living web. "Today the concept of ʻohana is often extended to include unrelated persons, community groups, or church membership."[28] This is a corruption of the concept, Pukui maintains, as "The real *ʻohana* is a natural phenomenon" (173). It refers not to wishing for a relationship but to a unity of people due to their common ancestors living both in them and in the spirits who remain in palpable daily contact with the ʻohana.

If Deleuze and Guatarri are correct that, even before the invention of electronic texts, metropolitan thought needed to become more rhizomatic, then surely the new electronic media are increasing this need. Traditional Euroamerican searches for roots and foundations work but clumsily in cyberspace, at least when compared with rhizomatic thinking, which fits with the demands of hypertexts much more neatly. Native Hawaiians practicing their traditional narratives could perhaps find themselves more at ease in these new media than do those Euroamericans who continue to resist concepts that exhibit an extended interconnectedness accepting few boundaries of either time or space.

Invisibilities

The new media give increasing prominence to visual images, films, and videos, but because these will be digitalized, they may nonetheless encourage a transformation of what Martin Heidegger calls "the conquest of the world as picture."[29] This conquest has encouraged contemporary Euroamericans to identify the real with what can be seen and recorded by cameras. Films and television have abetted this conquest, but now, as these media become available for easy editing by consumers at home, it may be increasingly apparent to many that what is seen is not necessarily what is or was "there" as the camera recorded. The current trust in visual images may gradually erode as people experience for themselves how to alter not only the voices, faces, and composition of their own video recordings, but also to "morph"—transform—the private and commercial productions of others. An increasing suspicion of the reality of what is seen in cyberspace may be accompanied by an increasing acceptance of what is not seen there.

Ancestral presences and hundreds if not thousands of akua are said by many to be essential constituents of traditional Native Hawaiian culture. Invisible presences also seem to be much more easily represented in the new media than in traditional print and film. Even some Euroamericans who have been educated within a secular tradition report that their extended time within cyberspace has produced an increased sensitivity to invisible forces. Mark Pesce, for example, one of the creators of Virtual Reality Markup Language (VRML), an influential three-dimensional hyperspace for the World Wide Web, maintains that the Internet works through the action of "emergent properties," which have powers that should be understood as a form of magic.[30] Erik Davis summarizes the outlook of those who share Pesce's view:

> As computers blanket the world like digital kudzu, we surround ourselves with an animated webwork of complex, powerful, and unseen forces that even the "experts" can't totally comprehend. Our technological environment may soon appear to be as strangely sentient as the caves, lakes, and forests in which the first magicians glimpsed the gods. . . .
> Today, in the silicon crucible of computer culture, digital denizens are once again building bridges between logic and fantasy, math and myth, the inner and the outer worlds. (177)

Such conceptions may be familiar to some who spend much of their daily lives online, but the inner and invisible worlds remain disrespected by most metropolitan scholars. Despite two decades of theorizing about the need to escape the narrow discourse of reason spawned by the enlightenment project, most mainstream metropolitan writers remain wedded to very narrow notions of what they accept as real. Most scholars still dismiss as epiphenomenal the invisible forces that the majority of the world's people accept as influential daily presences. Within scholarly writing, it remains less than respectable to cite those like Pesce who find nonmaterial entities in cyberspace to be "strangely sentient." Euroamerican scholars thus seem unlikely soon to accept the reality of any invisible presences, even in cyberspace.

Those embracing a more traditional Native Hawaiian view, by contrast, may welcome any opportunities cyberspace offers for invoking invisible forces online. They may, like Pesce, seek to discover and interact with the new "emergent properties" cyberspace unveils, or they may simply find that the new hypermedia offer an effective means within which to represent ancestral spirits and the ten thousand, the forty thousand, the four hundred thousand Kanaka Maoli akua. Print, film, and videos have so far but poorly represented these presences, but the new hypermedia may provide improved possibilities for integrating invisibilities within the categories of the real.

POSSIBLE FUTURES

The new hypermedia by themselves cannot make anything happen, for good or ill. Technological innovations like books or the World Wide Web create possibilities only, not inevitabilities. Whether the new hypermedia will only increase the power and reach of multinationals or instead increase the vitality of various critical traditionalisms depends on how people use these media much more than on any traits analysts may claim inhere within the new media themselves.

It is a mistake, I believe, to participate too enthusiastically in general discussions of the new technologies separate from discussions of some particular circumstances of one or more clearly specified critical traditionalism. Such general discussions, like general discussions of most concepts, usually function mostly as exercises to demonstrate the subtlety and cleverness of the analyst. Monorhetorical writers are rewarded for producing such discussions, for composing novel statements about what the new technologies mean, or for predicting how these inventions will change social formations. We should instead focus on specific traditions and regions, thereby resisting the monorhetorical practice of creating generalizations that purport to apply to all peoples on the earth. This restraint helps create more opportunities for the different and distinct groups who constitute the world majority to speak about themselves. The new technologies create possibilities for more of these previously silenced people to be heard in the metropole and elsewhere around the globe. If these possibilities are realized, however, it will be because of people's choices and not because the new technologies themselves dictate any specific changes.

Coda

Among the hundreds of books and articles I have looked at while researching this study, some pages in Robert C. Schmitt's short article, "Early Crime Statistics of Hawaii," especially haunt me. These pages display several tables summarizing the criminal convictions adjudicated by the first Euroamerican-type courts in the islands. According to Schmitt, the earliest written record of these courts appeared in the Hawaiian-language publication *Ke Kumu Hawaii* on January 16, 1839, and included only the convictions pronounced by judges in the city of Honolulu in 1838 (see Coda Table 1). Almost half of these convictions (246 out of 522) were for the crime of moekolohe, a Hawaiian word the courts were just then appropriating to use to designate what nineteenth-century Americans called adultery and fornication. The next most frequent crime was hookamakama, a term adapted by the judges to label both lewdness and prostitution. There were 32 convictions for uhauha (riot and/or spendthriftiness), 30 for mahuka (desertion), and 18 for weawea (seduction or lewdness). These five "crimes" accounted for about 80 percent of all the criminal offenses that judges adjudicated in 1838. This new judicial system thus made criminals out of Kanaka Maoli for continuing practices they had enacted without opprobrium for centuries.[1]

Coda Table 1   Convictions for the city of Honolulu, 1838

Kanawai (offense)	Ka helu ana (Number)
Pepehikanaka (manslaughter)	4
Moekolohe (adultery)	246
Aihue (theft)	48
Hookamakama (lewdness)	81
Uhauha (riot)	32
Hoopunipuni (false witness)	48
Mahuka (desertion)	30
Weawea (seduction)	18
Olhani (mutiny)	15
Total	522

Translation from *The Hawaiian Spectator*, Vol 2, No. 2 (April 1839), p. 234. Moekolohe has also been translated as "fornication"; aihue as "larceny"; hookamakama as "prostitution"; uhauha as "spendthrift"; hoopunipuni as "perjury"; and weawea as "pimping."
Source: Schmitt, 1969, 234. Reprinted by permission of the Hawaiian Historical Society.

165

Schmitt's tables from subsequent years repeat this pattern: Moekolohe remains the leading crime for 1839, 1845, 1846, and 1847, and additional, traditional Kanaka Maoli customs continue also to receive frequent convictions, leading to imprisonment, fines, forced labor, and public humiliations.[2] The project of transforming traditional behaviors into "crimes" was closely associated with the newly arrived Euroamerican missionaries and their merchant partners. Why so many of the ali'i assisted foreigners in transforming traditional Kanaka Maoli lifeways into punishable offenses continues to perplex historians. Kame'eleihiwa's pioneering *Native Land and Foreign Desires* offers what is probably the best explanation we will have for some time. Kame'eleihiwa looks at the shift in guiding metaphors that changed the ali'i's perspective on what was pono, or proper. She points to religious conversions and "other factors, including disease and depopulation, capitalist intrusion, and Western imperialism" that contributed to the shift in metaphors.[3] "The real loss of Hawaiian sovereignty began with the 1848 *Mahele*, when the *Mo'i* and *Ali'i Nui* lost ultimate control of the *'āina*" (15). Perhaps loss of sovereignty could as well be traced to the earlier institution of a judicial system that made traditional Hawaiian lifeways into felonies.

What haunts me about these tables is not ali'i complicity, however, but how starkly the lists of offenses reveal ways settlers acquired power in the islands by seizing control of Native words. In chapter 1 I discussed some of the problems Kanaka Maoli faced once legislation stole their traditional right to name themselves, their children, and their local places in accordance with Native Hawaiian customs. Settler adaptation of the Hawaiian language, I argued there and again in chapter 3, often masqueraded as a validation of Native traditions, when the actual effect was to encourage their destruction. Similarly, these tables illustrate how established Hawaiian words were given new, harshly pejorative meanings in the early court system in Hawai'i. The negative consequences resounded mostly on Natives and seldom on settlers. It was principally Kanaka Maoli who were fined, taken from their families, thrown in jail, and forced to labor for weeks and months, because missionaries and their friends loudly proclaimed that dancing, flirting (lewdness), making love, sharing possessions (spendthriftiness), taking off clothes, drinking awa and sour potatoes were crimes. That Kanaka Maoli had practiced forms of these customs probably since before Jesus was born counted for nothing to the stern judges who self-righteously enforced the penalties.

Schmitt's pages present a past with many similarities to the Hawai'i I live in today. Contemporary summaries of convictions remain dominated by records of Kanaka Maoli being tried mostly for offending foreign-introduced ideas of what is proper. Hawai'i's expanding prison-industrial complex remains mostly in the control of settlers—Asian and Euroamerican—and Polynesians constitute the majority of prisoners, serving terms for living on beaches, for sleeping in public places, for using land Kanaka Maoli ancestors have always used, and, especially often, for seeking, trading, selling, and/or using intoxicating substances.

Coda 167

The use of laws against intoxication to terrorize Kanaka Maoli has its own long history. By 1852, as Schmitt's tables show, fornication and adultery had sunk to become only the second most frequently convicted offense in the islands, displaced by ona rama (drunkenness). (Intoxication-related offenses composed a little over a third of the convictions in the Kingdom of Hawaii in 1852, and sexual offenses added up to about an additional one-fourth; see Coda Table 2.) Foreigners controlling the criminal justice system in 1852 vigorously punished Kanaka Maoli for enjoying substances other foreigners were eagerly importing and encouraging them to buy. Today in Hawai'i, most criminal convictions remain connected to ona rama (now usually spelled 'ona lama), though the drunkenness is more often of a kind connected to nonalcoholic, mind-altering substances. Settler ideas of right and wrong still rule, and it is Kanaka Maoli who are most often convicted.

Coda Table 2   Convictions for Kingdom of Hawai'i, 1852

Offense	Number
Manslaughter	1
Drunkenness	1,114
Drinking awa	13
Fornication and adultery	730
Illicit cohabitation	12
Polygamy	7
Sodomy	19
Assault and battery	254
Riot	104
Larceny	213
Receiving stolen goods	5
Forgery	6
Perjury	5
Profanity	14
Violating the Sabbath	46
Idolatry	7
Gambling	12
Furious riding	298
Common nuisance	16
Smuggling	4
Selling spiritous liquors without license	20
Distilling spiritous liquors	3
Gross cheat	2
All other offenses	43
Total	2,948

Data from *First Annual Report of the Chief Justice of the Supreme Court* (1853), p. 109.
Source: Schmitt, 1969, 240. Reprinted by permission of the

Schmitt's list of convictions seems less important as a record of historic behaviors than as a statement about how missionaries and settlers used their im-
ported ideas to increase their power in the islands while subjugating Kanaka
Maoli. When I think of how quickly these settlers' ideas swept across the islands
in a few decades in the first half of the eighteenth century, I wonder: What could
happen to sweep them away again?

The Bishop Museum in Honolulu owns by far the world's largest collection of
Native Hawaiian artifacts. The museum's displays are generally accompanied by
monorhetorical texts that attempt to explain the traditional Kanaka Maoli meaning and use of the objects on view. These written explanations were for many
years offered exclusively in English but, in the past few years, a second interpretive language, Japanese, has been added as well. There are few Hawaiian-
language texts at the museum, and no acknowledgment or hint that either English
or Japanese might be inadequate for representing the meanings of the cultural
productions the museum's mostly non-Native curators choose to display. At the
Bishop Museum then, as elsewhere in Hawai'i, the displacement of Native
Hawaiians that began with Cook's voyages continues at the close of the twentieth
century.

Though beginning to be impacted by texts by some of the Native Hawaiian
scholars mentioned in this study, Hawaiian history remains prominently monorhetorical, shaped by Ralph S. Kuykendall's three-volume *The Hawaiian Kingdom* and by Gavan Daws's *Shoal of Time*.[4] Kuykendall's and Daws's books make
little use of the vast archival material available in the Hawaiian language that
might, in some measure, encourage the resurgence of an alternative, Native,
polyrhetorical history. *The Hawaiian Journal of History*, nearing thirty years of
publication, still rarely publishes documents by or even about Hawaiians, and
could be more accurately titled the *Journal of Euroamericans and Immigrants in
Hawai'i*. The largest department of history in the state, located at the University
of Hawai'i at Mānoa, employs more specialists in European, in Asian, and of
course in English and American history than specialists focused on Hawai'i and
Oceania.

The displacement of Native voices continues in these islands within literary
studies as well. Anthologies compiled by A. Grove Day, often with the help of Carl
Stroven, fill the mass-market paperback racks and guide the understanding of
many of Hawai'i's seven million tourists. Typical of these volumes is *The Spell of
Hawaii*, edited by Day and Stroven, a paperback in print now for thirty years. Its
cover promises that readers will discover the "exotic literary heritage of the
Hawaiian Islands." The anthology includes twenty-five selections, including pieces
by Michener, Twain, Bird, Stevenson, London, Murayama and others. Only one of
the twenty-five is by a Native Hawaiian, a short piece extracted from Samuel M.
Kamakau's *The Ruling Chiefs of Hawaii*. This lone Native selection presents
Kamakau's version of Captain Cook's death, suggesting that Hawaiians are most
of interest when they speak about Euroamericans.[5]

As Paul Lyons demonstrates in his study of Day, the writing in these ubiquitous anthologies assumes that touristic, literary, and scholarly texts complement and support each other.[6] This presumption continues to dominate not only what most of the general public reads about Hawai'i but also what most reviewers, scholars, and teachers write and teach as well. As I began this study, for example, one professor at the University of Hawai'i advised me enthusiastically to be sure to give special attention to Jack London. "He understood Hawai'i better than any other writer," I was told by this man, who has taught in the islands for nearly thirty years. My experience over two decades as a teacher and student on two islands shows me that similar praises for often racist, Euroamerican views are commonly presented to students of all races, at all grade levels, from elementary through graduate school, at public as well as at private schools.

What, then, should researchers and teachers in Hawai'i do? There are numerous possibilities, surely, though in this study I have concentrated essentially on only two. I have tried to explore how Euroamerican-trained scholars like myself can compose analyses that undermine their own and other outsider cultural productions that claim a privileged knowledge of Native Hawaiians. I have tried as well to encourage non-Natives to listen more attentively and often to Kanaka Maoli speaking for themselves.

Euroamericans are trained to translate their encounters with the Other into monorhetorical interpretations. This impulse must be actively resisted, I believe, as all such translations likely reinscribe the displacement of those who are thus represented. Writers and teachers can avoid such displacements by shifting the focus away from metropolitan and toward Native texts and other cultural productions. There is much material close at hand presently being ignored. Richard Hamasaki points out, for example, that there is an immense body of Kanaka Maoli work in the islands within the familiar genre of poetry that is generally ignored by critics and teachers. Hamasaki recommends more study of the outpouring of new compositions for modern hulas and "the ever-mounting repertoire of ancient and contemporary Hawaiian language chants and compositions," seldom discussed or taught, "despite the availability of impressive bilingual texts."[7] Māhealani Dudoit and colleagues' new press, Kuleana 'Ōiwi, publishers of *'Ōiwi: A Native Hawaiian Journal*, now provides a site specifically encouraging this and allied literary Kanaka Maoli work. Throughout these pages I have referred to many other, mostly nonliterary texts by Kanaka Maoli that also deserve more study.

It is my hope that Euroamerican writers and teachers will encourage the reproduction and distribution of Kanaka Maoli texts as well as other historical and contemporary Native productions without simultaneously posing as authorities and constructing seemingly "expert" monorhetorical analyses. I believe careful scholars can function as compilers and reporters, recording what Native Hawaiians say about their productions, thereby enabling Native voices to be better heard. Scholars can also examine how Native Hawaiian productions challenge Euroamerican ideas. They can explore the ways that the cultural productions of Native Hawaiians may act as a critical traditionalism or regionalism that, in Wilson's formulation, builds "some hybrid culture of resistance grounded in place, language, and the will to collective decolonization."[8]

There is a danger that such comparative work may seem to offer supposedly authoritative representations of the meaning of Native Hawaiian texts. The emphasis must be not on these representations themselves but rather on the way Euroamerican constructions of the Other can be used to intervene in metropolitan traditions. My construction of polyrhetoric has been intended to serve as an example of just such an intervention. Such an intervention will fail, however, if it seems aimed at transforming monorhetoric into a kama'āina version of polyrhetoric. By using monorhetoric to interrogate itself while simultaneously championing alternative traditions, monorhetoric can instead be encouraged to metamorphose into some alternative form that no longer displaces the very people and places it represents. There is probably as much or more benefit for non-Natives as for Natives in such work.

Notes

ORIENTATION. RECOVERING HAWAIIAN WINDS

1. Moses K. Nakuina, *The Wind Gourd of La'amaomao*, translated by Esther K. Mookini and Sarah Nākoa (Honolulu: Kalamaku Press, 1990).
2. Nakuina, *Wind Gourd*, 50.
3. Ralph S. Kuykendall, *The Hawaiian Kingdom*, vol. 1, *1778–1854, Foundation and Transformation* (Honolulu: University of Hawaii Press, 1938); vol. 2, *1854–1874, Twenty Critical Years* (Honolulu: University of Hawaii Press, 1953); vol. 3, *1874–1893, The Kalakaua Dynasty* (Honolulu: University of Hawaii Press, 1967).
4. Capitalizing Native is a practice Haunani-Kay Trask helped pioneer; see her explanation in *From a Native Daughter, Colonialism and Sovereignty in Hawaii* (Monroe, Maine: Common Courage Press, 1993), 70. Lilikalā Kame'eleihiwa writes similarly: "The correct spelling of Hawaiian words and the selective capitalization of certain terms of our choosing, such as 'Native,' are signs of our incipient sovereignty. We will make the rules that govern spelling of our words. They are, after all, our words" (*Native Land and Foreign Desires* [Honolulu: Bishop Museum Press, 1992], 342).
5. Nakuina, *Wind Gourd*, vii.
6. For recent statistics on Native Hawaiians, see the Office of Hawaiian Affairs Native Hawaiian Data Book, available at <http//www.lava.net/~plnr>.
7. Edward Said, *Culture and Imperialism* (New York: Random House, 1993), 7.
8. Momi Kamahele, "Decolonizing Hawaiian Antiquities and Fragments of Hawaiian History," paper presented at the fifteenth Annual Meeting of the Association for Asian American Studies Conference, 1898–1998: Rethinking Asian and Pacific Colonial/Postcolonial Nations, Identities and Histories, Honolulu, Hawaii, 1998; Lilikalā Kame'eleihiwa, *Native Land and Foreign Desires*; George Hu'eu Sanford Kanahele, *Ku Kanaka: Stand Tall* (Honolulu: University of Hawaii Press, 1996), and *Waikīkī 100 B.C. to 1900 A.D.: An Untold Story* (Honolulu: University of Hawaii Press, 1995); Herb Kawainui Kane, "Comments," *Current Anthropology* 38, no. 2 (1997): 265–267; J. Kehaulani Kauanui, "Mapping the Native: Hawaiian Genealogical Reterritorialization of Land, Identity, and Sovereign Belonging," paper presented at the fifteenth Annual Meeting of the Association for Asian American Studies Conference, 1898–1998: Rethinking Asian and Pacific Colonial/Postcolonial Nations, Identities and Histories, Honolulu, Hawaii, 1998; Anne Kapulani Landgraf, *Na Wahi Pana O Ko'olau Poko, Legendary Places of Ko'olau Poko*, Hawaiian translated by Fred Kalani Meinecke (Honolulu: University of Hawaii Press, 1994); Davianna Pōmaika'i McGregor, "Waipi'o Valley, a Cultural Kīpuka in Early 20th

Century Hawai'i," *Journal of Pacific History* 30, no. 2 (1995): 194-209; Jon Osorio, "Protecting Our Thoughts," speech delivered at Voices of the Earth Conference held in Amsterdam, November 10, 1993—available from the Center for Hawaiian Studies, University of Hawaii, Mānoa, <http://www2.hawaii.edu/shaps/hawaii/osorio.html> (July 3, 1998); Noenoe K. Silva, "Ku'e!: Hawaiian Women's Resistance to the Annexation," *Social Process of Hawai'i* 38 (1997): 2–15; Amy Ku'uleialoha Stillman, "History Reinterpreted in Song: The Case of the Hawaiian Counterrevolution," *Hawaiian Journal of History* 23 (1989): 1–30, "Queen Kapi'olani's Lei Chants," *Hawaiian Journal of History* 30 (1996): 119–152, and *Sacred Hula: The Historical Hula 'Ā la'apapa* (Honolulu: Bishop Museum Press, 1998); Haunani-Kay Trask, *From a Native Daughter*, and "De-Colonizing Hawaiian Literature," in *Inside Out: Literature, Cultural Politics, and Identity in the New Pacific*, edited by Vilsoni Hereniko and Rob Wilson (Lanham, Md.: Rowman and Littlefield, 1999); Kanalu Young, *Rethinking the Hawaiian Past* (forthcoming).

9. Trask, *From a Native Daughter*, 115.

10. Dennis Kawaharada, "Toward an Authentic Local Literature in Hawai'i," in *Hawai'i Literature Conference: Reader's Guide*, edited by Lorna Hershinow (Honolulu: Hawai'i Literary Arts Council, 1994), 56–60; Richard Hamasaki, "Mountains in the Sea: The Emergence of Contemporary Hawaiian Poetry in English," in *Hawai'i Literature Conference: Reader's Guide*, edited by Lorna Hershinow (Honolulu: Hawai'i Literary Arts Council, 1994), 32–47.

11. Rob Wilson, "Blue Hawai'i: Bamboo Ridge and 'Critical Regionalism,'" in *Hawai'i Literature Conference: Reader's Guide*, edited by Lorna Hershinow (Honolulu: Hawai'i Literary Arts Council, 1994), 109–128, and *Reimagining the American Pacific: From 'South Pacific' to Bamboo Ridge and Beyond* (Durham, N.C.: Duke University Press, forthcoming); see also Rob Wilson and Arif Dirlik, "Introduction: Asia/Pacific as Space of Cultural Production," in *Asia/Pacific as Space of Cultural Production*, edited by Rob Wilson and Arif Dirlik (Durham, N.C.: Duke University Press, 1995), 1–14.

12. R. Douglas Herman, "Kalai'aina—Carving the Land: Geography, Desire and Possession in the Hawaiians Islands" (Ph.D. diss., University of Hawaii, 1995), and "The Dread Taboo, Human Sacrifice, and Pearl Harbor," *Contemporary Pacific* 8, no. 1 (Spring 1996): 81–126.

13. For an example of a non-Native scholar who interrogates Native claims for authenticity, see Roger Keesing, "Creating the Past: Custom and Identity in the Contemporary Pacific," *Contemporary Pacific* 1 (1989): 19–42. A good introductory discussion of this controversy can be found in Jeffrey Tobin, "Cultural Construction and Native Nationalism: Report from the Hawaiian Front," *Boundary* 2 21.1 (Spring 1994): 111–133.

14. McGregor, "Waipi'o Valley." McGregor ascribes the kīpuka concept to modern foresters. It seems these scientists in turn created this ecological model by borrowing a Hawaiian word and metaphor. That McGregor is now reclaiming this metaphor for use in constructing her Native narrative of Hawaiians illustrates the intertextuality one often finds in contemporary non-Native and Native writings about the islands. Page numbers to additional references from McGregor's article are included in the text.

15. Kanahele, *Ku Kanaka*.

16. See, e.g., Homi Bhabha, "Signs Taken for Wonders: Questions of Ambivalence and Authority Under a Tree Outside Delhi, May 1817," *Critical Inquiry* 12 (1985): 144–165, and "Sly Civility," *October* 34 (1985): 71–80; Roger Keesing, "Creating the Past."

CHAPTER ONE. THE VIOLENT RHETORIC OF NAMES

1. Haunani-Kay Trask, *From a Native Daughter: Colonialism and Sovereignty in Hawaii* (Monroe, Maine: Common Courage Press, 1993), 84.

2. In Archives of Hawaii, *Laws of His Majesty Kamehameha IV, King of Hawaiian Islands, Passed by the Nobles and Representatives at their Session*, 1860, 32; quoted in Mary Kawena Pukui, Samuel H. Elbert, and Esther T. Mookini, *Place Names of Hawaii* (Honolulu: University of Hawaii Press, 1974), 98.

3. Patricia Grimshaw, *Paths of Duty: American Missionary Wives in Nineteenth-Century Hawaii* (Honolulu: University of Hawaii Press, 1989), 156. See also Lilikalā Kame'eleihiwa, *Native Land and Foreign Desires* (Honolulu: Bishop Museum Press, 1992), especially 137–167; and Phyllis Turnbull and Kathey E. Ferguson, "Military Presence/Missionary Past: The Historical Construction of Masculine Order and Feminine Hawai'i," in *Women in Hawai'i: Sites, Identities, and Voices*, edited by Kathleen O. Kane, Joyce N. Chinen, and Ida M. Yoshinaga (Honolulu: Department of Sociology, University of Hawai'i, 1997), 94–107.

4. Mary Kawena Pukui, E. W. Haertig, and Catherine A. Lee, *Nānā I Ke Kumu (Look to the Source)*, vol. 1 (Honolulu: Queen Lili'uokalani Children's Center, 1972), 94.

5. Pukui, Elbert, and Mookini, *Place Names*, 258.

6. Quoted in R. Douglas K. Herman, "Kalai'aina—Carving the Land: Geography, Desire and Possession in the Hawaiian Islands" (Ph.D. diss., University of Hawaii, 1995), 7.

7. Herman, "Kalai'aina," 11.

8. George Hu'eu Sanford Kanahele, *Ku Kanaka: Stand Tall* (Honolulu: University of Hawaii Press, 1996), 208.

9. Samuel H. Elbert, "Preface," in *Place Names*, x.

10. Herman, "Kalai'aina," 357. See also Herman, "The Dread Taboo, Human Sacrifice, and Pearl Harbor," *Contemporary Pacific* 8, no. 1 (Spring 1996): 81–126, for an analysis of how the term "kapu" was transformed in Hawai'i from a concept marking Native relationships into a new "sacred principle" marking private property and foreign control. See especially page 84ff.

11. Kekuni Blaisdell, "'Hawaiian' vs. 'Kanaka Maoli' as Metaphors," *Hawaii Review* 13 (1989): 77–79. See also Kekuni Blaisdell and Noreen Mokuau, "Kānaka Maoli, Indigenous Hawaiians," in *Hawai'i Return to Nationhood*, edited by Ulla Hasager and Jonathan Friedman (Copenhagen: IWGIA, 1994), 49–67.

12. Blaisdell, "'Hawaiian' vs. 'Kanaka Maoli'," 79.

13. Marshal Sahlins, *What 'Natives' Think, About Captain Cook, for Example* (Chicago: University of Chicago Press, 1995); and Valerio Valeri, *Kingship and Sacrifice: Ritual and Society in Ancient Hawaii* (Chicago: University of Chicago Press, 1985).

14. Kekuni Blaisdell, "Water Diversion Is 'Genocide'," *Honolulu Advertiser*, 3 May 1998, B3. For more about the relationship between Hawaiians and kalo, see Kame'eleihiwa, *Native Land*, 23–24. Older examinations of the relationship can be found in David Malo, *Hawaiian Antiquities* (Honolulu: Bishop Museum Press, 1951), 244; and in E. S. Handy, C. Handy, and E. G. Handy, *Native Planters in Old Hawai'i* (Honolulu: Bishop Museum Press, 1972), 80–81. I return to this topic in chapter 8 below.

15. Mary Louise Pratt, "Arts of the Contact Zone," *Profession* 91 (1991): 139. See Pratt's use of the ideas contained in this essay in her *Imperial Eyes: Travel Writing and Transculturation* (New York: Routledge, 1992).

16. Arif Dirlik, "The Global in the Local," in *Global/Local: Cultural Production and the Transnational Imaginary*, edited by Rob Wilson and Wimal Dissanayake (Durham, N.C.: Duke University Press, 1996), 28.

17. Rob Wilson and Arif Dirlik, "Introduction," in *Asia/Pacific as Space of Cultural Production*, edited by Rob Wilson and Arif Dirlik (Durham, N.C.: Duke University Press, 1995), 8.

18. Pratt, "Arts," 139.

19. Joseph P. Balaz, *After the Drought* (Honolulu: Topgallant, 1985). Also see Balaz's poems in *Hoʻomānoa*, edited by Joseph P. Balaz (Honolulu: Ku Paʻa, 1989); Michael McPherson, *Singing with the Owls* (Honolulu: Petronium Press, 1982), "Glass Balls and Other Found Objects," in *Hawaiʻi Literary Conference: Reader's Guide*, edited by Lorna Hershinow (Honolulu: Hawaiʻi Literary Arts Council, 1994), 1–2, and "Kiholo Revisited," in *Hawaii Literature Conference*, edited by Lorna Hershinow (Honolulu: Hawaiʻi Literary Arts Council, 1994); Kiana Davenport, *Shark Dialogues* (New York: Macmillan, 1994).

20. For an important early discussion of these issues, see John Dominis Holt, *On Being Hawaiian* (Honolulu: Star-Bulletin Printing, 1964). For a more recent analysis, consult Trask, *From a Native Daughter*. David J. Baker, "*Ea* and Knowing in Hawaiʻi," *Critical Inquiry* 23, no. 3 (1997): 640–660, provides a summary of the major issues involved in the construction of contemporary Native Hawaiian identities. See also Candace Fujikane, "Between Nationalisms: Hawaiʻi's Local Nation and Its Troubled Racial Paradise," *Critical Mass* 1, no.2 (Spring/Summer 1994): 23–58.

21. John Dominis Holt, "Rev. of *Ku Kanaka*, by George Kanehele," *Hawaiian Journal of History* 21 (1987): 158.

22. Haunani-Kay Trask, "Natives and Anthropologists: The Colonial Struggle," *Contemporary Pacific* 2 (1991):165 n.1.

23. Trask, *From a Native Daughter*, 84.

24. Wilson and Dirlik, "Introduction," 7. "Critical regionalism" and "strategic localism" are sometimes used by Wilson, Dirlik and others as synonyms for critical localism.

25. Ashis Nandy, "Bearing Witness to the Future," *Futures* 28 (1996): 638.

26. Ashis Nandy, *Traditions, Tyranny and Utopias: Essays in the Politics of Awareness* (Delhi, India: Oxford University Press, 1987), 124. For an introduction to Nandy's thought, see the special issue of *Emergences*, nos. 7/8, titled *Plural Worlds, Multiple Selves: Ashis Nandy and the Postcolumbian Future*. See, especially, Ziauddin Sardar, "The A B C D (and E) of Ashis Nandy," *Emergences* 7/8 (1995-96): 125–145.

27. S. X. Goudie, "Theory, Practice and the Intellectual: A Conversation with Abdul R. JanMohamed," *Jouvert (Electronic Journal)*, 1997, <http://152.1.96.5/jouvert/issue2/Goudie.htm> (September 28, 1998). JanMohamed points out that the "assumption that epistemic resistance is automatically equivalent to political resistance" may support "Western hegemonic paradigms" as often as it resists them.

28. Nandy, "Bearing Witness," 638.

29. Paul Carter, *The Road to Botany Bay: An Essay in Spatial History* (Boston: Faber and Faber, 1987), 303.

30. See, for example, Ahmad Aijaz, *In Theory: Classes, Nations, Literatures* (New York: Verso, 1992); Arif Dirlik, *The Postcolonial Aura: Third World Criticism in the Age of Global Capitalism* (Boulder: Westview, 1997); Anne McClintock, "The Angel of Progress: The Pitfalls of the Term 'Post-colonialism'," *Social Text* 31, no. 3 (1992): 84–98;

Benita Parry, "Problems in Current Theories of Colonial Discourse," *Oxford Literary Review* 9 (1987): 27–58, and "The Postcolonial: Conceptual Category or Chimera," in *The Yearbook of English Studies: The Politics of Postcolonial Criticism*, edited by Andrew Gurr (London: W. S. Maney, 1997), 3–21; Robert J. C. Young, *Colonial Desire: Hybridity in Theory, Culture and Race* (New York: Routledge, 1995).

31. Jeffrey Tobin, "Cultural Construction and Native Nationalism: Report from the Hawaiian Front," *Boundary* 2 21, no. 1 (Spring 1994): 111–133. See also Tobin, "Savages, the Poor and the Discourse of Hawaiian Infanticide," *Journal of Polynesian Society* 106, no. 1 (March 1997): 65–92.

32. Nandy, *Traditions, Tyranny*, xvii; quoted in Dirlik, *After the Revolution*, 17.

CHAPTER TWO. CAPTAIN JAMES COOK, RHETORICIAN

1. Speaking in *Encounters with Paradise: Views of Hawaii and Its People, 1778–1941*, produced and directed by Richard J. Tibberts, Hawaii Public Television, 1992, videocassette.

2. James Cook and James King, *A Voyage to the Pacific Ocean: Undertaken by the Command of His Majesty, for Making Discoveries in the Northern Hemisphere. Performed under the Direction of Captains Cook, Clerke, and Gore, in His Majesty's Ships the* Resolution *and* Discovery; *in the Years 1776, 1777, 1778, 1779, and 1780. In Three Volumes, plus Folio* (London: Printed by H. Hughs for G. Nicol and T. Cadell, 1784).

3. Anthony Murray-Oliver, *Captain Cook's Hawaii: As Seen by His Artists* (Wellington, New Zealand: Millwood, 1975), 136–137.

4. O. A. Bushnell, "Aftermath: Britons' Responses to News of the Death of Captain James Cook," *The Hawaiian Journal of History* 25 (1991): 7. A summary of the Anglo-European reaction to the Cook and King volumes is also offered in *Captain James Cook and His Times*, edited by Robin Fisher and Hugh J.M. Johnston (Vancouver: Douglas and McIntyre, 1979); see especially the essays there by Michael E. Hoare, Rudiger Joppien, and Bernard Smith.

5. David W. Forbes and Honolulu Academy of Arts, *Encounters with Paradise: Views of Hawaii and Its People, 1778–1941* (Honolulu: Honolulu Academy of Arts, 1992), 54.

6. Concerning Webber's mythologizing. See also Rudiger Joppien and Bernard Smith, *The Art of Captain Cook's Voyages*, vol. 3, *The Voyage of the "Resolution" and "Discovery"* (New Haven: Yale University Press, 1988), 126. Herb Kawainui Kane's *Voyagers: Words and Images* (Bellevue, Wash.: WhaleSong, 1991), analyzes Webber's inaccuracies. Kane offers an alternative painting of Cook's death based on the historical record as Kane interprets it.

7. Bernard Smith, *European Vision and the South Pacific*, 2d ed. (New York: Oxford University Press, 1989), 112.

8. For discussions of the current iconography of these helmets, see Jocelyn Linnekin, "Consuming Cultures: Tourism and the Commoditization of Cultural Identity in the Island Pacific," in *Tourism, Ethnicity, and the State in Asian and Pacific Societies*, edited by Michaed Picard and Robert E. Wood (Honolulu: University of Hawaii Press, 1997), 215–250. For an analysis of Webber's method in creating his *Masked Paddlers At Kealakekua Bay*, see Kane, *Voyagers*, 92–3. Kane hypothesizes that the masks were worn by the priests of Ku during the makahiki season in deference to Lono and his priests.

9. Marshall Sahlins, *What 'Natives' Think, About Captain Cook, for Example* (Chicago: University of Chicago Press, 1995); Gananath Obeyesekere, *The Apotheosis of Captain Cook: European Mythmaking in the Pacific* (Princeton: Princeton University Press, 1992). See my comments on this quarrel in chapter 7.

10. See Samuel M. Kamakau's account of Keōua's death in *Ruling Chiefs of Hawaii* (Honolulu: Kamehameha Schools Press, 1961), 151–158. Cf. Ralph S. Kuykendall, *The Hawaiian Kingdom*, vol. 1, *1778–1854* (Honolulu: University of Hawaii Press, 1938), 37–38.

11. Beaglehole agrees with Captain Clerke's opinion that Cook's own murdering was the cause of his demise. Had Cook not fired first, according to Beaglehole, the Hawaiians in turn would not have killed him. See J. C. Beaglehole, "Introduction," in *The Journals of Captain James Cook on His Voyages of Discovery*, vol. 3, *The Voyage of the Resolution and Discovery, 1776–1780*, edited by J. C. Beaglehole (Cambridge: Cambridge University Press, 1967), clvi–clvii.

12. Stephen Greenblatt, *Marvelous Possessions* (Chicago: University of Chicago Press, 1991), 12–13.

13. Paul Carter, *The Road to Botany Bay: An Exploration of Landscape and History* (Chicago: University of Chicago Press, 1989), 18.

14. James Cook, *The Journals of Captain James Cook on his Voyages of Discovery*, vol. 1, *The Voyage of the Endeavor, 1769–1771, Charts & Views*. Edited by J. C. Beaglehole (Cambridge, Eng.: Cambridge University Press for the Hakluyt Society, 1955), 48.

15. R. Douglas Herman, "Kalai'aina—Carving the Land: Geography, Desire and Possession in the Hawaiian Islands" (Ph.D. diss., University of Hawaii, 1995), 57–61.

16. This emendation is Beaglehole's, in his 1967 edition of Cook's *Journals*. See note 17.

17. James Cook, *The Journals of Captain James Cook and his Voyages of Discovery*, Vol. 3, *The Voyage of the Resolution and Discovery 1776–1780, Parts One and Two*, edited by J. C. Beaglehole (Cambridge: Cambridge University Press, 1967), 263.

18. J. C. Beaglehole, *Cook the Writer* (Sydney: Sydney University Press, 1970), 7. See also Carter, *The Road*, 9–10, 41–42, for an analysis of Hawkesworth's influence on Cook's first book.

19. Beaglehole, "Introduction," clxxii.

20. Cook and King, *A Voyage*, volume 2, 549.

21. Cook, *Journals*, Vol. 3, 269.

22. For a summary of each of the many manuscripts that survive, see J. C. Beaglehole, "Textual Introduction," in *The Journals of Captain James Cook and his Voyages of Discovery*, Vol. 3, *The Voyage of the Resolution and Discovery 1776–1780, Parts One and Two*, edited by J. C. Beaglehole (Cambridge: Cambridge University Press, 1967), clxxi–ccx.

23. Quoted in Cook, *Journals*, Vol. 3, 132. Unless otherwise noted, page numbers for further citations from various members of Cook's crew will be cited from this same edition and volume of Cook's journals and will be given in the text.

24. Obeyesekere, *The Apotheosis*, 27ff, reviews several other eyewitness accounts of these events, providing further support for the view that Cook's journals suppress how often he personally led his troops in terrorizing and killing Pacific Island peoples.

25. Williamson's journal also emphasizes "the necessity of shedding blood" and is quoted in Cook (*Journals*, vol. 3):

I again repeated my orders to them [the seamen Williamson commanded] not to mind my firing (which I found I should be oblig'd to do) but wait until I told them, I then went forward to the man who had hold of the boat hook, offering him a nail, but he refus'd it, I then made a stroke at him with a small rifle barrel'd Gun which I had in my hand, but this he seemed not to mind, I was then going aft & the boats crew endeavouring to back the boat off, when one of the natives made a stroke at me, at the same time the bow man call'd out he must let go the boat hook, I again turned about, and with the greatest reluctance shot the indian who was struggling for the boat hook; . . . the man that was shot was a tall handsome man about 40 Years of age & seem'd to be a Chief, the ball entering under his right pap, he instantly dropt down dead in the water. (1348)

26. Beaglehole, "Introduction," cli.

27. Murray-Oliver, *Captain Cook's Hawaii*, 201. This was the first of repeated, indiscriminate killing sprees that Euroamericans would inflict on Hawaiians. A few years later, for example, in 1790, Captain Simon Metcalfe and his men murdered over a hundred Hawaiians in the waters off Maui in what is now known as the "Olowalu massacre." John Young, who would prove so influential to Hawaiian history, was kidnapped from the American whaler *Eleanora* by Kamehameha partially in retaliation for Metcalfe's murders.

28. Beaglehole, "Introduction," cliv.

29. James Watt provides an alternative apologia for Cook's behavior, illustrating to what extremes hagiographers will go to support continued worship of Europe's supposedly great men. Watt claims that on Cook's final voyage he was suffering from "a parasitic infection . . . probably of the lower ileum" (James Watt, "Medical Aspects and Consequences of Cook's Voyages," in *Captain James Cook and His Times*, edited by Robin Fisher and J. M. Johnston [Vancouver: Douglas and McIntyre, 1979], 155). This disease, Watt maintains, produces various physiological symptoms as well as "irritability" and a "change of personality" (155). Gananath Obeyesekere calls Watt's apologia a "pathetic attempt to exonerate Cook from responsibility for his actions" (*The Apotheosis*, 133) and points out, "Worms must have had a particular partiality for Cook, since none of the other officers seemed to have suffered from these symptoms, especially from a 'change of personality'" (224).

30. Quoted in Cook, *Journals*, vol. 3, ccxx.

31. See Cook's *Journals*, vol. 3, pages 188–189, 223, 286, and elsewhere for indications of how often England's competition with Spain was on his mind. See also Christon I. Archer, "The Spanish Reaction to Cook's Third Voyage," in *Captain James Cook and His Times*, 99–120.

32. See Carter, *Botany Bay*, for a discussion of the connections between naming and violence as allied acts of possession in the Pacific.

33. See Beaglehole, "Introduction," xliii, for a short summary of the political conditions extant when Cook sailed. See also David MacKay, *In the Wake of Cook: Exploration, Science and Empire, 1780–1801* (New York: St. Martin's, 1985) for an examination of how Cook "provided a model and methodology of scientific exploration" which was used in the second period of British imperialism after the loss of the American colonies ("Preface" n.p.).

34. Cook and King, *A Voyage*, vol. 2, 549.

35. Herman, "Kalai'aina," 66ff, provides a similar analysis of how European expeditions in the Pacific functioned as a veneer for colonialism. See also O.H.K. Spate, *Paradise Found and Lost* (Minneapolis: University of Minnesota Press, 1988), the third volume of Spate's series on the history of the Pacific since Magellan, in which Spate concludes: "Basically, then, the explorations of the Pacific [in Cook's time] represented the sparring for position by the superpowers of that day, Britain and France, in the disclosure of a new

world, as the superpowers today spar for a position in the new world of space. In both cases, scientific endeavor was at once a cover and a weapon" (79). Mary Louise Pratt, *Imperial Eyes: Travel Writing and Transculturation* (New York: Routledge, 1992), offers a related analysis of what she calls the "planetary consciousness" of the scientific explorations that accompanied European imperialism.

36. James Burney, first lieutenant on the *Discovery*, wrote similarly in his own journal the next day, "There was reason to apprehend, if these people got clear off, their success would encourage others who might be disposed to leave us" (quoted in Cook, *Journals*, vol. 3, 247, n. 2).

37. Quoted in Beaglehole, "Introduction," cxiiii.

38. Cook, *Journals*, Vol. 3, 23.

39. Captain George Vancouver, Cook's successor in Hawaii, continued both Cook's use of fireworks and his rhetoric of possession. In *The Death of William Gooch: A History's Anthropology* (Honolulu: University of Hawaii Press, 1995), Greg Dening notes that Vancouver took possession of Hawai'i on his third visit "in the name of King George III, but nobody seemed to notice or care" (32). Dening also details Vancouver's satisfaction at witnessing the murder of two innocent Native men aboard his ship. Vancouver interpreted these executions as evidence that the Hawaiian chiefs were beginning to comprehend that Cook, Vancouver, and other naval officers represented "a sovereignty and majesty greater than" any of the Hawaiian royalty themselves (41). Dening reminds us that the Native historian Samuel Kamakau would claim a few decades later it was the influence of Vancouver and other Euroamericans that precipitated an increasing violence by Hawaiian chiefs against their own people.

CHAPTER THREE. THE KAMA'ĀINA ANTI-CONQUEST

1. Armine Von Tempski, *Ripe Breadfruit* (1935; reprint, Woodbridge, Conn.: Ox Bow, 1992), 32.

2. Many customary Kanaka Maoli behaviors were labeled crimes, once the missionaries acquired sufficient power. See the tables summarizing convictions for some of these crimes in the "Coda" following chapter 8.

3. This extract from Stewart's journal appeared in Ephraim Eveleth, *History of the Sandwich Islands: With an Account of the American Mission Established There in 1820* (Philadelphia: American Sunday-School Union, 1830), and is quoted in R. Douglas Herman, "Kalai'aina—Carving the Land: Geography, Desire and Possession in the Hawaiians Islands" (Ph.D. diss., University of Hawaii, 1995), 171–172.

4. Hiram Bingham, *Residence of Twenty-One Years in the Sandwich Islands* (1847; reprint, Tokyo: Charles E. Tuttle, 1981), quoted in Gavan Daws, *Shoal of Time: A History of the Hawaiian Islands* (Honolulu: University of Hawaii Press, 1968), 64.

5. Quoted in Herman, "Kalai'aina," 176.

6. Patricia Grimshaw, *Paths of Duty: American Missionary Wives in Nineteenth-Century Hawaii* (Honolulu: University of Hawaii, 1989), 58.

7. Quoted in Grimshaw, *Paths of Duty*, 57–58.

8. Grimshaw, *Paths of Duty*, 172.

9. The two quotes from missionaries and Herman's comment can be found in Herman, "Kalai'aina," 177.

10. For a Kanaka Maoli perspective on these transformations, see Lilikalā Kameʻelei-hiwa, *Native Land and Foreign Desires* (Honolulu: Bishop Museum Press, 1992).

11. See Michel Foucault, *The Order of Things: An Archaeology of the Human Sciences*, translated by Alan Sheridan (London: Tavistock Publications, 1970), for a general discussion of the role of the social sciences in colonialism; Herman, "Kalaiʻaina," 136ff, applies this perspective specifically to the "science of race" and to its introduction into discourses in Hawaii.

12. Mark Twain, *Mark Twain's Letters from Hawaii*, edited by A. Grove Day (Honolulu: University of Hawaii Press, 1975), 282.

13. Jack London, *Stories of Hawaii* (Honolulu: Mutual, 1990), 52.

14. Mary Louise Pratt, *Imperial Eyes: Travel Writing and Transculturation* (New York: Routledge, 1992), 7.

15. Mary Kawena Pukui and Samuel H. Elbert, *Hawaiian Dictionary* (Honolulu: University of Hawaii Press, 1986).

16. "Our Literary Standard," *Paradise of the Pacific*, February 1909, 8; emphasis added.

17. Armine Von Tempski, *Born in Paradise* (New York: Duell Sloan and Pearce, 1940), 6. After the initial citation, further page numbers referring to Von Tempski's books are placed in the text.

18. Pratt, *Imperial Eyes*, 181.

19. Armine Von Tempski, *Hula: A Romance of Hawaii* (1927; reprint, Woodbridge, Conn.: Ox Bow, 1988), 236. After the initial citation, further page numbers referring to Von Tempski's books are placed in the text.

20. Von Tempski, *Ripe Breadfruit*, 241. After the initial citation, further page numbers referring to Von Tempski's books are placed in the text.

21. "Social Ambition," *Paradise of the Pacific*, June 1903, 23.

22. Ellen Bairos Luter, "Kamaaina Beach Home," *Paradise of the Pacific*, January 1955, 27.

23. Grimshaw, *Paths of Duty*, argues the missionaries sought to clothe Kanaka Maoli as much to keep them busy sewing, repairing, and cleaning as out of a puritanical desire to cover Native nakedness.

24. My reference to a contrasting Native view of objects is drawn primarily from three works: George Huʻeu Sanford Kanahele, *Ku Kanaka: Stand Tall* (Honolulu: University of Hawaii Press, 1986); Mary Kawena Pukui, E. W. Haertig, and Catherine A. Lee, *Nānā I Ke Kumu (Look to the Source)*, vol. 1 (Honolulu: Queen Liliʻuokalani Children's Center, 1972); and Haunani-Kay Trask, *From a Native Daughter: Colonialism and Sovereignty in Hawaii* (Monroe, Maine: Common Courage Press, 1993).

I emphasize these contemporary sources rather than nineteenth-century historians such as Iʻi, Kamakau, and Malo, as I am interested in pointing to a modern Kanaka Maoli perspective that offers a contemporary alternative to the usual kamaʻāina and corporate hotel view. See chapters 4 and 7 below for a more detailed discussion of contemporary Kanaka Maoli resistance.

25. Herb Kawainui Kane, for example, points out, "One cultural fact is the absence in the Polynesian language of equivalents for such Western religious terms as 'divine,' 'god,' 'adoration,' 'holy,' 'sacrifice,' 'supernatural,' and 'religion' " (Kane, "Comments," *Current Anthropology* 38, no. 2 [1997]: 265). When kamaʻānas claim to form relationships with Hawaiian gods, then, they should be understood to be speaking more about

beings or concepts brought from afar than about the akua Native Hawaiians know. For more about Euroamerican versus Kanaka Maoli conceptions of spirits, see chapter 7 below.

26. James Podgers reviews some of the legal questions in "Greetings from Independent Hawaii," *American Bar Association Journal* (June 1997), available online at <http://www.macmouse.com/freebumpy/abaj.html> (10 August 1998). Podgers writes:

> In the late 1940s the United States classified several possessions, including Hawaii, as "non-self-governing territories" under Article 73, of the U.N. Charter. In 1953, the U.N. General Assembly adopted Resolution 742, stating that independence is the primary form of self-rule for such territories unless another status is selected by the population under conditions of "absolute equality." Significantly, however, before Hawaiian residents voted for statehood in 1959, the United States had withdrawn Hawaii from the U.N list of non-self-governing territories. Accordingly, the vote asked Hawaiian residents concerned just one question: "Shall Hawaii immediately be admitted into the Union as a State?" Since the choice of independence was never offered, according to U.N. rules, Hawai'i was illegally absorbed as a state by the United States.

This illegality added further injustice to two previous unlawful acts: (1), the overthrow of the Hawaiian monarchy in 1893 by a small group of (mostly) American settlers who committed treason by breaking the oath of allegiance they earlier had taken to uphold the Hawaiian constitution; and (2), the annexation of the islands to the United States by a joint resolution in 1898 after protests from Kanaka Maoli (and others) convinced annexationists that a legitimate treaty of annexation would fail. The "joint resolution" did not and still does not constitute an agreement with nations or peoples beyond the borders of the United States.

These three unlawful acts are the basis for the increasingly common claim now heard in Hawai'i that annexation and statehood are not legally binding upon the island's Native people.

27. James A. Michener, *Hawaii* (New York: Random House, 1959).

28. Bibliographical information on films can be found in the Filmography at the end of this book.

29. Kanahele, *Ku Kanaka*; Trask, *From a Native Daughter*, 53.

30. Rob Wilson, "Blue Hawai'i: Bamboo Ridge and 'Critical Regionalism'," in *Hawai'i Literature Conference: Reader's Guide*, edited by Lorna Hershinow (Honolulu: Hawai'i Literary Arts Council, 1994), 114.

31. Richard Hamasaki, "Mountains in the Sea: The Emergence of Contemporary Hawaiian Poetry in English," in *Hawai'i Literature Conference: Reader's Guide*, edited by Lorna Hershinow (Honolulu: Hawai'i Literary Arts Council, 1994), 38.

32. Haunani-Kay Trask, "Indigenous Writers and Colonial Situations," *Pacific Islands Communication Journal* 13, no. 1 (1984); quoted in Hamasaki, "Mountains," 38. *'Ōiwi, A Native Hawaiian Journal*, a periodical newly founded by Māhealani Dudoit in 1998, hopes to provide a venue for Kanaka Maoli writers to encourage this continuing struggle against extinction.

33. Darrell H.K. Lum, "What Is Local Literature? Part 1," *Hawaii Literary Arts Council Newsletter* 73 (March 1984): 9.

34. Dennis Kawaharada, "Toward an Authentic Local Literature in Hawai'i," in *Hawai'i Literature Conference: Reader's Guide*, edited by Lorna Hershinow (Honolulu: Hawai'i Literary Arts Council, 1994), 58.

35. Stephen Sumida, *And the View from the Shore: Literary Traditions of Hawai'i* (Seattle: University of Washington Press, 1991); Henry B. Chapin, "Rev. of *And the View from the Shore: Literary Traditions of Hawai'i*, by Steve Sumida," *The Hawaiian Journal of History* 26 (1992): 267.

36. Wilson, "Blue Hawai'i," 116.

37. Milton Murayama, *All I Asking for Is My Body* (1975; reprint, Honolulu: University of Hawaii Press, 1988); John Dominis Holt, Waimea Summer (Honolulu: Topgallant, 1976).

DISORIENTATION. UNWRITABLE KNOWLEDGE

1. Jon Osorio, "Protecting Our Thoughts." A speech delivered at Voices of the Earth Conference held in Amsterdam, November 10, 1993. Available online from the Center for Hawaiian Studies, University of Hawaii, Mānoa, 1993; <http://www2.hawaii.edu/shaps/hawaii/osorio.html> (July 3, 1998). Further quotes from Osorio in the text are from this speech.

2. R. Douglas Herman, "Kalai'aina—Carving the Land: Geography, Desire and Possession in the Hawaiians Islands" (Ph.D. diss., University of Hawaii, 1995).

3. Sheldon Dibble, *History of the Sandwich Islands* (1843; reprint, Honolulu: Thos. G. Thrum, 1909), quoted in Herman, "Kalai'iana," 312–313.

4. Doris Sommer, "Textual Conquests: On Readerly Competence and 'Minority' Literature," in *The Uses of Literary History*, edited by Marshall Brown (Durham, N.C.: Duke University Press, 1995), 266.

5. Greg Dening, *Islands and Beaches: Discourse on a Silent Land: Marquesas, 1774–1880* (Chicago: Dorsey, 1988), 86. For a discussion of orality in the Pacific, see also Dening, *The Death of William Gooch: A History's Anthropology* (Honolulu: University of Hawaii Press, 1995); and P. M. Mercer, "Oral Tradition in the Pacific: Problems of Interpretation," *The Journal of Pacific History* 14, no. 2 (1979): 130–153.

6. Lilikalā K. Kame'eleihiwa, "Introduction," in *A Legendary Tradition of Kamapua'a, The Hawaiian Pig-God*, edited by Lilikalā K. Kame'eleihiwa (Honolulu: Bishop Museum Press, 1996), ix. Kame'eleihiwa discusses the importance of Native metaphors in constructing Native culture in *Native Land and Foreign Desires* (Honolulu: Bishop Museum Press, 1992).

7. The comment about the wide audience for Kame'eleihiwa's book is attributed to Dana Naone Hall. See the book jacket note on *A Legendary Tradition of Kamapua'a, The Hawaiian Pig-God*, cited in note 6 above. For further discussion on the problems of transforming Pacific oral traditions into written literature, see Houston Wood, "Preparing to Retheorize the Texts of Oceania," in *Inside Out: Literature, Cultural Politics, and Identity in the New Pacific*, edited by Rob Wilson and Vilsoni Hereniko (Lanham, Md.: Rowman and Littlefield, 1999).

8. Malcolm Naea Chun, "Introduction," in Davida Malo's *Ka Mo'olelo Hawai'i: Hawaiian Traditions*, translated by Malcolm Naea Chun (Honolulu: First People's Productions, 1996), ii.

9. Valerio Valeri, *Kingship and Sacrifice: Ritual and Society in Ancient Hawaii* (Chicago: University of Chicago Press, 1985), xxiv; quoted in Chun, "Introduction," ix.

10. Bob Krauss, "A Different Perspective on Work of Malo," *Honolulu Advertiser*, 25 May 1997, E3.

11. Tejaswini Niranjana, *Siting Translation: History, Post-Structuralism, and the Colonial Conquest* (Berkeley: University of California Press, 1992), 21.

12. As Niranjana points out, in *The Wretched of the Earth* (New York: Penguin, 1969) and elsewhere, Frantz Fanon warned at the very beginning of the decolonization process about the dangers of Native writers adopting Euroamerican representational apparatuses in an effort to try to create seemingly better or more accurate images of themselves. Niranjana concludes: "The missionaries' [i.e., Euroamerican] theology arises from a historicist model that sets up a series of oppositions between traditional and modern, undeveloped and developed. This kind of attempt to impose linear historical narratives on different civilizations obviously legitimizes and extends colonial domination" (20).

13. Anne Kapulani Landgraf, *Nā Wahi Pana O Ko'olau Poko Legendary Places of Ko'olau Poko*, Hawaiian translation by Fred Kalani Meinecke (Honolulu: University of Hawaii Press, 1994).

14. Haunani-Kay Trask, "Introduction," in Landgraf, *Nā Wahi Pana*, viii.

15. Joseph Bruchac, "Introduction," in the Association for Study of American Indian Literatures' (U.S.), *Returning the Gift: Poetry and Prose from the First North American Native Writers' Festival* (Tucson: University of Arizona Press, 1994), xix.

16. Cynthia G. Franklin, *Writing Women's Communities: The Politics and Poetics of Contemporary Multi-genre Anthologies* (Madison: University of Wisconsin Press, 1997), 221.

CHAPTER FOUR. DISPLACING PELE: HAWAI'I'S VOLCANOES IN A CONTACT ZONE

1. William Ellis, *Journal of William Ellis: Narrative of a Tour of Hawaii, or Owhyhe: With Remarks on the History, Traditions, Manners, Customs and Language of the Inhabitants of the Sandwich Islands* (1825; reprint, Rutland, Vt.: Tuttle, 1917), 164.

2. C. S. Stewart, *Journal of a Residence in the Sandwich Islands* (1828; reprint, Honolulu: University of Hawaii Press, 1970), 374.

3. Isabella L. Bird, *Six Months in the Sandwich Islands* (Honolulu: University of Hawaii Press for Friends of the Library of Hawaii, 1964), 54.

4. Mark Twain, *Mark Twain's Letters from Hawaii*, (1866; reprint edited by A. Grove Day, Honolulu: University of Hawaii Press, 1975), 295. Page numbers for further citations from these books are placed in the text.

5. Charles de Varigny, *Fourteen Years in the Sandwich Islands 1855–1868* (Honolulu: University of Hawaii Press, 1981); Alfons L. Korn, "Introduction," in Varigny, *Fourteen Years*, ix–xxiii.

6. Twain, *Letters*, 292.

7. Quoted in Thomas L. Wright and Takeo Jane Takahashi, *Observations and Interpretation of Hawaiian Volcanism and Seismicity, 1779–1955* (Honolulu: University of Hawaii Press, 1989), 28.

8. Quoted in Thomas L. Wright, Takeo Jane Takahashi, and J. D. Griggs, *Hawaii Volcano Watch: A Pictorial History, 1779–1991* (Honolulu: University of Hawaii Press, 1992), 29.

9. Twain, *Letters*, 297.

10. Rob Wilson, *The American Sublime: The Genealogy of a Poetic Genre* (Madison: University of Wisconsin Press, 1991).

11. Garrett Hongo, *Volcano: A Memoir of Hawaii* (New York: Knopf, 1995).

12. Neil Hertz, "The Notion of Blockage in the Literature of the Sublime," in *The End of the Line: Essays of Psychoanalysis and the Sublime*, edited by Neil Hertz (New York: Columbia University Press, 1985), 60.

13. Michel Foucault, "What Is an Author?" in *The Foucault Reader*, edited by Paul Rabinow (New York: Pantheon, 1984), 101–120.

14. Mary Louise Pratt, *Imperial Eyes: Travel Writing and Transculturation* (New York: Routledge, 1992), 15.

15. See R. Douglas Herman, "Kalai'aina—Carving the Land: Geography, Desire and Possession in the Hawaiians Islands" (Ph.D. diss., University of Hawaii, 1995) for discussion of this expedition, which Herman describes as "the mother-lode of material on American exploration in the islands" (41).

16. Pratt, *Imperial Eyes*, 23.

17. See notes 5 and 6 above.

18. Michel Foucault, *The Order of Things: An Archaeology of the Human Sciences* (London: Tavistock, 1970), 132.

19. Pratt, *Imperial Eyes*, 31.

20. Korns, "Introduction," xvii.

21. Varigny, *Fourteen Years*, xxviii.

22. Ellis, *Journal*, xxi.

23. Ellis spoke and understood Hawaiian much better than most of his Euroamerican contemporaries. One assumes, then, that Oani spoke in Hawaiian, as Ellis had that morning as he preached.

24. Ellis is shaken by the woman's accusations. Pages later he is still ruminating about it. It was "exceedingly painful," he writes, to hear her say that visitors from Christian countries "had been productive of consequences more injurious and fatal to the unsuspecting and unenlightened Hawaiians, than these dreadful phenomena of nature . . . and to know also that such a declaration was too true to be contradicted" (219).

25. Wright, Takahashi, and Griggs, *Hawaii Volcano Watch*, 45.

26. Pratt, *Imperial Eyes*, 6.

27. Quoted in Wright, Takahashi, and Griggs, *Hawaii Volcano Watch*, 63.

28. See Hugh Clark, "Kilauea Rangers Oppose Offerings by Outsiders," *Honolulu Advertiser*, 31 March 1995, A1. Also see Edwin Tanji, "Non-Hawaiian Religious Offerings Raise Concern on Maui," *Honolulu Advertiser*, 2 April 1995, A8.

29. Quoted in Tanji, "Non-Hawaiian," A8.

30. Linda Ching and Robin Stephens, *Powerstones: Letters to a Goddess* (Honolulu: Ching and Stephens, 1994), 10.

31. Michele Jamal, *Volcanic Visions: Encounters with Other Worlds* (New York: Arkana Penguin, 1991), xiii.

32. Michele Jamal, *Shape Shifters: Shaman Women in Contemporary Society* (London: Routledge and Kegan Paul, 1987).

33. Pualani Kanaka'ole Kanahele and Duke Kalani Wise, *Ka Honua Ola* (Honolulu: Center for Hawaiian Studies, University of Hawai'i at Manoa, 1992).

34. Tori Amos, *Boys for Pele* (Atlantic Recording Company: Atlantic, 1996). Compact sound disc.

35. Neil Spencer, "Goddess Pele Lifted Tori Out of Darkness," *Honolulu Star Bulletin*, 19 January 1996, D5.

36. James D. Houston, "Fire in the Night," in *World Between Waves*, edited by Frank Stewart (Washington, D.C.: Island Press, 1991), 117.

37. Quoted in Frank Stewart, *A Natural History of Nature Writing* (Washington, D.C.: Island Press, 1995), xix.

38. Quoted in Stewart, *A Natural History*, xxi.

39. Pamela Frierson's *The Burning Island: A Journey Through Myth and History in the Volcano Country, Hawai'i* (San Francisco: Sierra Club Books, 1991) is another example of a text that combines science and humanism in the manner that Stewart describes as typifying nature writing. See, for example, Frierson's invocation of "a nonhuman presence" and of "a vast mystery" in "Sacred Darkness," the epilogue to her otherwise very scientifically grounded book.

40. Quoted in *Pele: The Fire Within*, executive producer Phil Arnone and written by Stan Wentzel (Honolulu: Lee Enterprises), 1988. Videocassette.

41. Stewart, *World Between*, ix.

42. Quoted in *Pele: The Fire Within*.

43. David W. Forbes and Honolulu Academy of Arts, *Encounters with Paradise: Views of Hawaii and Its People, 1778–1941* (Honolulu: Honolulu Academy of Arts, 1992).

44. Homi Bhabha, "Signs Taken for Wonders: Questions of Ambivalence and Authority Under a Tree Outside Delhi, May 1817," *Critical Inquiry* 12 (1985): 144–165, "Sly Civility," *October* 34 (1985): 71–80; Epeli Hau'ofa, "Our Sea of Islands," in *A New Oceania: Rediscovering Our Sea of Islands*, edited by Eric Waddell et al. (Suva, Fiji: University of South Pacific, 1993), 1–18.

45. Annie E. Coombes explores how hybridity works in the contemporary rhetoric of the art world to encourage Euroamericans to continue to marginalize Native cultures in "Inventing the 'Postcolonial': Hybridity and Constituency in Contemporary Curating," *New Formations* 18 (Winter 1992). Coombes writes, "We need an account of difference which acknowledges the inequality of access to economic and political power" (50). In the new, mass-metropolitan culture that finds hybridity and the practice of bricolage everywhere, Coombes points out, the "specificity of experience" of Native peoples is denied.

46. Herb Kawainui Kane, "Comments," *Current Anthropology* 38, no. 2 (1997): 265.

47. E. S. Craighill Handy, *The Native Culture in the Marquesas* (Honolulu: Bishop Museum Bulletin 9, 1923), quoted in Kane, "Comments," 265.

48. Quoted in *Pele: The Fire Within*.

49. Pualani Kanaka'ole Kanahele in Kanahele and Wise, *Ka Honua Ola*, iii.

50. Haunani-Kay Trask, *From a Native Daughter: Colonialism and Sovereignty in Hawaii* (Monroe, Maine: Common Courage Press, 1993), 172.

CHAPTER FIVE. ECHO TOURISM: THE NARRATIVE OF NOSTALGIA IN WAIKĪKĪ

1. Glen Grant, *Waikiki Yesterday* (Honolulu: Mutual Publishing, 1996), inside front cover.

2. David Lodge, *Paradise News* (New York: Penguin, 1991), 4.

3. Stu Glauberman, "Attracting Isle Visitors," *Honolulu Advertiser*, 21 November 1994, D1.

4. George Hu'eu Sanford Kanehele, *Restoring Hawaiianness to Waikīkī* (Honolulu: Queen Emma Foundation, 1993), 1.

5. This and subsequent page numbers refer to Mark Twain, *Mark Twain's Speeches* (New York: Harper, 1923).

6. Michel Foucault, *The Order of Things: An Archaeology of the Human Sciences*, translated by Alan Sheridan (London: Tavistock, 1970); David Spurr, *The Rhetoric of Empire: Colonial Discourse in Journalism, Travel Writing, and Imperial Administration* (Durham, N.C.: Duke University Press, 1993).

7. Quoted in W. Storrs Lee, *Hawaii: A Literary Chronicle* (New York: Funk and Wagnalls, 1967), 350.

8. While in Hawai'i London also wrote two popular novels about dogs, *Jerry of the Islands* and *Michael, Brother of Jerry*, as well as the often reprinted short story, "To Build a Fire." Robert Louis Stevenson's wife, Frances Osbourne Stevenson, wrote a story in Hawai'i that combined the themes of mixed races and leprosy. Titled "The Half-White," it was published in *Scribner's Magazine* in 1891. A. Grove Day speculates that Frances Stevenson had her husband's help in the story's composition. See Day, "Introduction," in *Travels in Hawaii*, by Robert Louis Stevenson (Honolulu: University of Hawaii Press, 1973), xxxi.

9. London's stories of the islands are most easily available in an edition edited by A. Grove Day in Jack London, *Stories of Hawaii* (Honolulu: Mutual, 1990). References to page numbers in London's stories come from this edition.

10. Race dominated London's writing till the end. His final story, "Eyes of Asia," finished after his death by his wife, Charmian London, focuses on an orphaned baby with Asian looks who is raised in Hawai'i by haoles. She later rejects haole suitors and chooses instead to marry a Japanese man who takes her to Japan. As Day writes, this ending suggests that London "felt to the end that instinct is stronger than environment. The conclusion of 'Eyes of Asia,' a literary curiosity never printed in book form, is that blood still calls to blood." See Day, *Mad About Islands* (Honolulu: Mutual, 1987), 161.

11. James A. Michener, "Introduction," in *A Hawaiian Reader*, edited by A. Grove Day and Carl Stover (Honolulu: Mutual, 1984), xii.

12. James A. Michener, *Hawaii* (New York: Random House, 1959).

13. Stephen Sumida, *And the View from the Shore: Literary Traditions of Hawai'i* (Seattle: University of Washington Press, 1991), 72.

14. Rob Wilson demonstrates the central place a racial narrative occupies in Michener's *Tales of the South Pacific* and in the subsequent Broadway musical and film adaptations of Michener's stories. See Wilson, *Reimagining the American Pacific: From "South Pacific" to Bamboo Ridge and Beyond* (Durham, N.C.: Duke University Press, forthcoming).

15. Mark Twain, *Mark Twain's Letters from Hawaii*, edited by A. Grove Day (Honolulu: University of Hawaii Press, 1975), 52–53.

16. Serge A. Marek, "Waikiki Virtual Reality: Space, Place, and Representation in the Waikiki Master Plan" (master's thesis, University of Hawaii, 1997), 127.

17. Jon Goss, "Disquiet on the Waterfront: Reflections on Nostalgia and Utopia in the Urban Archetypes of Festival Marketplaces," Department of Geography, University of Hawai'i, 1995, 3; Spencer Leineweber, "Honolulu: Bride of the Sea," paper presented at the City Views Lecture Series, University of Hawaii, 22 February 1995. See as well Ali Behdad, *Belated Travelers: Orientalism in the Age of Colonial Dissolution* (Durham, N.C.: Duke University Press, 1994), for an exploration of how the very concepts that cultural critics use display a type of echo tourism that Behdad calls "belated traveling."

18. I here paraphrase Marek's observation that the 1992 Waikiki Master Plan creates a "vision of Waikiki's future without the consent, opinion, or politics of contemporary Native Hawaiians." See Marek, "Waikiki Virtual Reality," 125–126. Further references to Marek are cited in the text.

19. George Hu'eu Sanford Kanehele, *Restoring Hawaiianness to Waikīkī*.

20. Albert Bigelow Paine, *Mark Twain: A Biography* (New York: Harper, 1912), quoted in A. Grove Day, *Mad About Islands* (Honolulu: Mutual, 1987), 102. Jack London was one of the first to quote this passage when he included it in a 1916 article for *Cosmopolitan*.

21. Quoted in Day, *Mad About Islands*, 102.

22. Mary Kawena Pukui, Samuel H. Elbert, and Esther T. Mookini, *Place Names of Hawai'i* (Honolulu: University Press of Hawaii, 1974), 44. Concerning Kahahana and his death, see Samuel M. Kamakau, *Ruling Chiefs of Hawaii* (Honolulu: Kamehameha Schools Press, 1961), 136ff.

23. John Urry, *The Tourist Gaze: Leisure and Travel in Contemporary Societies* (Newbury Park: Sage, 1990). The quote from Runcie appears in the book's front matter.

24. Quoted in Ralph S. Kuykendall and A. Grove Day, *Hawaii: A History* (1949; reprint, Englewood Cliffs, N.J.: Prentice-Hall, 1961), 137.

25. Twain, *Letters from Hawaii*, 52.

26. King David Kalakaua, *The Legends and Myths of Hawaii: The Fables and Folk-Lore of a Strange People* (1888; reprint, Rutland, Vt.: Tuttle, 1972), 64.

27. Barry Nakamura, "The Story of Waikiki and the 'Reclamation' Project" (master's thesis, University of Hawaii at Mānoa, 1979).

28. Don Hibbard and David Franzen, *The View from Diamond Head: Royal Residence to Urban Resort* (Honolulu: Editions Limited, 1986), 93.

29. George S. Kanahele, *Waikīkī 100 B.C. to 1900 A.D.: An Untold Story* (Honolulu: University of Hawaii Press, 1995); *Taking Waikiki from Self-sufficiency to Dependency*, produced by Carol Bain and Ed Coll (Surfing Education Association and Kauai Worldwide Communications), 1994; Nakamura, "Story of Waikiki," 1979.

30. Marek, "Waikiki Virtual," 116.

31. Stan Cohen, *The Pink Palace: The Royal Hawaiian Hotel* (Missoula, Mont.: Pictorial Histories Publishing Company, 1986); Stan Cohen, *The First Lady of Waikiki, A Pictorial History of Sheraton Maona Surfrider* (Missoula, Mont.: Pictorial Histories Publishing Company, 1995).

32. Urry, *Tourist Gaze*, 2.

33. Jon Goss explores the threat and management of Native Hawaiian alterity in "Placing the Market and Marketing the Place: Tourist Advertising of the Hawaiian Islands, 1972–92," *Environment and Planning D: Society and Space* 11 (1993): 663–688. How Hollywood films exploit and manage comparable frights associated with Hawai'i is discussed in chapter 6 below.

34. Marek, "Waikiki Virtual," 117.

35. Kehaulani Kauanui, "Mapping the Native: Hawaiian Genealogical Reterritorialization of Land, Identity, and Sovereign Belonging," paper presented at the fifteenth Annual Meeting of the Association for Asian American Studies, 1898–1998: Rethinking Asian and Pacific Colonial/Postcolonial Nations, Identities and Histories, Honolulu, Hawaii, 1998.

36. Haunani-Kay Trask, *From a Native Daughter: Colonialism and Sovereignty in Hawaii* (Monroe, Maine: Common Courage Press, 1993), 84.

37. Quoted in Stu Glauberman, "Attracting Isle Visitors," *Honolulu Advertiser*, 21 November 1994, D1.

38. Haunani-Kay Trask, *Light in the Crevice Never Seen* (Corvallis, OR: Calyx, 1994), 60.

39. Trask, *From a Native Daughter*, 137; "Colonization" appears in Trask, *Light in the Crevice*, 65.

40. Trask, *From a Native Daughter*, 65.

41. Trask, *From a Native Daughter*, 149.

CHAPTER SIX. SAFE SAVAGERY: HOLLYWOOD'S HAWAI'I

1. James Cook, *The Journals of Captain James Cook and his Voyages of Discovery*, vol. 3, *The Voyage of the* Resolution *and* Discovery, *1776–1780, Parts One and Two*, edited by J. C. Beaglehole (Cambridge: Cambridge University Press, for the Hakluyt Society, 1967), 486. This entry was written January 5, 1779.

2. Martin Heidegger, *The Question Concerning Technology and Other Essays*, translated by William Lovitt (New York: Harper, 1977), 116.

3. Laura Mulvey, "Visual Pleasure and Narrative Cinema," in *Contemporary Film Theory*, edited by Anthony Easthope (New York: Longman, 1993), 112. This influential article first appeared in Mulvey, "Visual Pleasure and Narrative Cinema," *Screen* 16, no. 3 (1975): 6–18. For further references to Mulvey's views, see note 13 below.

4. Though I concentrate mostly on sexual and related tropes, these films are rich sites for additional analyses. Rob Wilson, for example, points to another master narrative, how Hollywood constructs Hawai'i as a "natural" site for both war and commerce. (See Wilson, *Reimagining the American Pacific: From 'South Pacific' to Bamboo Ridge and Beyond* [Durham, N.C.: Duke University Press, forthcoming]); cf. Phyllis Turnbull and Kathy E. Ferguson, "Military Presence/Missionary Past: The Historical Construction of Masculine Order and Feminine Hawai'i," in *Women in Hawai'i: Sites, Identities, and Voices*, edited by Kathleen O. Kane, Joyce N. Chinen, and Ida M. Yoshinaga [Honolulu: Department of Sociology, University of Hawai'i, 1997], 94–107. Floyd Matson describes yet another motif of Hollywood's Hawai'i, what he labels "the Tropical Crime Wave formula" (40), exploited by the Charlie Chan films of the 1930s. This motif later metamorphosed into such television series as *Hawaiian Eye*, *Hawaii Five-0*, *Magnum P.I.*, and *Marker*. See Matson, "Hollywood Goes Hawaiian," in *Viewer's Guide: East-West International Film Festival* (Honolulu: East-West Film Festival, 1984), 40–41.

5. Matson, "Hollywood," 40.

6. All references to the films mentioned in this chapter will be found in the Filmography included at the end of this book. Dwight Damon at the Movie Museum in Honolulu has been my helpful guide and procurer for many of these productions. My discussion of films not currently available for viewing is based primarily on summaries provided in the *American Film Institute Catalog of Motion Pictures Produced in the United States, 1931–1940* (Berkeley: University of California Press, 1993); in Robert C. Schmitt's *Hawai'i in the Movies: 1898–1959* (Honolulu: Hawaiian Historical Society, 1988), and in *The New York Times* film reviews. Less frequently used sources are mentioned at the appropriate places in the text.

7. Glenn K.S. Man, "Hollywood Images of the Pacific," *East-West Film Journal* 5, no. 2 (1991): 16.

188 *Notes*

8. David Spurr, *The Rhetoric of Empire: Colonial Discourse in Journalism, Travel Writing, and Imperial Administration* (Durham. N.C.: Duke, 1993), 125ff.

9. This film was based on Armine Von Tempski's novel of the same name and generally reflects the character of Hula presented there. See chapter 3 above for further discussion of Von Tempski's racialized narratives.

10. Schmitt, *Hawaii in the Movies*, 40.

11. Catherine Belsey, *The Subject of Tragedy: Identity and Difference in Renaissance Drama* (New York: Methuen, 1985), 46.

12. Turnbull and Ferguson, "Military Presence," 98.

13. Mulvey, "Visual Pleasure," 123. For Mulvey's reconsideration of this article, see Mulvey, "Afterthoughts on 'Visual Pleasure and Narrative Cinema' inspired by King Vidor's *Duel in the Sun 1946*," in *Contemporary Film Theory*, edited by Anthony Easthope (New York: Longman, 1993), 125–134. Also see Teresa De Lauretis, *Alice Doesn't: Feminism, Semiotics, Cinema* (Bloomington: Indiana University Press, 1984); Mary Ann Doane, Patricia Mellencamp and Linda Williams, eds., *Re-Vision: Essays in Feminist Film Criticism* (Frederick, Md.: University Publications of America, 1984); E. Ann Kaplan, *Women and Film: Both Sides of the Camera* (New York: Methuen, 1983), especially chapter 1, "Is the Gaze Male?"; and Linda Williams, ed., *Viewing Positions: Ways of Seeing View* (New Bruswick, N.J.: Rutgers University Press, 1995).

14. See De Lauretis, *Alice Doesn't*.

15. Howard Thompson, "Review of 'Blue Hawaii'," *New York Times*, 22 February 1962, 20.

16. Spurr, *The Rhetoric of Empire*, 80.

17. Joseph Conrad, *Heart of Darkness and The Secret Sharer* (New York: Bantam, 1981).

18. Bosley Crowther, "'Bird of Paradise,' Portrayal in Technicolor of South Sea Island Customs, at Roxy," *New York Times*, 15 March 1951, 37.

19. Conrad, *Heart of Darkness*, 97.

20. Vincent Canby, "Rev. of 'Paradise, Hawaiian Style'," *New York Times*, 16 June 1966, 53.

21. Quoted in Spurr, *The Rhetoric of Empire*, 82.

22. Still another silent of this time, *Hidden Pearls* (1918), weds an American man to a Hawaiian "princess," but at the end of this film, the American learns he is the rightful king, through his mother, of a Hawaiian island.

23. American Film Institute, *American Film Institute Catalog of Motion Pictures Produced in the United States, 1931–1940* (Berkeley: University of California Press, 1993), 44.

24. Wanda Tuchock, who single-handedly wrote the musical *Hawaii Calls* (1938), was one of three people given credit on the screenplay for *Bird of Paradise*. Beulah Marie Dix wrote the 1918 production *Hidden Pearls*.

25. Matson, "Hollywood," 40. For one account of this incident, see Theon Wright, *Rape in Paradise* (New York: Hawthorn Books, 1966).

26. Bosley Crowther, "Rev. of 'Miss Tatlock's Millions'," *New York Times*, 25 November 1948, 47.

27. DeSoto Brown, lecture, "Introduction to *Waikiki Wedding*," sponsored by the Hawaiian Historical Society at Bishop Museum, Honolulu, 10 May 1995.

28. Reported in Wayne Harada, "A Monster of a Movie Project," *Honolulu Advertiser*, 13 March 1997, C1+.

29. See, for example, Maxine Marantz, *Hawaii's Tragic Princess Kaiulani* (Honolulu: Aloha Graphics, 1980); and Kristin Zambucka, *Princess Kaiulani: The Last Hope of Hawaii's Monarchy* (Honolulu: Mana, 1982).

30. Michel Foucault, *The Order of Things: An Archaeology of the Human Sciences*, translated by Alan Sheridan (London: Tavistock, 1970).

31. Belsey, *Subject of Tragedy*, 8.

32. The two recent independent local Hawai'i productions, *Picture Bride* and *Goodbye Paradise*, are both alternative films in my definition, as both seek to subvert the dominant culture's emphasis on Euroamerican subjectivities. Rob Wilson examines several of the ways that *Goodbye Paradise* operates as a subversive work in *Reimaging the American Pacific*. Both *Picture Bride* and *Goodbye Paradise* usefully interrogate some elements of the Hollywood construction of Hawai'i, but since neither film interrogates the notion that Native Hawaiians are peripheral to contemporary island life, neither subverts Hollywood's constructions of Hawaiians.

33. Vilsoni Hereniko, *Fine Dancing*, with Reena Owen as Hina, performed in Ala Moana Park, Honolulu, August 1997. Continuing efforts to transform this play into a film may lead to the production of the first indigenous feature film about Hawai'i.

REORIENTATION. NEW HISTORIES, NEW HOPES

1. J. C. Beaglehole, "Introduction," in *The Journals of Captain James Cook on His Voyages of Discovery*, vol. 3, *The Voyage of the* Resolution *and* Discovery *1776–1780*, edited by J. C. Beaglehole (Cambridge: Cambridge University Press, 1967), lxxxviii.

2. Raymond Williams, *The Country and the City* (New York: Oxford, 1973), 51.

3. Samuel M. Kamakau, *Ruling Chiefs of Hawaii* (Honolulu: Kamehameha Schools Press, 1961), 231.

4. Noel Kent, *Hawaii: Islands Under the Influence* (1983; reprint, Honolulu: University of Hawaii Press, 1993).

5. Lilikalā Kame'eleihiwa, *Native Land and Foreign Desires* (Honolulu: Bishop Museum Press, 1992), see especially chapters 3, 4, and 6.

CHAPTER SEVEN. KAHO'OLAWE IN POLYRHETORIC AND MONORHETORIC

1. Noa Emmett Aluli and Daviana Pomaika'i McGregor, "The Healing of Kaho'olawe," in *Hawai'i Return to Nationhood*, edited by Ulla Hasager and Jonathan Friedman (Copenhagen: IWGIA, 1994), 207.

2. Johannes Fabian, *Time and the Other: How Anthropology Makes Its Object* (New York: Columbia University Press, 1983).

3. Elizabeth Bentzel Buck, *Paradise Remade: The Politics of Culture and History in Hawai'i* (Philadelphia: Temple University Press, 1993), 13.

4. George S. Kanahele, *Waikīkī 100 B.C. to 1900 A.D.: An Untold Story* (Honolulu: University of Hawaii Press, 1995). See "Orientation," note 8, for a list of some additional decolonizing histories by Native scholars.

5. Marshall Sahlins, *Islands of History* (Chicago: University of Chicago Press, 1985), 20.

6. Sahlins, *Islands*, 20.

7. Edwin Tanji, "It'll Be a Daunting Job Even for an Old Hand," *Honolulu Advertiser*, 12 April 1998, A8. Aluli and McGregor point out in "The Healing" (see note 1, above) that the Navy "also conducted spectacular experiments like simulating an atomic blast on the island in 1965. 500 tons of TNT was blasted to test the impact on ships anchored offshore. It lightened up the sky like day on the neighbor island, Maui. The experiment cracked the water table on part of the island and created a salt water pond that nothing lives in" (198).

8. Pualani Kanaka'ole Kanahele, "Ke Au Lono i Kaho'olawe, Ho'i (The Era of Lono at Kaho'olawe, Returned)," *Mānoa* (Summer 1995): 155.

9. Noa Emmett Aluli, a member of the Protect Kaho'olawe 'Ohana, writes in his "Foreword" to *Nā Leo a Kanaloa* (Honolulu: Ai Pohaku Press, 1995), similarly: "On Kaho'olawe, we've been able to live together as Hawaiians. We've been able to practice the religion and to carry on the traditions we've learned from our *kūpuna*, our elders. In doing this, we connect to the land, and we connect to the gods. We call them back to the land and back to our lives" (xiv).

10. Pualani Kanaka'ole Kanahele, "He Koihonua No Kanaloa, He Moku (History for Kanaloa, An Island)," *Mānoa* (Summer 1995): 20–25.

11. Edward L. Kanahele, "Kanaka'ole, Edith K.," in *Hawaiian Music and Musicians*, edited by George S. Kanahele (Honolulu: University of Hawaii Press, 1979), 207.

12. Rowland Reeves, *Kaho'olawe: Nā Leo Kanaloa: Chants and Stories of Kaho'olawe* (Honolulu: Ai Pohaku Press, 1995).

13. I rely here upon the first translation of Kanahele's oli, published in *Mānoa*. A second, different translation is offered in *Kaho'olawe: Nā Leo Kanaloa*. My own interpretation of this oli in this chapter is distant from its consequential performance on Kaho'olawe. If participating in the performance on Kaho'olawe constitutes a first level of understanding, then a second level appears to those who participate in reenactments of this performance. That level is not discussed here, nor is a third level, which is constituted by a metaphoric understanding of the Hawaiian language text. I speak in these pages instead only of one of Kanahele's two English translations of this composition, using the guidance she provides in her related essay previously reviewed. I write, it should be clear then, firmly from within a monorhetorical context about a polyrhetorical text.

14. Testimony quoted in Pam Smith, "Kaho'olawe: Hawaiians on Trial," *Hawai'i Observer*, 28 July 1977, 15.

15. Quoted in Smith, "Kaho'olawe," 15.

16. Jeffrey Tobin, "Cultural Construction and Native Nationalism: Report from the Hawaiian Front," *Boundary* 2 21.1 (Spring 1994): 111–133. The recent rulings on same sex marriage in Hawai'i, though precipitated by the state constitution, which prohibits sexual discrimination, resonates with the traditional Hawaiian flexibility about the nature of families and of childrearing. For a look at how these traditions have persisted, see Mary Kawena Pukui, E. W. Haertig, and Catherine A. Lee, *Nānā I Ke Kumu (Look To the Source)*, vol. 1 (Honolulu: Queen Lili'uokalani Children's Center, 1972).

17. Haunani-Kay Trask, *From a Native Daughter: Colonialism and Sovereignty in Hawaii* (Monroe, Maine: Common Courage Press, 1993), 53.

18. For example, in "What Do You Mean 'We,' White Man?" (reprinted in Trask, *From a Native Daughter*), Trask calls it a "racist assumption of foreigners" to "believe a few years training in an American university (or any other university) qualifies them to study, describe, and pass judgment upon Hawaiian culture and Hawaiian people" (164).

19. Richard Handler and Jocelyn Linnekin, "Tradition, Genuine or Spurious," *Journal of American Folklore* 97 (1984): 288. Quoted in Tobin, "Cultural," 120.

20. Roger Keesing, "Creating the Past: Custom and Identity in the Contemporary Pacific," *Contemporary Pacific* 1 (1989): 37; emphasis added.

21. Quoted in Gary T. Kubota, "Future: Questions Cloud the Visions," *Honolulu Star-Bulletin*, 23 August 1995, A8.

22. Quoted in Alan Matsuoka, "How a Split Second in 1976 Stirred the Hawaiian Spirit," *Honolulu Star-Bulletin*, 22 August 1995, A6.

23. Quoted in Kubota, "Future," A8.

24. George Hu'eu Sanford Kanahele, *Ku Kanaka: Stand Tall* (Honolulu: University of Hawaii Press, 1986). After publication of *Ku Kanaka*, Kanahele became involved in the controversial plan to "Hawaiiannize Waikiki," discussed in chapter 5. Nonetheless, Kanahele's earlier work, including editing *Hawaiian Music and Musicians: An Illustrated History* (Honolulu: University of Hawaii Press, 1979) and *Ku Kanaka*, remains widely respected. John Dominis Holt, for example, described the latter as a "treasure" and as "a source of mana and knowledge not previously found and pulled together in a single book" ("Rev. of *Ku Kanaka*, by George Kanehele," *Hawaiian Journal of History* 21 [1987]: 160).

25. Samuel H. Elbert, "Preface," in *Place Names of Hawaii*, edited by Mary Kawena Pukui, Samuel H. Elbert, and Esther T. Mookini (Honolulu: University of Hawaii Press, 1974), x.

26. Because Captain Cook and his men had abandoned their place and did not know their genealogies, they may have seemed to the Hawaiians they encountered to be "vagabonds," kanaka 'ae'a, shiftless people. Such people were, according to the early Hawaiian historian David Malo, the most despised class of people the Hawaiians knew. See Kanahele's discussion of kanaka 'ae'a in *Ku Kanaka* (182–183).

27. Martha Warren Beckwith, *Hawaiian Mythology* (Honolulu: University Press of Hawaii, 1976); quoted in Kanahele, *Ku Kanaka*, 70.

28. Michael Kioni Dudley, *Man, Gods, and Nature, Hawaiian Nation*, vol. 1 (Honolulu: Nā Kāne O Ka Malo Press, 1990), 75.

29. Translation in Martha W. Beckwith, *The Kumulipo: A Hawaiian Creation Chant* (Chicago: University of Chicago Press, 1951), 114.

30. Rowland Reeve, "Kaho'olawe: Ka Makupuni O Kanaloa," *Mānoa* 7, no. 1 (Summer 1995): 203–222, and *Kaho'olawe: Nā Leo*, see note 12 above.

31. David Malo, *Hawaiian Antiquities (Mo'olelo Hawai'i)*, translated by Nathaniel B. Emerson (Honolulu: Bishop Museum Press, 1951), 3–4; quoted in Kanahele, *Ku Kanaka*, 55–56.

32. In *Chanting the Universe: Hawaiian Religious Culture* (Honolulu: Emphasis International, 1983), John Charlot argues similarly: "Hawaiian religion was and still is in a ferment of constant rivalry and polemic" (23). Charlot explains, "Hawaiian awareness of this diversity is clearly expressed in the proverbial response to anyone too insistent on his own tradition or views: *'A'ole i pau ka 'ike i kāu hālau*. Knowledge is not exhausted in your hall of learning" (35).

33. This version was printed without attribution to any author as *He Pule Hoolaa Alii: He Kumlipo no Ka-I-imaomao, a ia Alapai Wahine* (Honolulu: Pa'iia e ka Hui Pa'ipalapala Elele, 1889).

34. Beckwith, *Kumulipo*, 311.

192   *Notes*

35. Kimo Campbell, "Preface," in *The Kumulipo: An Hawaiian Creative Myth*, edited by Lililuokalani (Kentfield, Calif.: Pueo, 1978).

36. Liluokalani, "Introduction," *On an Account of the Creation of the World According to Hawaiian Tradition* (Boston: Lee and Shepard, 1897).

37. Critical regionalism, critical localism, and strategic localism are related terms for critical traditionalism. See chapter 1, "The Violent Rhetoric of Names," above.

38. Arif Dirlik, "The Global in the Local," in *Global/Local: Cultural Production and the Transnational Imaginary*, edited by Rob Wilson and Wimal Dissanayake (Durham, N.C.: Duke University Press, 1996), 28.

39. Rob Wilson, "Blue Hawai'i: Bamboo Ridge and 'Critical Regionalism'," in *Hawai'i Literature Conference: Reader's Guide*, edited by Lorna Hershinow (Honolulu: Hawaii Literary Arts Council, 1994).

40. Arif Dirlik, *After the Revolution: Waking to Global Capitalism* (Hanover, Mass.: Wesleyan University Press, published by University Press of New England, 1994), 79.

41. Elizabeth Bentzel Buck, *Paradise Remade: The Politics of Culture and History in Hawai'i* (Philadelphia: Temple University Press, 1993).

42. Arif Dirlik, "Three Worlds or One, or Many? The Reconfiguration of Global Relations Under Contemporary Capitalism," *Nature, Society and Thought* 7, no. 1 (1995): 19–42.

43. Arif Dirlik, "The Past as Legacy and Project: Postcolonial Criticism in the Perspective of Indigenous Historicism," *American Indian Culture and Research* 20, no. 2 (1996): 19.

44. Mary Louise Pratt, *Imperial Eyes: Travel Writing and Transculturation* (New York: Routledge, 1992).

45. These purported similarities between polyrhetoric and postmodernism result in part from the fact that I interpret Native Hawaiian texts through the categories of postmodernism, a perspective I have internalized as a consequence of being educated in the contemporary Euroamerican tradition. Some implications of this are discussed below.

46. Michel Foucault, *The Order of Things: An Archaeology of the Human Sciences, World of Man* (London: Tavistock, 1970), 136.

47. Fabian, *Time and the Other*, see especially chapter 4, "The Other and Eye: Time and the Rhetoric of Vision," 105–141.

48. Martin Heidegger, *The Question Concerning Technology and Other Essays*, translated by William Lovitt (New York: Harper, 1977).

49. W.J.T. Mitchell, *Iconology: Image, Text, Ideology* (Chicago: University of Chicago Press, 1986); and *Picture Theory: Essays on Verbal and Visual Representation* (Chicago: University of Chicago Press, 1994).

50. Frank Tillman, "What Pictures Do to Words, What Words Do to Pictures," presented at the Image and Word Lecture Series, University of Hawai'i, 1995, paper. Some of the ways that networked computers in cyberspace may be changing the rhetoric of visual imaging will be explored in chapter 8, "Hawai'i in Cyberspace."

51. Roland Barthes, *Camera Lucida: Reflections of Photography* (New York: Farrar, Straus and Giroux, 1980), 87.

52. Quoted in Susan Sontag, *On Photography*, 2d ed. (New York: Anchor, 1989), 188.

53. William Gaddis, *The Recognitions* (New York: Harcourt Brace, 1955).

54. Michael Keith and Steve Pile, "Introduction," in *Place and the Politics of Identity*, edited by Michael Keith and Steve Pile (New York: Routledge, 1993), 6.

55. Edward Soja and Barbara Hooper, "The Space that Difference Makes," in *Place and the Politics of Identity*, 189.

56. Fredric Jameson, "Postmodernism, or, the Cultural Logic of Late Capitalism," *New Left Review* (1984): 71.

57. Edward Said, *Culture and Imperialism* (New York: Random House, 1993), 7.

58. Neil Smith and Cindi Katz, "Grounding Metaphor: Towards a Spatialized Politics," in *Place and the Politics of Identity*, 68.

59. David Bell and Gill Valentine, *Mapping Desires: Geographies of Sexualities* (New York: Routledge, 1995), 321.

60. Gillian Rose, *Feminism and Geography: The Limits of Geographical Knowledge* (Minneapolis: University of Minnesota Press, 1993); Doreen Massey, *Space, Place and Gender* (Minneapolis: University of Minnesota Press, 1994); Paul Rodaway, *Sensuous Geographies: Body, Sense, Place* (New York: Routledge, 1994).

61. Michel Foucault, "Questions of Geography," in *Power/Knowledge: Selected Interviews and Other Writings 1972–1977*, edited by C. Gordon (New York: Pantheon, 1980), 70.

62. Michel Foucault, "Of Other Spaces," *Diacritics* 16 (1986): 22.

63. Lilikalā Kame'eleihiwa, *Native Land and Foreign Desires* (Honolulu: Bishop Museum Press, 1992), 22.

64. Edward Soja, *Postmodern Geographies: The Reassertion of Space in Critical Social Theory* (London: Verso, 1989); David Harvey, *The Condition of Postmodernity: An Enquiry into the Origins of Cultural Change* (Cambridge, Mass.: Blackwell, 1989).

65. Gillian Rose, "Rev. of *Postmodern Geographies* by Edward W. Soja, and *The Condition of Modernity* by David Harvey," *Journal of Historical Geography* 17 (1991): 118.

66. Keith and Pile, "Introduction," in *Place and the Politics of Identity*, 6.

67. Smith and Katz, "Grounding Metaphor," 80.

68. Haunani-Kay Trask, *From a Native Daughter: Colonialism and Sovereignty in Hawaii* (Monroe, Maine: Common Courage Press, 1993), 168.

69. Ward Churchill, *Indians are Us? Culture and Genocide in Native North America* (Monroe, Maine: Common Courage Press, 1994); and Dirlik, "The Past as Legacy and Project."

70. Gayatri Chakravorty Spivak, "Can the Subaltern Speak? Speculations on Widow Sacrifice," in *Marxism and the Interpretation of Culture*, edited by Cary Nelson and Lawrence Grossberg (New York: Macmillan, 1988), 271–313. For Spivak's later thoughts, see her *Outside in the Teaching Machine* (New York: Routledge, 1993). For a valuable introduction to the Linnekin-Trask debate, see Tobin, "Cultural Construction."

71. Gananath Obeyesekere, *The Apotheosis of Captain Cook: European Mythmaking in the Pacific* (Princeton: Princeton University Press, 1992), 21. A valuable evaluation of the Obeyesekere and Sahlins dispute, along with commentaries from the principles, is available in Robert Borofsky, "Cook, Lono, Obeyesekere, and Sahlins," *Current Anthropology* 38, no. 2 (April 1997): 255–265, and 265ff.

72. In "An Offering of Words: The Landscape of N. Scott Momaday" (Department of English, University of Hawai'i, 1997), Kanaka Maoli essayist D. Māhealani Dudoit offers a nuanced examination of the claim that Native Americans and Native Hawaiians share similar perspectives. See also Dudoit's "Voyages of Return: Essays of Hawaiian Cultural Rediscovery" (master's thesis, University of Hawaii, 1996) and *'Ōiwi, A Native Hawaiian Journal*, the new periodical Dudoit has founded and is editing.

73. Marshall Sahlins, *How "Natives" Think, About Captain Cook, For Example* (Chicago: University of Chicago Press, 1995), ix.

74. For an earlier attempt at thinking more elaborately about how analysis creates its objects, see Hugh Mehan and Houston Wood, *The Reality of Ethnomethodology* (New York: Wiley, 1975), especially 192–224. Melvin Pollner traces some of the archeology of this tradition of reflexive thinking in "Left of Ethnomethodology: The Rise and Decline of Radical Reflexivity," *American Sociological Review* 56, no. 3 (June 1991): 370–380.

75. Marshall Sahlins, *Islands*, vii. For an overview of Sahlins's theory, see the "Introduction" in *Islands*, vii–xix.

76. Tobin, "Cultural Construction," points to the lack of reflexivity among all theorists he calls cultural constructionists. Tobin writes: "I question, however, whether cultural constructionists are as tenacious about contextualizing their own discourse as they are at contexualizing that of others" (161).

77. This is perhaps some of what Kanahele means when he writes in *Ku Kanaka* about the freedom inherent in "the logic of polytheism," which guides Kanaka Maoli values (76). See also Greg Dening, "Sharks that Walk on the Land: The Death of Captain Cook," *Meanjin* 41 (1982): 427–437, for an early discussion of the elasticity of Kanaka Maoli cultural structures. In *Chanting the Universe*, John Charlot also points out that Native Hawaiians generally have more intellectual independence and freedom of thought than their Euroamerican interpreters.

78. Kanahele, "He Koihonua No Kanaloa," 23–24. "Ua kāhea ʻiaʻo Lono i ka makahiki hou / Ma ka Hale Mua o Lono i kāhea ʻia ai / Ua kanaloa ʻo Kanaloa i Kohemālamala / Puka hou aʻe ka mana o Kanaloa / Ua kani ka leo pahu i ka māama o Hoku / Kuwāwāi ka houpo a Laka."

CHAPTER EIGHT. HAWAIʻI IN CYBERSPACE

An earlier version of chapter 8 appeared online under the title "Hawaiians in Cyberspace," <http://www.fas.nus.edu.sg/staff/conf/poco/paper2.html> as a part of the 1997 First Online Postcolonial Conference (at <http://www.fas.nus.edu.sg/staff/conf/poco/1st-conf.html>).

1. Roberto Verzola, *Towards a Political Economy of Information*, November 1995, <http://www.solinet.org/THIRDWORLD/obet1.htm> (September 20, 1998).

2. Sven Birkerts, *The Gutenberg Elegies: The Fate of Reading in an Electronic Age* (Boston: Faber and Faber, 1994). These citations from Birkerts can be found in *The Fate of the Book*, Text21 Conference, 16 September 1995 (Listserv: TEXT21-L@bigvax.alfred.edu) (November 6, 1995).

3. Nicholas Baran, "Computers and Capitalism: A Tragic Misuse of Technology," *Monthly Review* (September 1995): 40.

4. See, for example, Benedict Anderson, *Imagined Communities: Reflections on the Origin and Spread of Nationalism*, rev. and extended ed. (New York: Verso, 1991) and Tzvetan Todorov, *The Conquest of America: The Question of the Other*, translated by Richard Howard (New York: Harper, 1984). For an overview of writing and printing in Anglo-Europe, see Henri-Jean Martin, *The History and Power of Writing*, translated by Lydia G. Cochrane (Chicago: University of Chicago Press, 1994).

5. "Technology's Role in the Revival of the Hawaiian Language," May 1998, <http://www.readingonline.org/electronic/hawaii/techrol.htm> (September 14, 1998). See also Mark Warschaueer and Keola Donaghy, "Leokī: A Powerful Voice of Hawaiian Language Revitalization," in the journal *Computer Assisted Language Learning* (forthcoming).

6. Mark Poster, *Cyberdemocracy: Internet and the Public Sphere*, <http://www.hnet. uci.edu/mposter/writings/democ.html> (May 27, 1998).

7. Calvin F. Exoo, *Democracy Upside Down: Public Opinion and Cultural Hegemony in the United States* (New York: Praeger, 1987).

8. Ed Rampell, "Polynesian Political Prisoner or Dennis the Menace to Society," 1996 <http://www.aloha.net/nation/polynesian.html> (June 27, 1996).

9. James Podgers, "Greetings from independent Hawaii," *American Bar Association Journal* (June 1997); reprinted 1997 at <http://hawaii-nation.org/abaj.html> (January 22, 1999).

10. Nicholas Negroponte, "Message 26: Bit by Bit," 1996 <http://nicholas.www.media. mit.edu/people/nicholas/WIRED3-08.htm) (June 22, 1996).

11. See Steven Johnson's extended speculation on how the new technologies may transform information and information users in *Interface Culture: How New Technology Transforms the Way We Create and Communicate* (New York: Harper*Edge*, 1997).

12. Scott Crawford and Kekula Crawford, "Self-Determination in the Information Age," 1996 <http://info.isoc.org/HMP/PAPER/230/html/paper.htm#cont> (June 27, 1996).

13. The Internet has already become an important tool for many diasporic Pacific Islanders. Saari Kitalong and Tino Kitalong, for example, illustrate how "Palauan-made Internet spaces" enable these Pacific islanders "to build community, teach and learn about their cultural heritage, and engage in important social action." See "Complicating the Tourist Gaze: Literacy and the Internet as Catalysts for Articulating a Post-Colonial Palauan Identity," in *Global Literacies*, edited by Cynthia L. Slefe and Gail A. Hawisher (New York: Routledge, forthcoming).

14. The Nation of Hawai'i is only one of several Kanaka Maoli groups offering self-representations of Native Hawaiians on the Web. The Web sites of several other groups also seeking Native Hawaiian sovereignty provide alternative sources of information. For example, one can view Poka Laenui's site at <http://www.ohana.com/sovereignty>; Ka Lahui Hawai'i can be viewed at <http://kalahui.org>; a group working for the restoration of the Hawaiian monarchy has a site also, at <http://www.pixi.com/~kingdom>. For an updated list of such sites, see <http://hawaii-nation.org/links.htm>.

15. Richard Griggs; quoted in Crawford and Crawford, "Self-Determination in the Information Age."

16. The group of Native Americans from several tribes interviewed by Glen Martin share the Crawfords' view of this promise of cyberspace. As Martin summarizes the position of these Native Americans, "they see computers and wire as the best and brightest chance of reestablishing tribal bonds that were sundered with the massacre of Wounded Knee, an event remembered as ending all organized Indian resistance in North America." In Glen Martin, "Internet Indian Wars," *Wired* (December 1995), 116.

17. Quoted in Martin, "Internet Indian Wars," 117.

18. Nicholas Negroponte, "Message 19: Bits and Atoms," 1996 <http://nicholas.www. media.mit.edu/people/nicholas/WIRED3-01.html> (June 22, 1996).

19. George P. Landow, "What's a Critic to Do: Critical Theory in the Age of Hypertext," in *Hyper/Text/Theory*, edited by George P. Landow (Baltimore, Md.: Johns Hopkins University Press, 1994), 36.

20. Eric A. Havelock, *The Literate Revolution in Greece and Its Cultural Consequences* (Princeton: Princeton University Press, 1982); Richard A. Lanham, *The Electronic Word: Democracy, Technology, and the Arts* (Chicago: University of Chicago Press, 1993).

21. Joseph Gibaldi and Modern Language Association of America, *MLA Handbook for Writers of Research Papers*, 4th ed. (New York: Modern Language Association of America, 1995), 165.

22. Lanham, *Electronic Word*, 5.

23. Quoted in George Hu'eu Sanford Kanahele, *Ku Kanaka: Stand Tall* (Honolulu: University of Hawaii Press, 1986), 55. Kanahele's discussion of the *Kumulipo* begins on page 54. See chapter 7 for references to additional discussions of the *Kumulipo*.

24. Lilikalā Kame'eleihiwa, *Native Land and Foreign Desires* (Honolulu: Bishop Museum Press, 1992), 2; emphasis added.

25. See, for example, Gilles Deleuze and Félix Guattari, *Anti-Oedipus: Capitalism and Schizophrenia* (New York: Viking, 1977). Rob Wilson and Arif Dirlik point to Deleuze and Guattari's invocation of Oceanic rhizomatics in "Introduction: Asia/Pacific as Space of Cultural Production" in *Asia/Pacific as Space of Cultural Production*, edited by Rob Wilson and Arif Dirlik (Durham, N.C.: Duke University Press, 1995), 1–14. See also Charles J. Stivale, "The Rhizomatics of Cyberspace," in the Deleuze-Guattari Archive, database online, <gopher://jefferson.village.virginia.edu/00/pubs/listservs/spoons/deleuze-guattari.archive/papers/stiv.rhizcyber> (April 14, 1994).

26. Kame'eleihiwa, *Native Land*, 24.

27. Many Hawaiian proverbs use words for people and for kalo metonymically. Mary Kawena Pukuii, in *'Olelo No'eau: Hawaiian Proverbs and Poetical Sayings* (Honolulu: Bishop Museum Press, 1983), for example, includes: "Pūali kalo i ka wai 'ole," translated as "Taro, for lack of water, grows misshapen," and said to refer to people becoming ill from lack of care (296); also, "Ua 'ai i ke kāi-koi o 'Ewa," translated as "He has eaten the kāi-koi taro of 'Ewa," with the taro here understood to refer to a youth or maiden of 'Ewa (305). Similar examples can be found throughout Pukui's collection.

28. Mary Kawena Pukui, E. W. Haertig, and Catherine A. Lee, *Nānā I Ke Kumu (Look To the Source)*, vol. 1 (Honolulu: Queen Lili'uokalani Children's Center, 1972), 173.

29. Martin Heidegger, *The Question Concerning Technology and Other Essays*, translated by William Lovitt (New York: Harper, 1977), 134.

30. Quoted in Erik Davis, "Technopagans: May the Astral Plane Be Reborn in Cyberspace," *Wired* (July 1995): 131.

CODA

1. Robert C. Schmitt, "Early Crime Statistics of Hawaii," in *Hawaii Historical Review: Selected Readings*, edited by Richard A. Greer (Honolulu: Hawaiian Historical Society, 1969), 230–240.

2. For the criminalization of behaviors associated with marriage, see Robert C. Schmitt and Rose C. Strombel, "Marriage and Divorce in Hawaii Before 1870," in *Hawaii Historical Review*, 241–245.

3. Lilikalā Kame'eleihiwa, *Native Land and Foreign Desires* (Honolulu: Bishop Museum Press, 1992), 14.

4. Ralph S. Kuykendall, *The Hawaiian Kingdom*, vol. 1, *1778–1854, Foundation and Transformation* (Honolulu: University of Hawaii Press, 1938); *The Hawaiian Kingdom*, vol. 2, *1854–1874, Twenty Critical Years* (Honolulu: University of Hawaii Press, 1953); *The Hawaiian Kingdom*, vol. 3, *1874–1893, The Kalakaua Dynasty* (Honolulu: University

of Hawaii Press, 1967); Gavan Daws, *Shoal of Time: A History of the Hawaiian Islands* (Honolulu: University of Hawaii Press, 1968). For a list of some of the Kanaka Maoli scholars challenging these Eurocentric histories, see "Orientation," note 8.

5. A. Grove Day and Carl Stroven, *The Spell of Hawaii* (New York: Meredith Press, 1968).

6. Paul Lyons, "Pacific Scholarship, Literary Criticism, and Touristic Desire: The Specter of A. Grove Day," *Boundary 2* 24.2 (1997): 47–78.

7. Richard Hamasaki, "Mountains in the Sea: The Emergence of Contemporary Hawaiian Poetry in English," in *Hawai'i Literature Conference: Reader's Guide*, edited by Lorna Hershinow (Honolulu: Hawai'i Literary Arts Council, 1994), 41.

8. Rob Wilson, "Blue Hawai'i: Bamboo Ridge and 'Critical Regionalism'," in *Hawai'i Literature Conference: Reader's Guide*, edited by Lorna Hershinow (Honolulu: HLAC, 1994), 113.

Bibliography

Aijaz, Ahmad. *In Theory: Classes, Nations, Literatures*. New York: Verso, 1992.

Aluli, Noa Emmett. "Forward." In *Nā Leo a Kanaloa*. Honolulu: Ai Pohaku Press, 1995.

Aluli, Noa Emmett, and Davianna Pōmaikaʻi McGregor. "The Healing of Kahoʻolawe." In *Hawaiʻi Return to Nationhood*, edited by Ulla Hasager and Jonathan Friedman, 197–208. Copenhagen: IWGIA, 1994.

American Film Institute. *American Film Institute Catalog of Motion Pictures Produced in the United States, 1931–1940*. Berkeley: University of California Press, 1993.

Amos, Tori. *Boys for Pele*. Atlantic Recording Corporation, 1996. Compact sound disc.

Anderson, Benedict. *Imagined Communities: Reflections on the Origin and Spread of Nationalism*. Rev. and extended ed. New York: Verso, 1991.

Archer, Christon I. "The Spanish Reaction to Cook's Third Voyage." In *Captain James Cook and His Times*, edited by Robin Fisher and Hugh Johnson, 99–120. Seattle: University of Washington Press, 1979.

Baker, David J. "*Ea* and Knowing in Hawaiʻi." *Critical Inquiry* 23, no. 3 (1997): 640–660.

Balaz, Joseph P. *After the Drought*. Honolulu: Topgallant, 1985.

———, ed. *Hoʻomānoa*. Honolulu: Ku Paʻa, 1989.

Baran, Nicholas. "Computers and Capitalism: A Tragic Misuse of Technology." *Monthly Review* (September 1995): 40–46.

Barthes, Roland. *Camera Lucida: Reflections of Photography*. New York: Farrar, Straus and Giroux, 1980.

Beaglehole, J. C. *Cook the Writer, George Arnold Wood Memorial Lecture*. Sydney: Sydney University Press, 1970.

———. "Introduction." In *The Journals of Captain James Cook on His Voyages of Discovery*. Vol. 3, *The Voyage of the* Resolution *and* Discovery*, 1776–1780*, edited by J. C. Beaglehole, xxix–clxx. Cambridge: Cambridge University Press, 1967.

———. "Textual Introduction." In *The Journals of Captain James Cook on His Voyages of Discovery*. Vol. 3, *The Voyage of the* Resolution *and* Discovery*, 1776–1780*, edited by J. C. Beaglehole, clxxi–ccx. Cambridge: Cambridge University Press, 1967.

Beckwith, Martha W. *Hawaiian Mythology*. Honolulu: University Press of Hawaii, 1976.

———. *The Kumulipo*. Translated by Martha Beckwith. Honolulu: University of Hawaii Press, 1972.

———. *The Kumulipo: A Hawaiian Creation Chant*. Chicago: University of Chicago Press, 1951.

Behdad, Ali. *Belated Travelers: Orientalism in the Age of Colonial Dissolution*. Durham, N.C.: Duke University Press, 1994.

Bell, David, and Gill Valentine. *Mapping Desires: Geographies of Sexualities*. New York: Routledge, 1995.

Belsey, Catherine. *The Subject of Tragedy: Identity and Difference in Renaissance Drama*. London; New York: Methuen, 1985.

Bhabha, Homi. "Signs Taken for Wonders: Questions of Ambivalence and Authority Under a Tree Outside Delhi, May 1817." *Critical Inquiry* 12 (1985): 144–165.

———. "Sly Civility." *October* 34 (1985): 71–80.

Bingham, Hiram. *Residence of Twenty-One Years in the Sandwich Islands*. 1847. Reprint, Tokyo: Charles E. Tuttle, 1981.

Bird, Isabella L. *Six Months in the Sandwich Islands*. Honolulu: University of Hawaii Press, for Friends of the Library of Hawaii, 1964.

Birkerts, Sven. *The Fate of the Book*. Text21 Conference, 16 September 1995 (listserv: TEXT21-L@bigvax.alfred.edu) (November 6, 1995).

———. *The Gutenberg Elegies: The Fate of Reading in an Electronic Age*. Boston: Faber and Faber, 1994.

Blaisdell, Kekuni. "'Hawaiian' vs. 'Kanaka Maoli' as Metaphors." *Hawaii Review* 13 (1989): 77–79.

———. "Water Diversion Is 'Genocide'." *Honolulu Advertiser*, 3 May 1998, B3.

Blaisdell, Kekuni, and Noreen Mokuau. "Kānaka Maoli, Indigenous Hawaiians." In *Hawai'i Return to Nationhood*, edited by Ulla Hasager and Jonathan Friedman, 49–67. Copenhagen: IWGIA, 1994.

Borofsky, Robert. "Cook, Lono, Obeyesekere, and Sahlins." *Current Anthropology* 38, no. 2 (April 1997): 255–265.

Brown, DeSoto. Lecture, "Introduction to *Waikiki Wedding*." Sponsored by the Hawaiian Historical Society, Bishop Museum, Honolulu, 10 May 1995.

Bruchac, Joseph, and Association for Study of American Indian Literatures (U.S.). *Returning the Gift: Poetry and Prose from the First North American Native Writers' Festival*. Tucson: University of Arizona Press, 1994.

Buck, Elizabeth Bentzel. *Paradise Remade: The Politics of Culture and History in Hawai'i*. Philadelphia: Temple University Press, 1993.

Bushnell, O. A. "Aftermath: Britons' Responses to News of the Death of Captain James Cook." *The Hawaiian Journal of History* 25 (1991): 1–20.

Campbell, Kimo. "Preface." In *The Kumulipo: An Hawaiian Creative Myth*, edited by Lililuokalani. Kentfield, Calif.: Pueo, 1978.

Canby, Vincent. "Rev. of '*Paradise, Hawaiian Style*'." *New York Times*, 16 June 1966, 53.

Carter, Paul. *The Road to Botany Bay: An Exploration of Landscape and History*. Chicago: University of Chicago Press, 1989.

Chapin, Henry B. "Rev. of *And the View from the Shore: Literary Traditions of Hawai'i*, by Steve Sumida." *The Hawaiian Journal of History* 26 (1992): 267–269.

Charlot, John. *Chanting the Universe: Hawaiian Religious Culture*. Honolulu: Emphasis International, 1983.

Ching, Linda, and Robin Stephens. *Powerstones: Letters to a Goddess*. Honolulu: Ching and Stephens, 1994.

Chun, Malcolm Naea. "Introduction." In *Ka Mo'olelo Hawai'i: Hawaiian Traditions*, by Davida Malo, ii–ix. Honolulu: First People's Productions, 1996.

Churchill, Ward. *Indians are Us? Culture and Genocide in Native North America*. Monroe, Maine: Common Courage Press, 1994.

Clark, Hugh. "Kilauea Rangers Oppose Offerings by Outsiders." *Honolulu Advertiser*, 31 March 1995, A1.

Cohen, Stan. *The First Lady of Waikiki, A Pictorial History of Sheraton Moana Surfrider.* Missoula, Mt.: Pictorial Histories Publishing Company, 1995.

————. *The Pink Palace: The Royal Hawaiian Hotel.* Missoula, Mt.: Pictorial Histories Publishing Company, 1986.

Conrad, Joseph. *Heart of Darkness and The Secret Sharer.* New York: Bantam, 1981.

Cook, James. *The Journals of Captain James Cook on his Voyages of Discovery.* Vol. 1. *The Voyage of the* Endeavor, *1769–1771, Charts & Views.* Edited by J. C. Beaglehole. Cambridge: Cambridge University Press (for the Hakluyt Society), 1955.

————. *The Journals of Captain James Cook on his Voyages of Discovery.* Vol. 3. *The Voyage of the* Resolution *and* Discovery, *1776–1780, Parts One and Two.* Edited by J. C. Beaglehole. Cambridge: Cambridge University Press (for the Hakluyt Society), 1967.

Cook, James, and James King. *A Voyage to the Pacific Ocean: Undertaken by the Command of His Majesty, for Making Discoveries in the Northern Hemisphere. Performed under the Direction of Captains Cook, Clerke, and Gore, in His Majesty's Ships the Resolution and Discovery; in the Years 1776, 1777, 1778, 1779, and 1780. In Three Volumes Plus Folio.* London: Printed by H. Hughs for G. Nicol and T. Cadell, 1784.

Coombes, Annie E. "Inventing the 'Postcolonial': Hybridity and Constituency in Contemporary Curating." *New Formations* 18 (Winter 1992): 39–52.

Crawford, Scott, and Kekula Crawford. "Self-Determination in the Information Age." 1996. <http://www.info.isoc.org/HMP/PAPER/230/html/paper.htm#cont> (June 27,1996).

Crowther, Bosley. "'Bird of Paradise,' Portrayal in Technicolor of South Sea Island Customs, at Roxy." *New York Times*, 15 March 1951, 37.

————. "Rev. of 'Miss Tatlock's Millions'." *New York Times*, 25 November 1948, 47.

Davenport, Kiana. *Shark Dialogues.* New York: Macmillan, 1994.

Davis, Erik. "Technopagans: May the Astral Plane Be Reborn in Cyberspace." *Wired* (July 1995): 127ff.

Daws, Gavan. *Shoal of Time: A History of the Hawaiian Islands.* Honolulu: University of Hawaii Press, 1968.

Day, A. Grove. "Introduction." In *Travels in Hawaii.* By Robert Louis Stevenson, xi–xlv. Honolulu: University of Hawaii Press, 1973.

————. *Mad About Islands.* Honolulu: Mutual, 1987.

Day, A. Grove, and Carl Stroven. *The Spell of Hawaii.* New York: Meredith Press, 1968.

De Lauretis, Teresa. *Alice Doesn't: Feminism, Semiotics, Cinema.* Bloomington: Indiana University Press, 1984.

Deleuze, Gilles, and Felix Guattari. *Anti-Oedipus: Capitalism and Schizophrenia.* New York: Viking, 1977.

Dening, Greg. *The Death of William Gooch: A History's Anthropology.* Honolulu: University of Hawaii Press, 1995.

————. *Islands and Beaches: Discourse on a Silent Land: Marquesas, 1774–1880.* Chicago: Dorsey, 1988.

————. "Sharks that Walk on the Land: The Death of Captain Cook." *Meanjin* 41 (1982): 427–437.

Dibble, Sheldon. *History of the Sandwich Islands.* 1843. Reprint, Honolulu: Thos. G. Thrum, 1909.

Dirlik, Arif. *After the Revolution: Waking to Global Capitalism*. Hanover, Mass.: Wesleyan University Press, published by University Press of New England, 1994.

―――. "The Global in the Local." In *Global/Local: Cultural Production and the Transnational Imaginary*, edited by Rob Wilson and Wimal Dissanayake, 21–45. Durham, N.C.: Duke University Press, 1996.

―――. "The Past as Legacy and Project: Postcolonial Criticism in the Perspective of Indigenous Historicism." *American Indian Culture and Research Journal* 20, no. 2 (1996): 1–32.

―――. *The Postcolonial Aura: Third World Criticism in the Age of Global Capitalism*. Boulder: Westview, 1997.

―――. "Three Worlds or One, or Many? The Reconfiguration of Global Relations Under Contemporary Capitalism." *Nature, Society and Thought* 7, no. 1 (1995): 19–42.

Doane, Mary Ann, Patricia Mellencamp, and Linda Williams, eds. *Re-Vision: Essays in Feminist Film Criticism*. Frederick, Md.: University Publications of America, 1984.

Dudley, Michael Kioni. *Man, Gods, and Nature, Hawaiian Nation*. vol.1. Honolulu: Nā Kāne O Ka Malo Press, 1990.

Dudoit, D. Māhealani. "An Offering of Words: The Landscape of N. Scott Momaday." Department of English, University of Hawaii, 1997. Photocopy.

―――. "Voyages of Return: Essays of Hawaiian Cultural Rediscovery." Master's thesis, University of Hawaii, 1996.

Elbert, Samuel H. "Preface." In *Place Names of Hawaii*, edited by Mary Kawena Pukui, Samuel H. Elbert, and Esther T. Mookini, ix–xiii. Honolulu: University of Hawaii Press, 1974.

Ellis, William. *Journal of William Ellis*. 1825. Reprint, Rutland, Vt.: Charles E. Tuttle, 1979.

Eveleth, Ephraim. *History of the Sandwich Islands: With an Account of the American Mission Established There in 1820*. Philadelphia: American Sunday-School Union, 1830.

Exoo, Calvin F. *Democracy Upside Down: Public Opinion and Cultural Hegemony in the United States*. New York: Praeger, 1987.

Fabian, Johannes. *Time and the Other: How Anthropology Makes Its Object*. New York: Columbia University Press, 1983.

Fanon, Frantz. *The Wretched of the Earth*. New York: Penguin, 1969.

Fisher, Robin, and Hugh J.M. Johnston, eds. *Captain James Cook and His Times*. Vancouver: Douglas & McIntyre, 1979.

Forbes, David W., and Honolulu Academy of Arts. *Encounters with Paradise: Views of Hawaii and Its People, 1778–1941*. Honolulu: Honolulu Academy of Arts, 1992.

Foucault, Michel. "Of Other Spaces." *Diacritics* 16 (1986): 22–27.

―――. *The Order of Things: An Archaeology of the Human Sciences*. Translated by Alan Sheridan. London: Tavistock, 1970.

―――. "Questions of Geography." In *Power/Knowledge: Selected Interviews and Other Writings 1972–1977*, edited by C. Gordon, 63–77. New York: Pantheon, 1980.

―――. "What Is an Author?" In *The Foucault Reader*, edited by Paul Rabinow, 101–120. New York: Pantheon, 1984.

Franklin, Cynthia G. *Writing Women's Communities: The Politics and Poetics of Contemporary Multi-genre Anthologies*. Madison: University of Wisconsin Press, 1997.

Frierson, Pamela. *The Burning Island: A Journey through Myth and History in the Volcano Country*. San Francisco: Sierra Club Books, 1991.

Fujikane, Candace. "Between Nationalisms: Hawai'i's Local Nation and Its Troubled Racial Paradise." *Critical Mass* 1, no.2 (Spring/Summer 1994): 23–58.

Gaddis, William. *The Recognitions*. New York: Harcourt Brace, 1955.

Gibaldi, Joseph, and Modern Language Association of America. *MLA Handbook for Writers of Research Papers*. 4th ed. New York: Modern Language Association of America, 1995.

Glauberman, Stu. "Attracting Isle Visitors." *Honolulu Advertiser*, 21 November 1994, D1–D2.

Goss, Jon. "Disquiet on the Waterfront: Reflections on Nostalgia and Utopia in the Urban Archetypes of Festival Marketplaces." Department of Geography, University of Hawai'i, 1995. Photocopy.

———. "Placing the Market and Marketing the Place: Tourist Advertising of the Hawaiian Islands, 1972–92." *Environment and Planning D: Society and Space* 11 (1993): 663–688.

Goudie, S. X. "Theory, Practice and the Intellectual: A Conversation with Abdul R. JanMohamed." *Jouvert (Electronic Journal)* (1997). <http://152.1.96.5/jouvert/issue2/Goudie.htm> (September 28, 1998).

Grant, Glen. *Waikiki Yesterday*. Honolulu: Mutual Publishing, 1996.

Greenblatt, Stephen. *Marvelous Possessions*. Chicago: University of Chicago Press, 1991.

Grimshaw, Patricia. *Paths of Duty: American Missionary Wives in Nineteenth-Century Hawaii*. Honolulu: University of Hawaii Press, 1989.

Hall, Dana Naone. "Book Jacket Note." In *A Legendary Tradition of Kamapua'a, The Hawaiian Pig-God*, edited by Lilikalā Kame'eleihiwa. Honolulu: Bishop Museum Press, 1996.

Hamasaki, Richard. "Mountains in the Sea: The Emergence of Contemporary Hawaiian Poetry in English." In *Hawai'i Literature Conference: Reader's Guide*, edited by Lorna Hershinow, 32–47. Honolulu: Hawai'i Literary Arts Council, 1994.

Handler, Richard, and Jocelyn Linnekin. "Tradition, Genuine or Spurious." *Journal of American Folklore* 97 (1984).

Handy, E. S. Craighill. *The Native Culture in the Marquesas*. Honolulu: Bishop Museum Bulletin 9, 1923.

Handy, E. S. Craighill, C. Handy, and E. G. Handy. *Native Planters in Old Hawai'i*. Honolulu: Bishop Museum Press, 1972.

Harada, Wayne. "A Monster of a Movie Project." *Honolulu Advertiser*, 13 March 1997 1997, C1.

Harvey, David. *The Condition of Postmodernity: An Enquiry into the Origins of Cultural Change*. Oxford, England; Cambridge, Mass.: Blackwell, 1989.

Hau'ofa, Epeli. "Our Sea of Islands." In *A New Oceania: Rediscovering Our Sea of Islands*, edited by Eric Waddell et al., 1–18. Suva, Fiji: University of South Pacific, 1993.

Havelock, Eric A. *The Literate Revolution in Greece and Its Cultural Consequences*. Princeton: Princeton University Press, 1982.

Heidegger, Martin. *The Question Concerning Technology and Other Essays*. Translated by William Lovitt. New York: Harper, 1977.

He Pule Hoolaa Alii: He Kumulipo no Ka-I-imamao, a ia Alapai Wahine. Honolulu: Pa'iia e ka Hui Pa'ipalapala Elele, 1889.

Hereniko, Vilsoni. *Fine Dancing*. Theatrical production. Honolulu, August 1997.

Herman, R. Douglas. "The Dread Taboo, Human Sacrifice, and Pearl Harbor." *Contemporary Pacific* 8, no. 1 (Spring 1996): 81–126.

———. "Kalai'aina—Carving the Land: Geography, Desire and Possession in the Hawaiian Islands." Ph.D. Diss., University of Hawaii, 1995.

Hertz, Neil. "The Notion of Blockage in the Literature of the Sublime." In *The End of the Line: Essays of Psychoanalysis and the Sublime*, edited by Neil Hertz, 40–60. New York: Columbia University Press, 1985.

Hibbard, Don, and David Franzen. *The View from Diamond Head: Royal Residence to Urban Resort.* Honolulu: Editions Limited, 1986.

Hoare, Michael E. "Two Centuries' Perceptions of James Cook: George Forster to Beaglehole." In *Captain James Cook and His Times*, edited by Robin Fisher and Hugh Johnson, 211–227. Seattle: University of Washington Press, 1979.

Holt, John Dominis. *On Being Hawaiian.* Honolulu: Star-Bulletin Printing, 1964.

———. "Rev. of *Ku Kanaka*, by George Kanahele." *Hawaiian Journal of History* 21 (1987): 158–160.

———. *Waimea Summer.* Honolulu: Topgallant, 1976.

Hongo, Garrett. *Volcano: A Memoir of Hawaii.* New York: Knopf, 1995.

Houston, James D. "Fire in the Night." In *World Between Waves*, edited by Frank Stewart, 115-121. Washington, D.C.: Island Press, 1991.

Jamal, Michele. *Shape Shifters: Shaman Women in Contemporary Society.* London: Routledge and Kegan Paul, 1987.

———. *Volcanic Visions: Encounters with Other Worlds.* New York: Arkana Penguin, 1991.

Jameson, Fredric. "Postmodernism, or, the Cultural Logic of Late Capitalism." *New Left Review* (1984): 53–92.

Johnson, Steven. *Interface Culture: How New Technology Transforms the Way We Create and Communicate.* New York: Harper*Edge*, 1997.

Joppien, Rudiger, and Bernard Smith. *The Art of Captain Cook's Voyages.* Vol. 3, *The Voyage of the "Resolution" and "Discovery."* New Haven: Yale University Press, 1988.

Kalakaua, King David. *The Legends and Myths of Hawaii: The Fables and Folk-Lore of a Strange People.* 1888. Reprint, Rutland, Vt.: Charles E. Tuttle, 1972.

Kamahele, Momi. "Decolonizing Hawaiian Antiquities and Fragments of Hawaiian History." Paper presented at the Fifteenth Annual Meeting of the Association for Asian American Studies, 1898–1998: Rethinking Asian and Pacific Colonial/Postcolonial Nations, Identities and Histories, Honolulu, Hawaii, 1998.

Kamakau, Samuel M. *Ruling Chiefs of Hawaii.* Honolulu: Kamehameha Schools Press, 1961.

Kame'eleihiwa, Lilikalā. "Introduction." In *A Legendary Tradition of Kamapua'a*, edited by Lilikalā Kamele'eihiwa, vii–xix. Honolulu: Bishop Museum Press, 1996.

———. *Native Land and Foreign Desires.* Honolulu: Bishop Museum Press, 1992.

Kanahele, Edward L. "Kanaka'ole, Edith K." In *Hawaiian Music and Musicians*, edited by George S. Kanahele, 205–208. Honolulu: University of Hawaii Press, 1979.

Kanahele, George Hu'eu Sanford. *Ku Kanaka: Stand Tall.* Honolulu: University of Hawaii Press, 1986.

———. *Restoring Hawaiianness to Waikīkī.* Honolulu: Queen Emma Foundation, 1993.

———. *Waikīkī 100 B.C. to 1900 A.D.: An Untold Story.* Honolulu: University of Hawaii Press, 1995.

———, ed. *Hawaiian Music and Musicians: An Illustrated History.* Honolulu: University of Hawaii Press, 1979.

Kanahele, Pualani Kanakaʻole. "He Koihonua No Kanaloa, He Moku (History for Kanaloa, An Island)." *Mānoa* (Summer 1995): 20–25.

———. "Ku Au Lono i Kahoʻolawe, Hoʻi (The Era of Lono at Kahoʻolawe, Returned)." *Mānoa* (Summer 1995): 152–167.

Kanahele, Pualani Kanakaʻole, and Duke Kalani Wise. Ka Honua Ola. Honolulu: Center for Hawaiian Studies, University of Hawaiʻi at Mānoa, 1992.

Kane, Herb Kawainui. "Comments." *Current Anthropology* 38, no. 2 (1997): 265–267.

———. *Voyagers: Words and Images.* Bellevue, Wash.: WhaleSong, 1991.

Kaplan, E. Ann. *Women and Film: Both Sides of the Camera.* New York: Methuen, 1983.

Kauanui, J. Kehaulani. "Mapping the Native: Hawaiian Genealogical Reterritorialization of Land, Identity, and Sovereign Belonging." Paper presented at the Fifteenth Annual Meeting of the Association for Asian American Studies, 1898–1998: Rethinking Asian and Pacific Colonial/Postcolonial Nations, Identities and Histories, Honolulu, Hawaii, 1998.

Kawaharada, Dennis. "Toward an Authentic Local Literature in Hawaiʻi." In *Hawaiʻi Literature Conference: Reader's Guide*, edited by Lorna Hershinow, 56–60. Honolulu: Hawaiʻi Literary Arts Council, 1994.

Keesing, Roger. "Creating the Past: Custom and Identity in the Contemporary Pacific." *Contemporary Pacific* 1 (1989): 19–42.

Keith, Michael, and Steve Pile. "Introduction." In *Place and the Politics of Identity*, edited by Michael Keith and Steve Pile, 1–40. New York: Routledge, 1993.

Kent, Noel. Hawaii: *Islands Under the Influence.* 1983. Reprint, Honolulu: University of Hawaii Press, 1993.

Kitalong, Saari, and Tino Kitalong. "Complicating the Tourist Gaze: Literacy and the Internet as Catalysts for Articulating a Post-Colonial Palauan Identity." In *Global Literacies*, edited by Cynthia L. Slefe and Gail A. Hawisher. New York: Routledge, forthcoming.

Korn, Alfons L. "Introduction." In *Fourteen Years in the Sandwich Islands 1855–1868*, edited by Charles de Varigny, ix–xxiii. Honolulu: University of Hawaii Press, 1981.

Krauss, Bob. "A Different Perspective on Work of Malo." *Honolulu Advertiser*, 25 May 1997, E3.

Kubota, Gary T. "Future: Questions Cloud the Visions." *Honolulu Star-Bulletin*, 23 August 1995, A1.

Kuykendall, Ralph S. *The Hawaiian Kingdom.* Vol. 1, *1778–1854, Foundation and Transformation.* Honolulu: University of Hawaii Press, 1938.

———. *The Hawaiian Kingdom.* Vol. 2, *1854–1874, Twenty Critical Years.* Honolulu: University of Hawaii Press, 1953.

———. *The Hawaiian Kingdom.* Vol. 3, *1874–1893, The Kalakaua Dynasty.* Honolulu: University of Hawaii Press, 1967.

Kuykendall, Ralph S., and A. Grove Day. *Hawaii: A History.* 1948. Reprint, Englewood Cliffs, N.J.: Prentice-Hall, 1961.

Landgraf, Anne Kapulani. *Nā Wahi Pana O Koʻolau Poko, Legendary Places of Koʻolau Poko.* Hawaiian translation by Fred Kalani Meinecke. Honolulu: University of Hawaii Press, 1994.

Landow, George P. "What's a Critic to Do: Critical Theory in the Age of Hypertext." In *Hyper/Text/Theory*, edited by George P. Landow, 1–52. Baltimore, Md.: Johns Hopkins University Press, 1994.

Lanham, Richard A. *The Electronic Word: Democracy, Technology, and the Arts.* Chicago: University of Chicago Press, 1993.

Lee, W. Storrs. *Hawaii: A Literary Chronicle*. New York: Funk and Wagnalls, 1967.

Leineweber, Spencer. "Honolulu: Bride of the Sea." Paper presented at the City Views Lecture Series, University of Hawaii, February 22, 1995.

Liliuokalani. "Introduction." In *An Account of the Creation of the World According to Hawaiian Tradition*. Boston: Lee and Shepard, 1897.

Linnekin, Jocelyn. "Consuming Cultures: Tourism and the Commoditization of Cultural Identity in the Island Pacific." In *Tourism, Ethnicity, and the State in Asian and Pacific Societies*, edited by Michael Picard and Robert E. Wood, 215–250. Honolulu: University of Hawaii Press, 1997.

Lodge, David. *Paradise News*. New York: Penguin, 1991.

London, Jack. *Stories of Hawaii*, edited by A. Grove Day. Honolulu: Mutual, 1990.

Lum, Darrell H.K. "What Is Local Literature? Part 1." *Hawaii Literary Arts Council Newsletter* 73 (March 1984): 9.

Luter, Ellen Bairos. "Kamaaina Beach Home." *Paradise of the Pacific* (January 1955): 20–21, 27.

Lyons, Paul. "Pacific Scholarship, Literary Criticism, and Touristic Desire: The Specter of A. Grove Day." *Boundary* 2 24, no. 2 (1997): 47–78.

MacKay, David. *In the Wake of Cook: Exploration, Science and Empire, 1780–1801*. New York: St. Martin's, 1985.

Malo, David. *Hawaiian Antiquities (Moʻolelo Hawaiʻi)*. Translated by Nathaniel B. Emerson. Honolulu: Bishop Museum Press, 1951.

———. *Ka Moʻolelo Hawaiʻi: Hawaiian Traditions*. Translated by Malcolm Naea Chun. Honolulu: First People's Productions, 1996.

Man, Glenn K.S. "Hollywood Images of the Pacific." *East-West Film Journal* 5, no. 2 (1991): 16–29.

Marantz, Maxine. *Hawaii's Tragic Princess Kaiulani*. Honolulu: Aloha Graphics, 1980.

Marek, Serge A. "Waikiki Virtual Reality: Space, Place, and Representation in the Waikiki Master Plan." Master's thesis, University of Hawaii, 1997.

Martin, Glen. "Internet Indian Wars." *Wired* (December 1995): 108–117.

Martin, Henri-Jean. *The History and Power of Writing*. Translated by Lydia G. Cochrane. Chicago: University of Chicago Press, 1994.

Massey, Doreen. *Space, Place and Gender*. Minneapolis: University of Minnesota Press, 1994.

Matson, Floyd. "Hollywood Goes Hawaiian." In *Viewer's Guide: East-West International Film Festival*, 40–41. Honolulu: East-West Film Festival, 1984.

Matsuoka, Alan. "How a Split Second in 1976 Stirred the Hawaiian Spirit." *Honolulu Star-Bulletin*, 22 August 1995, A1.

McClintock, Anne. "The Angel of Progress: The Pitfalls of the Term 'Post-colonialism'." *Social Text* 31, no. 3 (1992): 84–98.

McGregor, Davianna Pōmaikaʻi. "Waipiʻo Valley, a Cultural Kīpuka in Early 20th Century Hawaiʻi." *Journal of Pacific History* 30, no. 2 (1995): 194–209.

McPherson, Michael. "Glass Balls and Other Found Objects." In *Hawaiʻi Literary Conference: Reader's Guide*, edited by Lorna Hershinow, 1–2. Honolulu: Hawaii Literary Arts Council, 1994.

———. "Kiholo Revisited." In *Hawaiʻi Literature Conference*, edited by Lorna Hershinow, 3. Honolulu: Hawaii Literary Arts Council, 1994.

———. *Singing with the Owls*. Honolulu: Petronium, 1982.

Mehan, Hugh, and Houston Wood. *The Reality of Ethnomethodology*. New York: Wiley, 1975.

Mercer, P. M. "Oral Tradition in the Pacific: Problems of Interpretation." *Journal of Pacific History* 14, no. 2 (1979): 130–153.

Michener, James A. *Hawaii*. New York: Random House, 1959.

———. "Introduction." In *A Hawaiian Reader*, edited by A. Grove Day and Carl Stover, xii–xvii. Honolulu: Mutual, 1984.

Mitchell, W.J.T. *Iconology: Image, Text, Ideology*. Chicago: University of Chicago Press, 1986.

———. *Picture Theory: Essays on Verbal and Visual Representation*. Chicago: University of Chicago Press, 1994.

Mulvey, Laura. "Afterthoughts on 'Visual Pleasure and Narrative Cinema' inspired by King Vidor's *Duel in the Sun 1946*." In *Contemporary Film Theory*, edited by Anthony Easthope, 125–134. New York: Longman, 1993.

———. "Visual Pleasure and Narrative Cinema." *Screen* 16, no. 3 (1975): 6–18. Reprinted in *Contemporary Film Theory*, edited by Anthony Easthope, 111–124. New York: Longman, 1993.

Murayama, Milton. *All I Asking for Is My Body*. 1975. Reprint, Honolulu: University of Hawaii Press, 1988.

Murray-Oliver, Anthony. *Captain Cook's Hawaii: As Seen by His Artists*. Wellington, New Zealand: Millwood, 1975.

Nakamura, Barry. "The Story of Waikiki and the Reclamation Project." Master's thesis, University of Hawaii at Mānoa, 1979.

Nakuina, Moses K. *The Wind Gourd of La'amaomao*. Translated by Esther K. Mookini and Sarah Nākoa. Honolulu: Kalamaku Press, 1990.

Nandy, Ashis. "Bearing Witness to the Future." *Futures* 28 (1996): 636–639.

———. *Traditions, Tyranny and Utopias: Essays in the Politics of Awareness*. Delhi, India: Oxford University Press, 1987.

Negroponte, Nicholas. "Message 19: Bits and Atoms." 1996. <http://www.media.mit.edu/~nicholas/Wired/WIRED3-01.html > (June 22, 1996).

———. "Message 26: Bit by Bit." 1996. <http://www.media.mit.edu/~nicholas/Wired/WIRED3-08.html> (June 22, 1996).

Niranjana, Tejaswini. *Siting Translation: History, Post-Structuralism, and the Colonial Conquest*. Berkeley: University of California Press, 1992.

Obeyesekere, Gananath. *The Apotheosis of Captain Cook: European Mythmaking in the Pacific*. Princeton: Princeton University Press, 1992.

Osorio, Jon. "Protecting Our Thoughts." Speech delivered at Voices of the Earth Conference held in Amsterdam, November 10, 1993. Reprinted <http://www2.hawaii.edu/shaps/hawaii/osorio.html> July 3, 1998.

———. "Songs of Our Natural Selves, the Enduring Voice of Nature in Hawaiian Music." Paper presented at the eighth Pacific History Association Conference, 1990.

"Our Literary Standard." *Paradise of the Pacific* (February 1909): 7–8.

Paine, Albert Bigelow. *Mark Twain: A Biography*. New York: Harper, 1912.

Parry, Benita. "The Postcolonial: Conceptual Category or Chimera." In *The Yearbook of English Studies: The Politics of Postcolonial Criticism*, edited by Andrew Gurr, 3–21. London: W. S. Maney, 1997.

———. "Problems in Current Theories of Colonial Discourse." *Oxford Literary Review* 9 (1987): 27–58.

Podgers, James. "Greetings from Independent Hawaii." *American Bar Association Journal* (June 1997). Reprinted 1997 at <http://hawaii-nation.org/abaj.html> January 22, 1999.

Pollner, Melvin. "Left of Ethnomethodology: The Rise and Decline of Radical Reflexivity." *American Sociological Review* 56 no. 3 (June 1991): 370–380.

Poster, Mark. *Cyberdemocracy: Internet and the Public Sphere.* <http://www.hnet.uci.edu/mposter/writings/democ.html> (May 27, 1996).

Pratt, Mary Louise. "Arts of the Contact Zone." *Profession* 91 (1991): 137–144.

———. *Imperial Eyes: Travel Writing and Transculturation.* London; New York: Routledge, 1992.

Pukui, Mary Kawena, and Samuel H. Elbert. *Hawaiian Dictionary.* Honolulu: University of Hawaii Press, 1986.

Pukui, Mary Kawena, Samuel H. Elbert, and Esther T. Mookini. *Place Names of Hawai'i.* Honolulu: University of Hawaii Press, 1974.

Pukui, Mary Kawena, E. W. Haertig, and Catherine A. Lee. *Nānā I Ke Kumu (Look to the Source).* Vol. 1. Honolulu: Queen Lili'uokalani Children's Center, 1972.

Pukui, Mary Kawena, and Dietrich Varez. *'Ōlelo No'eau: Hawaiian Proverbs and Poetical Sayings.* Honolulu: Bishop Museum Press, 1983.

Rampell, Ed. "Polynesian Political Prisoner or Dennis the Menace to Society." 1996. <http://www.aloha.net/nation/polynesian.html> (June 27, 1996).

Reeve, Rowland B. "Kaho'olawe: Ka Makupuni O Kanaloa." *Mānoa* 7, no. 1 (Summer 1995): 203–222.

———. Kaho'olawe: *Nā Leo Kanaloa: Chants and Stories of Kaho'olawe.* Honolulu: Ai Pohaku Press, 1995.

Rodaway, Paul. *Sensuous Geographies: Body, Sense, Place.* New York: Routledge, 1994.

Rose, Gillian. *Feminism and Geography: The Limits of Geographical Knowledge.* Minneapolis: University of Minnesota Press, 1993.

———. "Rev. of *Postmodern Geographies* by Edward W. Soja, and *The Condition of Modernity* by David Harvey." *Journal of Historical Geography* 17 (1991): 118–121.

Sahlins, Marshall. *Islands of History.* Chicago: University of Chicago Press, 1985.

———. *What 'Natives' Think, About Captain Cook, for Example.* Chicago: University of Chicago Press, 1995.

Said, Edward. *Culture and Imperialism.* New York: Random House, 1993.

Sardar, Ziauddin. "The A B C D (and E) of Ashis Nandy." *Emergences* 7/8 (1995–96): 125–145.

Schmitt, Robert C. "Early Crime Statistics of Hawaii." In *Hawaii Historical Review: Selected Readings,* edited by Richard A. Greer, 230–240. Honolulu: Hawaiian Historical Society, 1969.

———. *Hawaii in the Movies: 1898–1959.* Honolulu: Hawaiian Historical Society, 1988.

Schmitt, Robert C., and Rose C. Strombel. "Marriage and Divorce in Hawaii Before 1870." In *Hawaii Historical Review,* edited by Richard C. Greer, 241–245. Honolulu: Hawaiian Historical Society, 1969.

Silva, Noenoe K. "Ku'e!: Hawaiian Women's Resistance to the Annexation." *Social Process of Hawai'i* 38 (1997): 2–15.

Smith, Bernard. *European Vision and the South Pacific.* 2d ed. New York: Oxford University Press, 1989.

Smith, Neil, and Cindi Katz. "Grounding Metaphor: Towards a Spatialized Politics." In *Place and the Politics of Identity*, edited by Michael Keith and Steve Pile, 67–83. New York: Routledge, 1993.

Smith, Pam. "Kaho'olawe: Hawaiians on Trial." *Hawai'i Observer*, 28 July 1977, 15.

"Social Ambition." *Paradise of the Pacific* (June 1903): 23–24.

Soja, Edward. *Postmodern Geographies: The Reassertion of Space in Critical Social Theory*. London: Verso, 1989.

Soja, Edward, and Barbara Hooper. "The Space that Difference Makes." In *Place and the Politics of Identity*, edited by Michael Keith and Steve Pile, 183–205. New York: Routledge, 1993.

Sommer, Doris. "Textual Conquests: On Readerly Competence and 'Minority' Literature." In *The Uses of Literary History*, edited by Marshall Brown, 255–267. Durham, N.C.: Duke University Press, 1995.

Sontag, Susan. *On Photography*. 2d ed. New York: Anchor, 1989.

Spate, O.H.K. *Paradise Found and Lost*. Minneapolis: University of Minnesota Press, 1988.

Spencer, Neil. "Goddess Pele Lifted Tori Out of Darkness." *Honolulu Star Bulletin*, 19 January 1996, D5.

Spivak, Gayatri Chakravorty. "Can the Subaltern Speak? Speculations on Widow Sacrifice." In *Marxism and the Interpretation of Culture*, edited by Cary Nelson and Lawrence Grossberg, 271–313. New York: Macmillan, 1988.

———. *Outside in the Teaching Machine*. New York: Routledge, 1993.

Spurr, David. *The Rhetoric of Empire: Colonial Discourse in Journalism, Travel Writing, and Imperial Administration*. Durham, N.C.: Duke University Press, 1993.

Stewart, C. S. *Journal of a Residence in the Sandwich Islands*. 1828. Reprint, Honolulu: University of Hawaii Press, 1970.

Stewart, Frank. *A Natural History of Nature Writing*. Washington, D.C.: Island Press, 1995.

Stillman, Amy Ku'uleialoha. "History Reinterpreted in Song: The Case of the Hawaiian Counterrevolution." *Hawaiian Journal of History* 23 (1989): 1–30.

———. "'Na Lei O Hawai'i': On Hula Songs, Floral Emblems, Island Princesses, and *Wahi Pana*." *Hawaiian Journal of History* 28 (1994): 87–108.

———. "Queen Kapi'olani's Lei Chants," *Hawaiian Journal of History* 30 (1996): 119–152.

———. *Sacred Hula: The Historical Hula 'Ā la'papa*. Honolulu: Bishop Museum Press, 1998.

Stivale, Charles J. "The Rhizomatics of Cyberspace." Available in the Deleuze-Guattari Archive, database online <gopher://jefferson.village.virginia.edu/00/pubs/listservs/spoons/deleuze-guattari.archive/papers/stiv.rhizcyber> (April 14, 1994).

Sumida, Stephen. *And the View from the Shore: Literary Traditions of Hawai'i*. Seattle: University of Washington Press, 1991.

Tanji, Edwin. "It'll be a Daunting Job Even for an Old Hand." *Honolulu Advertiser*, 12 April 1998, A8.

———. "Non-Hawaiian Religious Offerings Raise Concern on Maui." *Honolulu Advertiser*, 2 April 1995, A8.

"Technology's Role in the Revival of the Hawaiian Language." International Reading Associations. 1998. <http://www.readingonling.org/electronic/hawaii/techrol.htm> (September 20, 1998).

Thompson, Howard. "Review of 'Blue Hawaii'." *New York Times*, 22 February 1962, 20.

Tillman, Frank. "What Pictures Do to Words, What Words Do to Pictures." Paper presented at the Image and Word Lecture Series, University of Hawaii, 1995.

Tobin, Jeffrey. "Cultural Construction and Native Nationalism: Report from the Hawaiian Front." *Boundary* 2 21.1 (Spring 1994): 111–133.

———. "Savages, the Poor and the Discourse of Hawaiian Infanticide." *Journal of Polynesian Society* 106, no. 1 (March 1997): 65–92.

Todorov, Tzvetan. *The Conquest of America: The Question of the Other.* Translated by Richard Howard. New York: Harper, 1984.

Trask, Haunani-Kay. *From a Native Daughter: Colonialism and Sovereignty in Hawaii.* Monroe, Maine: Common Courage Press, 1993.

———. "Indigenous Writers and Colonial Situations." *Pacific Islands Communication Journal* 13, no. 1 (1984).

———. "Introduction." In *Nā Wahi Pana O Koʻolau Poko Legendary Places of Koʻolau Poko,* vii–viii. Honolulu: University of Hawaii Press, 1994.

———. *Light in the Crevice Never Seen.* Corvallis, Ore.: Calyx, 1994.

———. "Natives and Anthropologists: The Colonial Struggle." *Contemporary Pacific* 2 (1991): 159–167.

———. "Politics in the Pacific Islands: Imperialism and Native Self-Determination." *Amerasia* 16 (1990): 15–16.

———. "Returning the gift." In *Returning the Gift: Poetry and Prose from the First North American Native Writers' Festival,* edited by the Association for Study of American Indian Literatures, 290. Tucson: University of Arizona Press, 1994.

Turnbull, Phyllis, and Kathy E. Ferguson. "Military Presence/Missionary Past: The Historical Construction of Masculine Order and Feminine Hawaiʻi." In *Women in Hawaiʻi: Sites, Identities, and Voices,* edited by Kathleen O. Kane, Joyce N. Chinen, and Ida M. Yoshinaga, 94–107. Honolulu: University of Hawaiʻi, 1997.

Twain, Mark. *Mark Twain's Letters from Hawaii.* 1866. Reprint, edited by A. Grove Day. Honolulu: University of Hawaii Press, 1975.

———. *Mark Twain's Speeches.* New York: Harper, 1923.

Urry, John. *The Tourist Gaze: Leisure and Travel in Contemporary Societies.* Newbury Park, Calif.: Sage, 1990.

Valeri, Valerio. *Kingship and Sacrifice: Ritual and Society in Ancient Hawaii.* Chicago: University of Chicago Press, 1985.

Varigny, Charles de. *Fourteen Years in the Sandwich Islands 1855–1868.* Honolulu: University of Hawaii Press, 1981.

Verzola, Roberto. *Towards a Political Economy of Information.* 1995. <http://www.solinet. org/THIRDWORLD/obet1.htm> (September 20, 1998).

Von Tempski, Armine. *Born in Paradise.* New York: Duell Sloan and Pearce, 1940.

———. *Hula: A Romance of Hawaii.* 1927. Reprint, Woodbridge, Conn.: Ox Bow, 1988.

———. *Ripe Breadfruit.* 1935. Reprint, Woodbridge, Conn.: Ox Bow, 1992.

Warschaueer, Mark, and Keola Donaghy. "Leokī: A Powerful Voice of Hawaiian Language Revitalization." *Computer Assisted Language Learning* (forthcoming).

Watt, James. "Medical Aspects and Consequences of Cook's Voyages." In *Captain James Cook and His Times,* edited by Robin Fisher and Hugh Johnston, 159–185. Seattle: University of Washington Press, 1979.

Williams, Linda, ed. *Viewing Positions: Ways of Seeing View.* New Brunswick, N.J.: Rutgers University Press, 1995.

Williams, Raymond. *The Country and the City*. New York: Oxford, 1973.

Wilson, Rob. *The American Sublime: The Genealogy of a Poetic Genre*. Madison: University of Wisconsin Press, 1991.

———. "Blue Hawai'i: Bamboo Ridge and 'Critical Regionalism'." In *Hawai'i Literature Conference: Reader's Guide*, edited by Lorna Hershinow, 109–128. Honolulu: Hawaii Literary Arts Council, 1994,

———. *Reimagining the American Pacific: From 'South Pacific' to Bamboo Ridge and Beyond*. Durham, N.C.: Duke University Press. Forthcoming.

Wilson, Rob, and Arif Dirlik. "Introduction: Asia/Pacific as Space of Cultural Production." In *Asia/Pacific as Space of Cultural Production*, edited by Rob Wilson and Arif Dirlik, 1–14. Durham, N.C.: Duke University Press, 1995.

Wilson, Rob, and Wimal Dissanayake. *Global/Local: Cultural Production and the Transnational Imaginary*. Durham, N.C.: Duke University Press, 1996.

Wood, Houston. "Preparing to Retheorize the Texts of Oceania." In *Inside Out: Literature, Cultural Politics, and Identity in the New Pacific*, edited by Rob Wilson and Vilsoni Hereniko. Lanham, Md.: Rowman and Littlefield, 1999.

Wright, Theon. *Rape in Paradise*. New York: Hawthorn Books, 1966.

Wright, Thomas L., and Takeo Jane Takahashi. *Observations and Interpretation of Hawaiian Volcanism and Seismicity, 1779–1955*. Honolulu: University of Hawaii Press, 1989.

Wright, Thomas L., Takeo Jane Takahashi, and J. D. Griggs. *Hawaii Volcano Watch: A Pictorial History, 1779–1991*. Honolulu: University of Hawaii Press, 1992.

Young, Kanalu. *Rethinking the Hawaiian Past*. Forthcoming.

Young, Robert J.C. *Colonial Desire: Hybridity in Theory, Culture and Race*. New York: Routledge, 1995.

Zambucka, Kristin. *Princess Kaiulani: The Last Hope of Hawaii's Monarchy*. Honolulu: Mana, 1982.

Filmography

Aloha. Dir. Albert Rogell. Rogell Productions. 1931.

Aloha Oe. Dir. G. P. Hamilton or Thomas H. Ince. KP for Triangle/Ince. 1915.

Big Jim McClain. Dir. Edward Ludwig. With John Wayne. Wayne-Fellows for Warner Bros. 1952.

Bird of Paradise. Dir. King Vidor. With Dolores Del Rio and Joel McCrea. 1932.

Bird of Paradise. Dir. Delmar Davis. With Louis Jourdan, Jeff Chandler, and Debra Paget. 20th Century-Fox. 1951.

Blue Hawaii. Dir. Norman Taurog. Prod. Hal Wallis. With Elvis Presley. Paramount. 1961.

Encounters with Paradise: Views of Hawaii and Its People, 1778–1941. Dir. and prod. by Richard J. Tibberts. Hawaii Public Television. 1992.

Fallen Idol. A. Dir. Kenean Buel. Fox Film Corp. 1919.

Flirtation Walk. Dir. Frank Borzage. With Dick Powell and Ruby Keeler. First National/ Warner Bros. 1934.

Gidget Goes Hawaiian. Dir. Paul Endkos. With Deborah Walley and James Darren. Columbia Pictures. 1961.

Goodbye Paradise. With Joe Moore, Pat Morita. Latitude 20 Pictures. 1992.

Hawaii Calls. Dir. Edward F. Cline. Principle Production. 1938.

Hawaiian Nights. Dir. Albert S. Rogell. Universal. 1939.

Hidden Pearls. Dir. George H. Melford. Jesse S. Lasky Features. 1918.

Honolulu. Dir. Edward Buzzell. With Eleanor Powell and Robert Young. Metro-Goldwyn-Mayer. 1939.

Hula. Dir. Victor Fleming. With Clara Bow. Paramount. 1927.

Hula Honeymoon. Dir. unknown. Circa 1927.

Miss Tatlock's Millions. Dir. Richard Haydn. With Hilo Hattie. Paramount. 1948.

Once Were Warriors. Dir. Lee Tamahori. With Rena Owen and Temurera Morrison. Communicado. 1994.

Paradise, Hawaiian Style. Dir. Michael Moore. With Elvis Presley. Paramount. 1966.

Pele: The Fire Within. Phil Arnone, executive producer, and Stan Wentzel, writer. Honolulu: Lee Enterprises, 1988. Videocassette.

Picture Bride. Dir. Kayo Hatta. Thousand Crane Filmworks. 1995.

Song of the Islands. Dir. Walter Lang. With Betty Grable, Victor Mature, and Hilo Hattie. 20th Century-Fox. 1942.

Tabu. Dir. R. W. Murnau. Motion Picture Sales Corp. 1931.

Taking Waikiki from Self-sufficiency to Dependency. Prod. Carol Bain and Ed Coll. Surfing Education Association and Kauai Worldwide Communications. 1994.

Vengeance of the Deep. Dir. A. B. Barringer. American Releasing Company. 1923.

Waikiki Wedding. Dir. Frank Tuttle. With Bing Crosby, Shirley Ross, and Martha Raye. Paramount. 1937.

White Heat. Dir. Lois Weber. Seven Seas. 1934.

Index

Law, John, 30
Lee, Catherine A., 11
Lee, Christopher Paul, 118
legacy and project, 139, 140, 146
Legendary Tradition of Kamapua'a, The Hawaiian Pig-God, A, 55
Legends and Myths of Hawaii, The, 97
Likelike, Mariam, 97
Lili'uokalani, 9, 87–88, 97, 119, 138, 154
Linnekin, Jocelyn, 133, 134, 146–47
local literature, 48–52
Lodge, David, 85, 95
London, Jack, 40, 88–90, 169
Lono, 147–148
Lum, Darrell H.K., 50
Lyons, Paul, 168

male gaze, 106–9
Malo, David, 56, 137
Man, Glenn K.S., 104, 105
Maori, 42, 119–20
Marek, Serge A., 92, 94, 95, 99, 100
Massey, Doreen, 143
Matson, Floyd, 104, 115
McClintock, Anne, 19
McCrea, Joel, 110–11
McGregor, Davianna Pōmaika'i, 3, 4–5, 129, 134
McPherson, Michael, 16
Metcalfe, Simon, 177n27
Michener, James A., 48, 90, 91, 94, 168
mimicry, 82–83. *See also* hybridity
missionaries, 41, 83, 96, 136, 182n12; as criminal law makers, 166–68; and Hawaiian language, 12, 54, 166; and rhetoric of revulsion, 37–39; as volcano observers, 68–70, 73
Miss Tatlock's Millions, 115
Mitchell, W.J.T., 141
monorhetoric: accuracy and totality of, 5, 16, 17, 54, 55, 121, 139, 144, 145; in cyberspace, 161, 164; defined, 15, 129; and knowledge, 18, 59, 142, 168, 169–70;

polyrhetoric, compared to, 130–34, 136–37, 140–41, 146–49
Mookini, Esther T., 1, 55, 94
Mulvey, Laura, 103, 107
Murayama, Milton, 51
Murray-Oliver, Anthony, 21, 30

Nakamura, Barry, 98
Nākoa, Sarah, 1, 55
Nakuina, Moses K., 1, 3, 55
naming practices. *See* Kanaka Maoli, naming practices
Nandy, Ashis, 17–19, 139
Naone, Lyons Kapi'ioho, 74–75
Nāpākā, Nathan, 99
Nation of Hawai'i, 153–56, 157
Native Land and Foreign Desires, 56, 161, 166
Native-Net, 157
Native Web, 156
Natural History of Nature Writing, A, 80
nature writing, 78–81
Nā Wahi Pana O Ko'olau Poko, Legendary Places of Ko'olau Poko, 57–59
Negroponte, Nicholas, 155, 158
Niranjana, Tejaswini, 57, 58

Oani, 72, 80
Obeyesekere, Gananath, 23, 147–49
Observations and Interpretation of Hawaiian Volcanism and Seismicity, 1779–1955, 68–69
'Ōiwi: A Native Hawaiian Journal, 169
Okamura, Reggie, 80
oli, 131–132, 150, 190n13
Olowalu massacre, 9, 177n27
ona rama, 167
Once Were Warriors, 119–121
On the Makaloa Mat, 89
Order of Things, The: An Archaeology of the Human Sciences, 141
Osorio, Jon, 3, 53–54

Pacific Commercial Advertiser, 73
Pacific Islanders, 34–36, 82
Paine, Albert Bigelow, 93
Papa, 132

About the Author

Houston Wood began his career as a sociologist then spent several years as an indigenous Hawaiian tree planter and macadamia nut farmer on the island of Hawaiʻi. He now works in downtown Honolulu where he is an assistant professor and academic coordinator for English at Hawaii Pacific University. Wood's previous publications include studies of contemporary Pacific literature and *The Reality of Ethnomethodology*, written with Hugh Mehan.